Medical Insurance for Pharmacy Technicians

Janet McGregor Liles, CPhT

Arkansas State University, Beebe, Arkansas

Cynthia Newby, CPC

Mc Graw Hill **Higher Education**

Boston   Burr Ridge, IL   Dubuque, IA   New York   San Francisco   St. Louis
Bangkok   Bogotá   Caracas   Kuala Lumpur   Lisbon   London   Madrid   Mexico City
Milan   Montreal   New Delhi   Santiago   Seoul   Singapore   Sydney   Taipei   Toronto

Higher Education

MEDICAL INSURANCE FOR PHARMACY TECHNICIANS
Published by McGraw-Hill, a business unit of The McGraw-Hill Companies, Inc., 1221 Avenue of the Americas,
New York, NY, 10020. Copyright © 2010 by The McGraw-Hill Companies, Inc. All rights reserved. No part of
this publication may be reproduced or distributed in any form or by any means, or stored in a database or
retrieval system, without the prior written consent of The McGraw-Hill Companies, Inc., including, but not
limited to, in any network or other electronic storage or transmission, or broadcast for distance learning.

Some ancillaries, including electronic and print components, may not be available to customers outside the
United States.

This book is printed on acid-free paper.

Printed in the United States of America.

8 9 0 QVS/QVS 17 16 15

ISBN   978-0-07-337416-1
MHID   0-07-337416-4

Vice president/Editor in chief: *Elizabeth Haefele*
Vice president/Director of marketing: *John E. Biernat*
Senior sponsoring editor: *Debbie Fitzgerald*
Director of development, Allied Health: *Patricia Hesse*
Executive marketing manager: *Roxan Kinsey*
Lead media producer: *Damian Moshak*
Media producer: *Marc Mattson*
Director, Editing/Design/Production: *Jess Ann Kosic*
Project manager: *Marlena Pechan*
Senior production supervisor: *Janean A. Utley*

Designer: *Marianna Kinigakis*
Media project manager: *Mark A. S. Dierker*
Outside development house: *Derek H. Noland,*
  Chestnut Hill Enterprises
Cover design: *Ellen Pettengell*
Interior design: *Kay Lieberherr*
Typeface: *10.5/13*
Compositor: *Aptara®, Inc.*
Printer: *Quad/Graphics Versailles*
Cover credit: ©Comstock Images/PictureQuest

Library of Congress Cataloging-in-Publication Data

Liles, Janet McGregor.
    Medical insurance for pharmacy technicians / Janet McGregor Liles, Cynthia Newby.
       p. ; cm.
    Includes index.
    ISBN-13: 978-0-07-337416-1 (alk. paper)
    ISBN-10: 0-07-337416-4 (alk. paper)
    1. Pharmaceutical services insurance—United States. 2. Pharmacy technicians. I. Newby,
Cynthia. II. Title.
    [DNLM: 1. Insurance, Pharmaceutical Services—United States. 2. Fees and Charges—United
States. 3. Insurance Claim Reporting—United States. 4. Pharmacists' Aides—United States.
W 265 AA1 L728m 2010]
    HG9391.5.U6L55 2010
    368.38'200246151—dc22

                                    2008053880

The Internet addresses listed in the text were accurate at the time of publication. The inclusion of a Web site
does not indicate an endorsement by the authors or McGraw-Hill, and McGraw-Hill does not guarantee the
accuracy of the information presented at these sites.

All brand or product names are trademarks or registered trademarks of their respective companies.

CPT codes are based on CPT 2009
ICD-9-CM codes are based on ICD-9-CM 2009

CPT five-digit codes, nomenclature, and other data are copyright 2008 American Medical Association. All rights
reserved. No fee schedules, basic unit, relative values, or related listings are included in the CPT. The AMA
assumes no liability for the data contained herein.

All names, situations, and anecdotes are fictitious. They do not represent any person, event, or medical record.

All screen shot images of pharmacy management programs or software in this textbook depict McKesson's
EnterpriseRx™ software and are the property of McKesson Corporation or its subsidiaries and protected by
copyright and other applicable laws.

www.mhhe.com

Brief Contents

Contents

Welcome to *Medical Insurance for Pharmacy Technicians.* This text provides you with an introduction to medical insurance in the pharmacy environment. The goal of this program is to give you the knowledge you will need to process insurance claims in the pharmacy. Whether you plan to work in a small community pharmacy, a large retail chain pharmacy, a hospital, or any other setting which processes prescriptions and dispenses medication, this book is addressed to you.

Your Career as a Pharmacy Technician

Pharmacy technician is one of the fastest-growing allied health occupations, with employment expected to increase by 32 percent from 2006 to 2016 (Source: *Occupational Outlook Handbook 2008–09 Edition,* Bureau of Labor Statistics.) This employment growth is the result of the increased medical needs of an aging population—who use more prescription drugs than younger people—as well as a steady flow of new medications to treat diseases. When there are more prescriptions to be filled, more pharmacy technicians are needed.

Pharmacy technicians perform a number of important tasks as they assist licensed pharmacists provide medication to patients. While the specific duties may be determined by State rules and regulations, technicians are usually involved in clinical and administrative tasks. Clinical tasks may include retrieving, counting, weighing, measuring, and sometimes mixing the medication, preparing prescription labels, and selecting a container for the medication. Once the prescription is filled, it is reviewed by a pharmacist before it is dispensed to the patient. Technicians also perform important administrative tasks, such as answering phones, entering patient and prescription information in a computer, verifying electronic prescriptions, determining patient eligibility, responding to claim denials, and operating cash registers.

Pharmacy technician is a challenging, interesting position, where you are compensated according to your level of skills and how effectively you put them to use. Those with the right combination of skills and abilities may have the opportunity to advance to supervisory positions. Education, coupled with certification, brings more employment options and advancement opportunities.

Overview of This Textbook

This text provides you with an introduction to medical insurance as it pertains to the job of the pharmacy technician. It gives you a solid understanding of many topics in medical insurance. The program focuses on three key aspects of the position of pharmacy technician:

1. Knowledge of procedures—including and an understanding of the different types of prescription plans and of administrative duties important to the financial well-being of a pharmacy.

2. Health information technology skills—understanding the role of technology in the pharmacy billing cycle, from electronic prescriptions to electronic remittance advice.
3. Communication skills—working with patients, pharmacists, and payers to obtain the information necessary to process prescriptions safely and efficiently.

To the Student

The chapter content in *Medical Insurance for Pharmacy Technicians* is as follows:

Chapter 1 discusses the importance of pharmacy benefits to patients, providers, and the pharmacy practice. The main types of medical insurance plans that provide coverage for patients are described, and the steps in the pharmacy billing cycle are explained.

Chapter 2 focuses on the HIPAA legislation and its impact on the pharmacy practice, including the HIPAA Privacy Rule, HIPAA Security Rule, HIPAA Electronic Health Care Transactions and Code Sets standards and National Identifiers, and the Health Care Fraud and Abuse Control Program and related laws.

Chapter 3 describes the major types of health insurance plans, and the patient's financial responsibilities under each type of plan. Concepts specific to the pharmacy are explained, including formularies and tiers. Students also practice calculating patients' payments.

Chapter 4 introduces students to the four parts of the government-based Medicare program. The concepts of participating and nonparticipating physicians and medically unnecessary services are presented. The chapter describes the differences between the pharmacy benefit provided by the Original Medicare Plan and the Medicare Advantage plan, and provides practice calculating payments due from Medicare patients.

Chapter 5 describes prescription coverage under Medicaid, TRICARE, CHAMPVA, Workers' Compensation, and Discount Card Programs. The chapter focuses on the eligibility, benefits, and payments associated with each type of plan.

Chapter 6 focuses on the types of information that are required to complete a pharmacy claim. The chapter content includes coordination of benefits, dispense as written (DAW) codes, prescription pricing, electronic claims, and the methods used to bill for medication therapy management (MTM). This chapter also includes hands-on computer exercises with a pharmacy management system.

Chapter 7 explains the process of payer adjudication of claims, including the criteria for reimbursement. Topics include common administrative and safety edits and the electronic remittance advice used for pharmacy claims. Point-of-sale payment collections, resubmitting and appealing claims, and the need for account reconciliation are also discussed. This chapter also includes hands-on computer exercises with a pharmacy management system.

What Every Instructor Needs to Know

Welcome to Medical Insurance for Pharmacy Technicians!

The pharmacy field that you are training students to enter is changing, as technology changes the way in which prescriptions are received and processed. As you know, the field of health care is in the midst of an enormous transition from paper-based systems to computer-based systems. Your students are entering the field at an exciting time, and you are teaching at an exciting time. While the demand for graduates of pharmacy technician programs exceeds the supply, students entering the field today also need a basic understanding of medical insurance and the technology used to process and receive payment for prescriptions. That is the purpose of this text, which was developed specifically for students in pharmacy technician programs.

Teaching Supplements

For the Instructor
Instructor's Manual, posted to the Online Learning Center, www.mhhe.com/LilesMedInsPharmTech includes:

- Course overview
- Chapter-by-chapter lesson plans
- Tech Check, Your Turn, and end-of-chapter solutions

Instructor Productivity Center assets posted to the Online Learning Center, www.mhhe.com/LilesMedInsPharmTech includes:

- Instructor's PowerPoint® presentation of Chapters 1 through 7.
- Electronic testing program featuring McGraw-Hill's EZ Test. This flexible and easy-to-use program allows instructors to create tests from book specific items. It accommodates a wide range of question types and instructors may add their own questions. Multiple versions of the test can be created and any test can be exported for use with course management systems such as WebCT, Blackboard, or PageOut.
- Instructor's Manual.

Online Learning Center (OLC), www.mhhe.com/LilesMedInsPharmTech, Instructor Resources include:

- Instructor's Manual in Word and PDF format
- PowerPoint® files for each chapter
- Links to professional associations
- PageOut link

For the Student
Online Learning Center (OLC), www.mhhe.com/LilesMedInsPharmTech includes additional chapter quizzes and other review activities.

Janet McGregor Liles, CPhT

Janet is a seasoned 24 year pharmacy veteran. Her passion of the pharmacy profession has grown and flourished.

At the beginning of her career in pharmacy, third party insurance billing of pharmacy claims was virtually non existent. Times have changed, and so have the billing needs of pharmacy. Pharmacies filed less than 1% of claims forms in the 1980's, while now pharmacies bill ~90% of all claims on behalf of the patient.

Janet's pharmacy career has grown and changed with the times. She understands the need for all pharmacy personnel to be engaged in the business of pharmacy, as well as the outcome of that engagement. It is through experience and education that she offers future pharmacy technicians and other pharmacy personnel her knowledge and expertise in the area of third party billing.

CYNTHIA NEWBY, CPC

Cynthia has developed and written text programs for McGraw-Hill for over eighteen years. She is the author of *From Patient to Payment, Medical Insurance Coding Workbook, HIPAA for Allied Health Careers,* and *Medical Insurance.* Cynthia is certified as a professional coder by the American Academy of Professional Coders, and is a graduate of Hood College.

Many tools to help you learn have been integrated into your text.

Chapter Features

Learning Outcomes

present a list of the most important points you should focus on in the chapter.

Key Terms

list the important vocabulary words alphabetically to build your insurance terminology. Key terms are highlighted and defined when introduced in the text.

Chapter Outline

gives you an overview of the key concepts and organization.

HIPAA Tips, Billing Tips, and Compliance Tips

connect you to the real world of medical insurance. These tips on HIPAA rules, billing points, and ensuring compliance are located in the margins near the related chapter topics.

---

chapter
1

From Prescription to Payment:
Becoming a Pharmacy Technician Insurance Specialist

 Learning Outcomes

After completing this chapter, you will be able to define the key terms and:

1-1. Discuss the importance of pharmacy benefits to patients, providers, and the pharmacy practice.

1-2. Discuss the key features of medical insurance.

1-3. Describe the main types of medical insurance plans that provide coverage for patients.

1-4. Describe the ten steps in the pharmacy billing cycle.

1-5. Discuss the effects of billing errors on the success of the pharmacy practice.

Chapter Outline

The Importance of Pharmacy Benefits
Medical Insurance Basics
The Pharmacy Practice Billing Cycle
Procedures, Communication, and Information Technology in the Pharmacy Billing Cycle
Effects of Pharmacy Claim Errors

Key Terms

accounts receivable (AR)
adjudication
benefits
billing cycle
coinsurance
copayment
deductible
EDI (electronic data interchange)
electronic prescribing (eRx)
explanation of benefits (EOB)
formulary
health plan
insurance payers
managed care
managed care organization (MCO)
maximum benefit limit
medical insurance
medically necessary
noncovered (excluded) services
pharmacy benefit
pharmacy claim
pharmacy management (PM) system
pharmacy technician insurance specialist
point of sale (POS)
policyholder
preferred drug list
premium
prescription drug list (PDL)
provider
remittance advice (RA)

 HIPAA Tip

45 CFR Parts 160 and 164

The HIPAA Privacy Rule is also often referred to b
in the *Federal Reg*
45 CFR Parts 160

 Billing Tip

State-Mandated Benefits

States may require be
are not mandated in f
regulations. For exam
states mandate covere
infertility treatments fo

Compliance Guideline

Staying Current with HIPAA

HIPAA laws undergo a lengthy review process before being released as final rules. Future changes are expected. Pharmacy technician insurance specialists need to stay current with HIPAA regulations that affect their areas of responsibility.

Figures, Tables, and Screen Captures
illustrate the key concepts in the chapter visually.

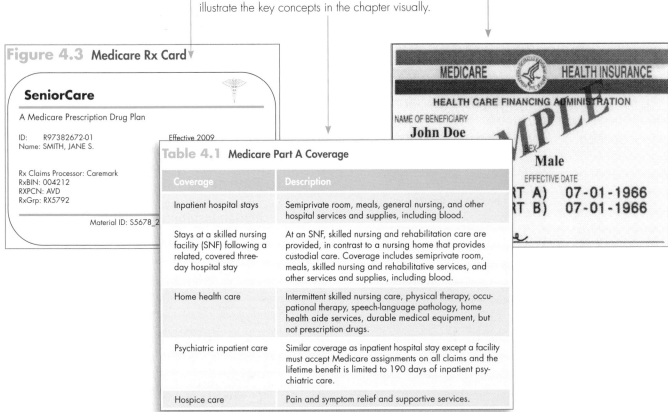

Figure 4.3 Medicare Rx Card

SeniorCare

A Medicare Prescription Drug Plan

ID: R97382672-01
Name: SMITH, JANE S.

Rx Claims Processor: Caremark
RxBIN: 004212
RXPCN: AVD
RxGrp: RX5792

Effective 2009

Material ID: S5678_2

MEDICARE   HEALTH INSURANCE

HEALTH CARE FINANCING ADMINISTRATION
NAME OF BENEFICIARY
John Doe

Male

EFFECTIVE DATE

RT A)   07-01-1966

RT B)   07-01-1966

Table 4.1 Medicare Part A Coverage

Coverage	Description
Inpatient hospital stays	Semiprivate room, meals, general nursing, and other hospital services and supplies, including blood.
Stays at a skilled nursing facility (SNF) following a related, covered three-day hospital stay	At an SNF, skilled nursing and rehabilitation care are provided, in contrast to a nursing home that provides custodial care. Coverage includes semiprivate room, meals, skilled nursing and rehabilitative services, and other services and supplies, including blood.
Home health care	Intermittent skilled nursing care, physical therapy, occupational therapy, speech-language pathology, home health aide services, durable medical equipment, but not prescription drugs.
Psychiatric inpatient care	Similar coverage as inpatient hospital stay except a facility must accept Medicare assignments on all claims and the lifetime benefit is limited to 190 days of inpatient psychiatric care.
Hospice care	Pain and symptom relief and supportive services.

Tech Checks

challenge you to stop and think through the questions that are posed at major points in the chapter.

 Tech Check

What are the terms for the two entities that form an agreement, that makes medical insurance available to people?

What does a policyholder pay to a health plan in order to receive benefits?

What are the possible sources of medical insurance?

FYI

"For Your Information Boxes" with interesting bits of information about topics in the text.

 Electronic Prescribing

Most pharmacies are equipped to accept electronic prescriptions sent by physicians. The use of eRx has several advantages: it eliminates the problem of illegible prescriptions; allows the use of clinical decision support to reduce preventable errors such as drug-drug interactions, drug-allergy reactions, dosing errors, and therapeutic duplication; improves communication through all parts of the prescribing chain; and results in better records.

Your Turn

computer-based exercises introduce you to the features and functions of a pharmacy management system, McKesson's EnterpriseRx.

Your Turn 1

Review Prescription Details, Part 1

Instructions: Double-click Activity 1 and follow the on-screen instructions. Answer the questions listed below.

1. When was the prescription written?
2. Who is the prescriber?

 YOUR TURN

Chapter Review

Summary

provides a helpful review of the chapter's key concepts.

Review Questions

reinforce the important facts and points made in the chapter. Question formats include matching, true-false, completion, and short answer.

Internet Activities

describe relevant websites and direct you to use the Internet to research and report your findings. The goal of the activities is to extend your knowledge of the selected topics and to learn to use the Internet as a research tool.

Chapter Summary

1. With around $180 billion being spent on outpatient prescription medications annually in the United States and with expected growth in expenditures, paying for drugs is a matter of concern for patients, physicians, hospitals, pharmacists, and the health plans that help patients cover the costs. As a result, the role of the pharmacy technician insurance specialist is of the utmost importance to the success of a pharmacy.

2. To afford medical expenses, many people enter into agreements with health plans to receive medical insurance. The policyholder pays a premium to the health plan to receive benefits and care from providers—hospitals, physicians, and other medical staff members and facilities. The health plan informs the policyholder about which medical services are considered medically necessary and which are noncovered (excluded) services, the drugs available on its formulary, and the limitations placed on benefits.

3. Several main types of health insurance provide coverage to patients. Indemnity plans generally cover the medical costs policyholders incur when they receive treatment for accidents and illnesses. Managed care plans supervise medical care with the goal of ensuring that patients get needed services in the most appropriate, cost-effective setting. Medical insurance is available through private health plans and various state and federal government programs.

4. The steps in the pharmacy billing cycle are (a) receipt of prescription, (b) patient interview, (c) filling of prescription, (d) pharmacy claim transmittal, (e) payer adjudication, (f) point-of-sale patient payment, (g) calculation of payer claim balance, (h) accounts receivable follow-up, (i) payment processing, and (j) collections and problem resolution. These steps are designed to provide the best possible service for a patient at

Chapter Review

Multiple Choice

Read the question and select the best response.

1. Which of these terms refers to the selection of prescription medications offered by a health plan?
   A. formulary
   B. prescription drug list
   C. preferred drug list
   D. all of the above

2. What is the final step in the pharmacy billing cycle?
   A. collections and problem resolution
   B. payer adjudication
   C. payment processing
   D. accounts receivable follow-up

3. Which of these terms is the name of the document received by the pharmacy that shows the detail for

   A. copayment
   B. premium
   C. formulary
   D. pharmacy claim

7. A monetary amount imposed by a health plan after which benefits end is known by which term?
   A. remittance advice
   B. adjudication
   C. coinsurance
   D. maximum benefit limit

8. Which of the following is *not* a government health plan?
   A. Medicare
   B. workers' compensation
   C. adjudication
   D. CHAMPVA

Internet Activities

1. Using a search engine such as Google, review some of the various medical insurance plans that are available. Try using key words for your search, such as *insurance, medical, health,* and *plan.*

2. Use a search engine to research topics related to the jobs, training, and certifications available for pharmacy technician insurance specialists in your area and nationwide.

Glossary

The most important definitions are found at the back of the text for easy reference.

Glossary

A

abuse action that misuses money that the government has allocated

account reconciliation the act of comparing the total charges and amount owed with the reimbursement received from the insurer and the patient

accounts receivable (AR) remaining balance due after an initial payment has been made

adjudication payer's processing of claim data to decide whether a drug is covered by the patient's plan and properly utilized

administrative edits checks that typically indicate that additional information is required to process the claim or that some information has been entered incorrectly

advance beneficiary notice (ABN) of noncoverage form given to a patient before treatment when a provider thinks that Medicare will deem a procedure not reasonable and necessary and will not cover it

aging reports documents used to identify patient accounts with overdue outstanding balances

any willing provider state laws requiring pharmacy benefit

C

capitation fee usually paid monthly by a patient to the primary care physician regardless of the number of times the patient visits the physician

catastrophic cap limit on the total medical expenses a patient must pay in one year

categorically needy special group of Medicaid recipients whose needs are addressed under the Welfare Reform Act

Centers for Medicare and Medicaid Services (CMS) main federal government agency responsible for health care

CHAMPVA program that helps pay health care costs for families of veterans who are totally and permanently disabled because of service-related injuries

Claim Adjustment Group Codes codes that describes the type of needed claim adjustment

Claim Adjustment Reason Codes (CARC) mandatory codes used to specify reasons for adjustments to claims

clearinghouses companies that help providers handle electronic transactions such as pharmacy claims

closed formulary type of formulary that will not provide coverage for unlisted drugs without an authorized medical

Online Learning Center (OLC)

www.mhhe.com/LilesMedInsPharmTech The OLC offers additional learning and teaching tools.

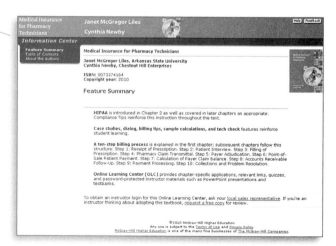

Acknowledgments

For insightful reviews and helpful suggestions, we would like to acknowledge the following:

Larry M. Allen, Ph.D., MBA, R.Ph.
Arapahoe Community College

Jeffrey A. Baird, MBA, CPhT
Great Lakes Institute of
Technology

Mandy Chapple, BA
Granite Technical Institute

Karen Davis, CPhT
Southeastern Technical College

Cristal M. Greene, BA
Hutchinson Community College

Coelle Lynette Harper Deaton,
BSE
Career Centers of Texas

Michael M. Hayter, Pharm. D.,
MBA
Virginia Highlands Community
College

Susan Helfter, PharmD, RPh
Hibbing Community College

Mindy Koppel, CPhT
Pennsylvania Institute of
Technology

Monica Lashway, CPhT
Western Career College

Marcy May, MEd, CPhT
Austin Community College

Michelle C. McCranie, AAS
Ogeechee Technical College

Kelly Meyer, BS
Cisco Junior College

Nicole Motes, CPhT
Pikes Peak Community College

Nancy L. Needham, CPhT, MA Ed
American Career College

Jean A. Oldham, MS, BS, ABD
for EDD
St. Catharine College

Marsha M. Sanders, BS
Jones County Junior College

Becky Schonscheck, CPhT
High-Tech Institute

Michael Spencer, PharmD
Modesto Junior College

Cardiece Sylvan, CPhT
MedVance Institute of Baton
Rouge

Dawn M. Tesner, CPhT, BS,
MSHA
Mid Michigan Community
College

Joseph A. Tinervia, CPhT, MBA
Tulsa Job Corps—Pharmacy &
Tulsa Community College

Sandi Tschritter, BA, CPhT
Spokane Community College

Marvin L. Walker, JR, AAS
Austin Community College

Marsha Lynn Wilson,
Clarian Health Sciences
Education Center

Michele Wootton, BA, RPhT
Western Career College

From Prescription to Payment:
Becoming a Pharmacy Technician Insurance Specialist

 Learning Outcomes

After completing this chapter, you will be able to define the key terms and:

1-1. Discuss the importance of pharmacy benefits to patients, providers, and the pharmacy practice.

1-2. Discuss the key features of medical insurance.

1-3. Describe the main types of medical insurance plans that provide coverage for patients.

1-4. Describe the ten steps in the pharmacy billing cycle.

1-5. Discuss the effects of billing errors on the success of the pharmacy practice.

Chapter Outline

The Importance of Pharmacy Benefits

Medical Insurance Basics

The Pharmacy Practice Billing Cycle

Procedures, Communication, and Information Technology in the Pharmacy Billing Cycle

Effects of Pharmacy Claim Errors

Key Terms

accounts receivable (AR)
adjudication
benefits
billing cycle
coinsurance
copayment
deductible
EDI (electronic data interchange)
electronic prescribing (eRx)
explanation of benefits (EOB)
formulary
health plan
insurance payers
managed care
managed care organization (MCO)
maximum benefit limit
medical insurance
medically necessary
noncovered (excluded) services
pharmacy benefit
pharmacy claim
pharmacy management (PM) system
pharmacy technician insurance specialist
point of sale (POS)
policyholder
preferred drug list
premium
prescription drug list (PDL)
providers
remittance advice (RA)

The Importance of Pharmacy Benefits

In an average year, according to the U.S. Department of Health and Human Services Agency for Health Research and Quality, Americans spend around $180 billion on outpatient prescription medications. Of this total, $32 billion is spent on cardiovascular drugs, $25 billion on hormones, and $24 billion on central nervous system drugs. Cholesterol-lowering medications and antidepressants round out the top five with costs of about $20 billion each. This expenditure is growing and is expected to continue to increase. In addition, for the first time, more than half of Americans are taking prescription medicines regularly for chronic health problems.

Paying for these vital drugs is a matter of concern to patients, physicians, hospitals, pharmacists, and the health plans that help patients cover the costs. This chapter describes the basics of pharmacy benefits as a component of health insurance, the work flow in the pharmacy practice that supplies and bills for the prescriptions, and especially the role of the **pharmacy technician insurance specialist.** This title describes the vital job of getting paid for prescriptions, whether in a large pharmacy practice where individuals specialize in various tasks or a small practice where the same individual may handle this role, as well as others, such as filling prescriptions.

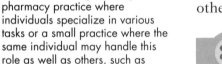

 Tech Check

About how much do Americans spend on outpatient prescription medications in an average year?

What groups are particularly concerned with paying for prescription drugs?

pharmacy technician insurance specialist job title that describes the vital job of getting paid for prescriptions, whether the setting is a large pharmacy practice where individuals specialize in various tasks or a small practice where the same individual may handle this role as well as others, such as filling prescriptions

medical insurance agreement between a person and a health plan that enables individuals to be able to afford medical expenses

policyholder individual who enters into an agreement with a health plan to receive medical insurance

health plan organization that offers financial protection in case of illness or accidental injury (also known as *insurance payer*)

insurance payers organizations that offer financial protection in case of illness or accidental injury (also known as *health plans*)

premium fee paid monthly to a health plan by a person who buys medical insurance

benefits payments made by a health plan for medical services

providers hospital, physician, and other medical staff members and facilities that offer medical services

Medical Insurance Basics

Everyone, no matter how healthy, needs medical care at some time. People need preventive care, such as routine checkups and vaccinations, to stay healthy. They also need medications and treatment for sicknesses, accidents, and injuries. A person who receives health care owes a charge for the medical services and supplies, such as prescription drugs, that are involved.

To be able to afford the charges, many people in the United States have **medical insurance,** which is an agreement between a person, who is called the **policyholder,** and a **health plan.** Health plans, also known as **insurance payers** (or *carriers*), are organizations that offer financial protection in case of illness or accidental injury. Medical insurance helps pay for the policyholder's medical treatment.

The Insurance Contract

A person who buys medical insurance pays a **premium** to a health plan. In exchange for the premium, the health plan agrees to pay amounts, called **benefits,** for medical services. Medical services include the care supplied by **providers**—hospitals, physicians, and other medical staff members and facilities. Benefits usually start once the policyholder has paid a certain amount each year, called the **deductible.** Some contracts, do not demand deductibles, providing *first-dollar-coverage* that begins with the first charge of the year.

What Is Medically Necessary?

The health plan issues the policyholder an insurance policy that contains a list of covered medical services that is called a *schedule of benefits.* Benefits commonly include payment of medically necessary medical treatments received by policyholders and their dependents. The Health Insurance Association of America defines the insurance term **medically necessary** as "medical treatment that is appropriate and rendered in accordance with generally accepted standards of medical practice." In general, these conditions surrounding medical procedures and medications must be met to be considered necessary:

- They match the patient's illness.
- They are not elective. They are required to treat a condition, rather than being elected to be done by the patient.
- They are not experimental. The procedures or medications must be approved by the appropriate federal regulatory agency, such as the Food and Drug Administration (FDA).
- They are furnished at an appropriate level. Simple diagnoses usually require simple procedures or medications; complex conditions may require multiple medications for effective control.

What Is Covered?

Insurance may cover a number of different items, including primary medical care, emergency care, and surgery. Many health plans also cover preventive medical services, such as annual physical examinations, pediatric and adolescent immunizations, prenatal care, and routine cancer screening procedures such as mammograms. The policies list treatments that are covered at different rates and medical services that are not covered. For example, a plan may pay 80 percent of most treatments but a smaller percentage of the charges for vision services such as eyeglasses.

Policies that have a **pharmacy benefit** usually provide coverage for a selection of prescription medications. The plan's **prescription drug list (PDL)**—which is also known as a **preferred drug list** or a **formulary**—contains the FDA-approved brand-name and generic medications the plan covers. It also describes the permitted sources of the PDL, which may include local pharmacies and online (Internet) or mail suppliers.

The medical insurance policy also describes **noncovered (excluded) services**—what it does not pay for. For example, dental care is generally not included in the medical insurance policy; however, separate dental insurance plans are available for purchase. Also, if a new policyholder has a medical condition that was diagnosed before the policy was written—known as a *preexisting condition*—a health plan may not cover medical services for its treatment.

What Are the Limitations?

Plans often have a **maximum benefit limit** (also called a lifetime limit), a monetary amount after which benefits end, and they may also impose

deductible amount paid by a policyholder each year before benefits from a health plan will start

medically necessary insurance term referring to appropriate medical treatment given under generally accepted standards of medical practice

pharmacy benefit feature of a policy that provides coverage for selection of prescription medications

prescription drug list (PDL) list containing the Food and Drug Administration (FDA)-approved brand-name and generic medications a plan covers (also known as a *formulary* or *preferred drug list*)

preferred drug list list containing the Food and Drug Administration (FDA)-approved brand-name and generic medications a plan covers (also known as a *formulary* or *prescription drug list*)

formulary list containing the Food and Drug Administration (FDA)-approved brand-name and generic medications a plan covers (also known as a *preferred drug list* or *prescription drug list*)

noncovered (excluded) services services that a medical insurance policy does not pay for

maximum benefit limit monetary amount after which a plan's benefits end

lifetime limits for particular conditions. For example, the plan may have a $500,000 lifetime limit on all benefits covered under the plan for any policyholder and a $2,000 limit on benefits provided for a specific health condition of an individual policyholder. Some plans may also have an annual benefit limit that restricts the amount payable in a given year.

Most health plans have cost-containment practices to help control costs. For example, patients may be required to choose from a specific group of physicians and hospitals for all medical care. A visit to a specialist may require a referral from the patient's primary care physician. A second physician's opinion may be required before surgery can be reimbursed. Also, many services that previously involved overnight hospital stays are now covered only if done during daytime clinic visits, with patients recuperating at home. Pharmacy benefit plans have similar restrictions.

Types of Plans

Indemnity Plans

In the past, most medical insurance policies in the United States were *indemnity* plans, which cover the medical costs policyholders incur when they receive treatment for accidents and illnesses. If a policyholder or a covered *dependent* (a spouse, child, or other relative specified in the insurance policy) gets sick, the health plan pays most of the bill.

coinsurance percentage of the fees owed by the policyholder

The policy of an indemnity plan lists the services that are paid for and the amounts that are paid. The benefit may be for all or part of the charges. In many cases, the policyholder owes a percentage of the fees, usually called **coinsurance.** For example, the schedule of benefits in a medical insurance policy may say that it pays 80 percent of the fees for surgery performed in a hospital and that the policyholder must pay 20 percent. Under this contract, if the policyholder has surgery in the hospital and the bill is $2,000, the health plan pays 80 percent of $2,000, or $1,600. The policyholder is responsible for the coinsurance—the other 20 percent, or $400 in this example.

Managed Care Plans

managed care method of supervising medical care with the goal of ensuring that patients get needed services in the most appropriate, cost-effective setting

managed care organization (MCO) plan that establishes links among provider, patient, and payer by combining the delivery of services with the financing and management of health care

Under indemnity plans, it is difficult for insurance payers to control costs because there are few restrictions on how much providers can charge, especially for new technology, drugs, and procedures. To counter this trend, the concept of **managed care** was introduced. Managed care is a way of supervising medical care with the goal of ensuring that patients get needed services in the most appropriate, cost-effective setting.

To accomplish the goal of managed care, financing and management of health care are combined with the delivery of services. A **managed care organization (MCO)** establishes links among provider, patient, and payer. Instead of only the patient's having a policy with the health plan, under managed care *both* the patient and the provider have agreements with the MCO. The patient agrees to the payments for the services, and the provider agrees to accept the fees the MCO offers for services. This arrangement gives the managed care plan more control over the services the provider performs and the fees the plan pays.

Managed care is the leading type of health plan, and many different kinds of managed care programs are available. These are covered in detail in Chapter 3. In some cases, patients pay fixed premiums at regular time periods, such as monthly, that cover all services and medications that will be received. A patient may also pay a **copayment**—a small fixed fee, such as $10 for a generic drug. In some plans, the *copay* is a percentage of the amount the provider receives. In either case, the copayment must always be paid by the patient at the time of service.

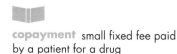

copayment small fixed fee paid by a patient for a drug

Sources of Medical Insurance

Some patients are covered by private insurance; others qualify for programs sponsored by state or federal governments.

Private Plans

Private health plans offer a variety of types of medical insurance coverage. Most people enrolled in private insurance are covered under group contracts—policies bought by employers or other organizations to cover employees or those who belong to the organization. Other plans are policies purchased by people who do not qualify as members of a group. Private insurance plans are covered in Chapter 3.

Government Programs

The following are the most common government plans in effect in the United States:

- *Medicare:* Medicare is a federal health plan that covers most citizens aged sixty-five and over, people with disabilities, people with end-stage renal disease (ESRD), and dependent widows.
- *Medicaid:* Low-income people who cannot afford medical care are covered by Medicaid, which is cosponsored by the federal and state governments. Medicaid is run by the state, and matching federal dollars are available for states that satisfy certain requirements, such as providing prenatal care and child vaccinations. Qualifications and benefits vary by state.
- *TRICARE (formerly CHAMPUS):* TRICARE covers expenses for dependents of active-duty members of the uniformed services and for retired military personnel. It also covers dependents of military personnel who were killed while on active duty.
- *CHAMPVA:* The Civilian Health and Medical Program of the Department of Veterans Affairs is a program for veterans with permanent service-related disabilities and their dependents. It also covers surviving spouses and dependent children of veterans who died from service-related disabilities.
- *Workers' compensation:* People with job-related illnesses or injuries are covered under workers' compensation insurance through their employers. Workers' compensation benefits vary according to state law.

These government health plans, as well as state-sponsored drug coverage programs, are described in Chapters 4 and 5.

Tech Check

What are the terms for the two entities that form an agreement, that makes medical insurance available to people?

What does a policyholder pay to a health plan in order to receive benefits?

What are the possible sources of medical insurance?

The Pharmacy Practice Billing Cycle

point of sale (POS) drug plan benefits received at the time the pharmacy technician insurance specialist processes a person's prescriptions

billing cycle ten-step work flow followed at a pharmacy to care for patients' financial matters

People who are covered by a drug plan receive their benefits when the pharmacy technician insurance specialist processes their prescriptions at the **point of sale (POS).** The **billing cycle** for a patient's pharmacy bene-fits follows a ten-step work flow, as shown in Table 1.1 and explained below.

Step 1: Receipt of Prescription

The receipt of a prescription order starts the pharmacy billing cycle. This step—for either a new prescription or a refill—may occur through several means:

electronic prescribing (eRx) use of software by a physician to transmit an order

- The patient or caregiver personally phones in the prescription or pres-ents it at a face-to-face meeting.
- The physician or physician representative phones in the prescription.
- The physician or physician representative faxes the prescription.
- In a small percentage of transactions, the physician uses software to transmit an order via **electronic prescribing (eRx).**

Table 1.1 Pharmacy Billing Cycle

1	Receipt of Prescription
2	Patient Interview
3	Filling of Prescription
4	Pharmacy Claim Transmittal
5	Payer Adjudication
6	Point-of-Sale Patient Payment
7	Calculation of Payer Claim Balance
8	Accounts Receivable Follow-Up
9	Payment Processing
10	Collections and Problem Resolution

 **Electronic Prescribing**

Most pharmacies are equipped to accept electronic prescriptions sent by physicians. The use of eRx has several advantages: it eliminates the problem of illegible prescriptions; allows the use of clinical decision support to reduce preventable errors such as drug-drug interactions, drug-allergy reactions, dosing errors, and therapeutic duplication; improves communication through all parts of the prescribing chain; and results in better records.

Step 2: Patient Interview

The second step in the billing work flow sets the stage for processing a prescription when an insurance plan is involved. During this step, the patient or the caregiver is interviewed to determine whether the patient is a returning or a new customer of the pharmacy and is covered by a prescription drug plan.

If the patient responds that prescription benefits apply, the insurance specialist asks to see the applicable insurance card and then asks a series of questions to help determine the status of coverage. The answers to these questions are entered or verified in the **pharmacy management (PM) system,** which stores, processes, transmits, and receives billing data (see Figure 1.1). The necessary information includes the following:

- First name, middle initial, and last name.
- Gender (*F* for female or *M* for male).

pharmacy management (PM) system system that stores, processes, transmits, and receives billing data

Figure 1.1 Sample screen from McKesson's EnterpriseRx, a pharmacy management system.

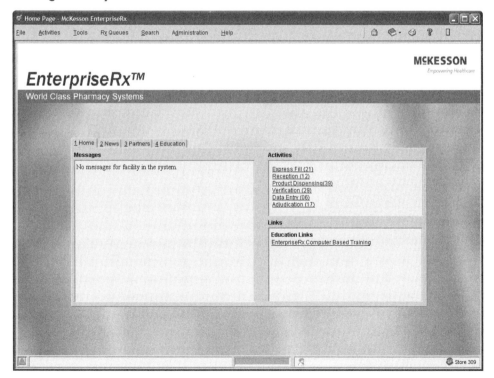

- Martial status (*S* for single, *M* for married, *D* for divorced, *W* for widowed).
- Birth date, using four digits for the year.
- Home address and telephone number (area code with seven-digit number).
- If the patient is a minor (under the age of majority according to state law) or has a medical power of attorney in place (such as a person who is handling the medical decisions of another person), the responsible person's name, gender, marital status, birth date, address, Social Security number, telephone number, and employer information. For a school-child, the status of full-time or part-time student is recorded. In most cases, the responsible person is a parent, guardian, adult child, or someone else acting with legal authority to make health care decisions on behalf of the patient.
- The name of the patient's drug plan and identifying numbers, such as the group identification number.
- The plan policyholder's name and demographic information if not the patient (the policyholder may be a spouse, divorced spouse, guardian, or other relation).
- If the patient is covered by another drug plan, the name and policyholder information for that plan.
- Food and drug allergies.

Step 3: Filling of Prescription

The assigned pharmacy staff member fills the prescription order after drug utilization and drug interactions are reviewed by the pharmacist. Medication is filled properly utilizing the HIPAA-mandated NDC numbers (see Chapter 2) for correct product selection and payer prescription payments.

Step 4: Pharmacy Claim Transmittal

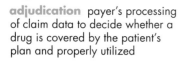

pharmacy claim information transmitted to a payer that identifies the policyholder, the prescriber, the pharmacy sending the claim, and the medications being supplied

EDI (electronic data interchange) claims that are sent electronically between the pharmacy management system and the payer

After the prescription is filled, information is sent to the payer to permit a payment decision. A **pharmacy claim** is "filed," or transmitted; it identifies the policyholder (and the patient, if he or she is not the policyholder), the prescriber (the licensed physician or other author of the prescription), the pharmacy that is sending the claim, and the medications that are being supplied. Most pharmacies file claims for their patients, and most claims are sent electronically by **EDI (electronic data interchange)** between the pharmacy management system and the payer, although in some cases the claim may be on paper, a *paper claim*.

Step 5: Payer Adjudication

adjudication payer's processing of claim data to decide whether a drug is covered by the patient's plan and properly utilized

In the fifth step, the claim is adjudicated by the payer. **Adjudication** means the payer's processing of claim data to determine whether the drug is covered by the patient's plan and is being properly utilized. The claim is monitored by the payer for the amount provided, overutilization, and correctly dispensed medications. If these points are correct, the payer then compares the charges with the terms of the patient's benefit plan and calculates what the patient owes, as well as what the insurance plan is going to pay.

This payment information is returned electronically to the pharmacy for the next step in the cycle. Because this transaction happens very quickly, usually in a matter of seconds, it is often referred to as *real-time claim adjudication (RTCA)*.

Step 6: Point-of-Sale Patient Payment

The next step is to give the patient the prescription and collect payment. This may be in the form of cash, a check, a credit card, or a debit card. Consultation by the pharmacist is offered on the proper administration of the drug. The patient may also sign an insurance log, establishing that he or she actually received the medication.

Step 7: Calculation of Payer Claim Balance

In the seventh step, the payer starts internal processing of the claim for payment to the pharmacy. The amount the patient paid is subtracted from the total the payer specified as the intended payment, and this amount is then due from the payer to the pharmacy. From the pharmacy's point of view, this balance due is an **accounts receivable (AR).**

accounts receivable (AR)
remaining balance due after an initial payment has been made

Step 8: Accounts Receivable Follow-Up

The balance due on the claim is likely to be paid thirty to sixty days after the date of service. An important job of the pharmacy technician insurance specialist is to follow up on balances due from payers. The AR needs to be collected as rapidly as possible to provide funds for the continued operation of the pharmacy practice.

Step 9: Payment Processing

Generally all prescriptions filled within a certain date range are paid electronically or by check in a single transaction. If the payment is received electronically, payment is made directly into the pharmacy's bank account. If the payment is received in the form of a check, the pharmacy must deposit the funds. The pharmacy also receives a document called a **remittance advice (RA)** (also called an **explanation of benefits,** or **EOB**) showing the detail for each claim. The RA is checked to verify that each claim reimbursed by a payer is correct according to the expected payment— a process called *reconciliation*.

remittance advice (RA)
document that comes to a pharmacy showing the details for a claim (also known as an *explanation of benefits*)

explanation of benefits (EOB)
document that comes to a pharmacy showing the details for a claim (also known as a *remittance advice*)

Step 10: Collections and Problem Resolution

In the processing of many transactions, it is possible that there will be payment problems. For example, the claim may not match the payer's payment, or the patient's check may not clear. In the case of hugely expensive *specialty drugs* such as some cancer treatments, patients may want to establish a payment plan so that the bill can be spread out over time.

In the rare case that a paper claim is filed, the claim is sent after the patient receives the prescription and is then paid by the payer. The payer requires that the claim form be legible and filed in a timely manner. When the payer issues payment on a paper claim, the claim form is matched to the remittance and reviewed for proper payment. Appropriate outstanding balances may then be billed to the patient.

The pharmacy technician insurance specialist follows up on all uncollected sums, tracks and solves problems, and works to ensure maximum appropriate payment for the pharmacy practice.

 Tech Check

List the steps of the pharmacy billing cycle in order.

What person working in a pharmacy is vital to the success of the pharmacy billing cycle?

Procedures, Communication, and Information Technology in the Pharmacy Billing Cycle

Each step of the billing process has three parts: (1) following procedures, (2) communicating effectively, and (3) using information technology.

Following Procedures

Each step in pharmacy practice billing cycle has procedures. Some procedures involve administrative duties, such as entering data and updating patients' records. Other procedures are done to comply with government regulations, such as keeping computer files secure from unauthorized viewing. In most pharmacies, policy and procedure manuals are available that describe how to perform major duties.

Communicating Effectively

Communication skills are as important as knowing about specific forms, codes, and regulations. A pleasant tone, a friendly attitude, and a helpful manner when gathering information increase patient satisfaction. Interpersonal skills enhance the billing process by establishing professional, courteous relationships with people of different backgrounds and communication styles. Effective communicators have the skill of empathy; their actions convey that they understand the feelings of others.

Equally important are effective communications with pharmacists and other staff members. Conversations must be brief and to the point, showing that the speaker values the provider's time. People are more likely to listen when the speaker is smiling and has an interested expression, so speakers should be aware of their facial expressions and should maintain moderate eye contact. In addition, good listening skills are important.

 Billing Tip

Pharmacy Management Programs: EnterpriseRx

In this text, McKesson's EnterpriseRx is used to illustrate typical PM data entry screens and printed reports.

Using the Pharmacy Management System

Pharmacy technician insurance specialists use information technology (IT)—computer hardware and software information systems—every day. For example, the use of billing programs that are part of a pharmacy management system streamlines the process of creating and following up on pharmacy claims sent to payers and following up on payments received.

A Note of Caution: What Information Technology Cannot Do

Although computers increase efficiency and reduce errors, they are not more accurate than the individuals who are entering the data. If people make mistakes while entering data, the information the computer produces will be incorrect. Computers are very precise and also very unforgiving. While the human brain knows that *flu* is short for *influenza,* the computer regards them as two distinct conditions. If a computer user accidentally enters a name as *ORourke* instead of *O'Rourke,* a human might know what is meant; the computer does not. It would probably respond with a message such as "No such patient exists in the database."

 Tech Check

What are the three parts of each step of the pharmacy billing process?

What limits the accuracy and efficiency of computers?

Effects of Pharmacy Claim Errors

Efficient and accurate completion of the pharmacy claim process helps a pharmacy practice run smoothly. The job of the pharmacy technician insurance specialist is especially important because much of the income of a pharmacy practice comes from insurance payments. Errors in filing claims slow the reimbursement process and interfere with other work. Filing inaccurate claims can also result in reduced payments or denials and problems with customers.

Lower Payment or Denied or Delayed Claims

A typographical error or incorrect code may communicate the wrong policyholder or medication to the payer. This can result in a lower benefit payment or in denial of the claim. If the health plan must request additional information, payment will be delayed. The payer's claims department can correct an error, but it takes time, so issuing the benefit payment will take longer.

Disruption of Other Work

When a pharmacy technician insurance specialist has to send a corrected claim or fill out a request for a review, the time spent means that new claims for other patients have to wait. Correcting information may also require the assistance of the pharmacist or other members of the office staff, who then must interrupt their activities.

Problematic Customer Relations

If a patient has already paid for services, errors in the claim process can slow reimbursement. The pharmacy technician insurance specialist or another member of the office staff may have to interrupt activities to handle inquiries and complaints.

Working as a Pharmacy Technician Insurance Specialist

Pharmacy technician insurance specialists are employed by community pharmacies, which may be independently owned or part of a chain. They also work in clinics, for health plans, for hospitals or nursing homes, and in other health care settings. Pharmacy technician insurance specialists analyze patients' prescriptions and collect payments for drugs from health plans and patients.

Pharmacy technician insurance specialists also handle the administrative work that is part of the payment process. These activities include preparing and sending pharmacy claims, communicating with health plans to follow up on claims, entering charges and payments in the pharmacy management program, and handling bill collection. They may gather information from patients and answer written or oral questions from both patients and payers, maintaining the confidentiality of patients' data.

Completion of a pharmacy technician insurance specialist or medical assisting program at a postsecondary institution is an excellent background for an entry-level position. Professional certification, additional study, and work experience contribute to advancement.

Tech Check

Where does much of the income of a pharmacy practice come from?

What three negative effects can errors in filing claims cause?

Chapter Summary

1. With around $180 billion being spent on outpatient prescription medications annually in the United States and with expected growth in expenditures, paying for drugs is a matter of concern for patients, physicians, hospitals, pharmacists, and the health plans that help patients cover the costs. As a result, the role of the pharmacy technician insurance specialist is of the utmost importance to the success of a pharmacy.

2. To afford medical expenses, many people enter into agreements with health plans to receive medical insurance. The policyholder pays a premium to the health plan to receive benefits and care from providers—hospitals, physicians, and other medical staff members and facilities. The health plan informs the policyholder about which medical services are considered medically necessary and which are noncovered (excluded) services, the drugs available on its formulary, and the limitations placed on benefits.

3. Several main types of health insurance provide coverage to patients. Indemnity plans generally cover the medical costs policyholders incur when they receive treatment for accidents and illnesses. Managed care plans supervise medical care with the goal of ensuring that patients get needed services in the most appropriate, cost-effective setting. Medical insurance is available through private health plans and various state and federal government programs.

4. The steps in the pharmacy billing cycle are (a) receipt of prescription, (b) patient interview, (c) filling of prescription, (d) pharmacy claim transmittal, (e) payer adjudication, (f) point-of-sale patient payment, (g) calculation of payer claim balance, (h) accounts receivable follow-up, (i) payment processing, and (j) collections and problem resolution. These steps are designed to provide the best possible service for a patient at

the pharmacy, while regulating the pharmacy's financial practices.

5. Efficient and accurate completion of pharmacy claims is very important; errors in filing claims slow the reimbursement process and interfere with other work. When errors are made, the consequences may also include lower payment or denied claims and problematic customer relations.

Chapter Review

Multiple Choice

Read the question and select the best response.

1. Which of these terms refers to the selection of prescription medications offered by a health plan?
   A. formulary
   B. prescription drug list
   C. preferred drug list
   D. all of the above

2. What is the final step in the pharmacy billing cycle?
   A. collections and problem resolution
   B. payer adjudication
   C. payment processing
   D. accounts receivable follow-up

3. Which of these terms is the name of the document received by the pharmacy that shows the detail for each claim?
   A. explanation of benefits
   B. remittance advice
   C. pharmacy claim
   D. both A and B

4. When a pharmacy files a patient's claim electronically by EDI, the data are sent between which two entities?
   A. the policyholder and the payer
   B. the pharmacy management system and the policyholder
   C. the pharmacy management system and the payer
   D. the prescriber and the policyholder

5. Which of the following would *not* result from inaccurately filing claims?
   A. lower payments
   B. easier customer relations
   C. denied/delayed claims
   D. disruption of work

6. What is the term for the money paid to a health plan by a patient to receive benefits?
   A. copayment
   B. premium
   C. formulary
   D. pharmacy claim

7. A monetary amount imposed by a health plan after which benefits end is known by which term?
   A. remittance advice
   B. adjudication
   C. coinsurance
   D. maximum benefit limit

8. Which of the following is *not* a government health plan?
   A. Medicare
   B. workers' compensation
   C. adjudication
   D. CHAMPVA

9. The payer's processing of claim data to decide whether a drug is covered by a patient's plan and is properly utilized is known by which name?
   A. adjudication
   B. coinsurance
   C. explanation of benefits
   D. pharmacy benefit

10. Which of the following types of information probably would *not* be stored in a pharmacy management system?
    A. the patient's marital status
    B. the patient's food preferences
    C. the patient's food allergies
    D. the name of the patient's drug plan and identifying numbers

11. Which of the following is *not* part of each step of the billing process?
    A. communicating effectively
    B. following procedures
    C. problem resolution
    D. using information technology

12. What is the program of supervising medical care with the goal of ensuring that patients get needed services in the most appropriate, cost-effective setting known as?

A. managed care plan

B. indemnity plan

C. coinsurance

D. government plan

13. Which of these groups owes a pharmacy the money known as *accounts receivable* after the patient has paid?

A. the provider

B. the payer

C. the policyholder

D. none of the above

14. What is the term for the money a policyholder may owe as a percentage of the fees paid by a health plan?

A. deductible

B. premium

C. benefit

D. coinsurance

15. Which of the following services would *not* be considered medically necessary?

A. procedures that match a patient's illness

B. procedures that are required, rather than elected by the patient

C. procedures that are experimental

D. procedures approved by the Food and Drug Administration

Matching

Match the key term with the appropriate definition.

____ 1. Hospital, physician, and other medical staff members and facilities that offer medical services

____ 2. Services that a medical insurance policy does *not* pay for

____ 3. Percentage of the fees owed by the policyholder

____ 4. Payments made by a health plan for medical services

____ 5. A small fixed fee paid by a patient for a generic drug

____ 6. An individual who enters into an agreement with a health plan to receive medical insurance

____ 7. Appropriate medical treatment given under generally accepted standards of medical practice

____ 8. Amount paid by a policyholder each year before benefits from a health plan will start

____ 9. Fee paid monthly to a health plan by a person who buys medical insurance

____ 10. Organizations that offer financial protection in case of illness or accidental injury

A. copayment

B. coinsurance

C. health plan

D. provider

E. premium

F. benefits

G. deductible

H. policyholder

I. noncovered (excluded) services

J. medically necessary

True/False

Indicate whether the following statements are true or false.

_____ 1. Experimental medical procedures are considered medically necessary.

_____ 2. An agreement between a health plan and a policyholder is known as medical insurance.

_____ 3. Pharmacy technician insurance specialists do *not* need to be concerned with the steps of the pharmacy billing cycle.

_____ 4. Much of the income of a pharmacy practice comes from insurance payments.

_____ 5. The maximum benefit limit set by a health plan is a monetary amount after which benefits end.

_____ 6. The role of the pharmacy technician insurance specialist is vital to the success of a pharmacy.

_____ 7. The three parts of each step of the billing process are following procedures, communicating effectively, and problem resolution.

_____ 8. Pharmacies do not file claims for their patients.

_____ 9. Health plans pay premiums to the policyholder for the benefits they receive.

_____ 10. Indemnity plans and managed care plans are both valid types of medical insurance.

Short Answer

Think carefully about the following questions, and write your answers in the space provided.

1. In what ways does the job of a pharmacy technician insurance specialist affect the success of a pharmacy? Explain your answer.

_____

_____

_____

2. Why is it important for pharmacy technician insurance specialists to follow the pharmacy billing cycle?

_____

_____

_____

Internet Activities

1. Using a search engine such as Google, review some of the various medical insurance plans that are available. Try using key words for your search, such as *insurance, medical, health,* and *plan*.

2. Use a search engine to research topics related to the jobs, training, and certifications available for pharmacy technician insurance specialists in your area and nationwide.

Medicolegal Issues and the Pharmacy

chapter

2

Learning Outcomes

After completing this chapter, you will be able to define the key terms and:

2-1. Explain the purpose of the HIPAA Privacy Rule.

2-2. Distinguish between a covered entity and a business associate under HIPAA.

2-3. Define protected health information (PHI).

2-4. Discuss patients' rights concerning the use and disclosure of their PHI.

2-5. Briefly describe the purpose of the HIPAA Security Rule.

2-6. Describe the HIPAA Electronic Health Care Transactions and Code Sets standards and National Identifiers.

2-7. Discuss some examples of legislative actions that affect pharmacy.

2-8. Explain the purpose of the Health Care Fraud and Abuse Control Program and related laws.

Chapter Outline

Health Care Regulation

Pharmacy Records

HIPAA Privacy Rule

HIPAA Security Rule

HIPAA Electronic Health Care Transactions and Code Sets

Other Legislation Affecting Pharmacy

Fraud and Abuse Regulations

Pharmacy Question and Answers

Key Terms

abuse
audit
authorization
business associates
Centers for Medicare and Medicaid Services (CMS)
clearinghouses
code set
compliance plans
corporate integrity agreement
covered entities
Current Procedural Terminology (CPT)
de-identified health information
designated record set (DRS)
encryption
fraud
Healthcare Common Procedure Coding System (HCPCS)
Health Care Fraud and Abuse Control Program
Health Insurance Portability and Accountability Act (HIPAA) of 1996
HIPAA Electronic Health Care Transactions and Code Sets (TCS)
HIPAA National Identifiers
HIPAA Privacy Rule
HIPAA Security Rule
ICD-9-CM
medical records
minimum necessary standard
National Provider Identifier (NPI)
NCPDP Provider Identification Number
Notice of Privacy Practices (NPP)
Office for Civil Rights (OCR)
Office of the Inspector General (OIG)
password
protected health information (PHI)
qui tam
relator
respondeat superior
subpoena
subpoena *duces tecum*
transactions
treatment, payment, and health care operations (TPO)

Health Care Regulation

To protect consumers' health, both the federal and state governments pass laws that affect the medical services that must be offered to patients. To protect the privacy of patients' health information, additional laws cover the way health care plans and providers such as pharmacies exchange this information as they conduct business. Under these laws, pharmacy technician insurance specialists can share patients' information for payment purposes if they observe the proper procedures to ensure the security of the data. Sharing information incorrectly can lead to serious consequences. This chapter covers the information pharmacy technicians need to correctly handle patients' health information.

CMS Home Page

www.cms.hhs.gov

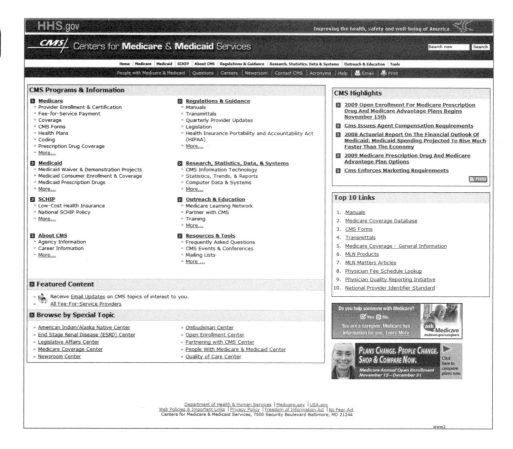

Centers for Medicare and Medicaid Services (CMS)
main federal government agency responsible for health care

Federal Regulation

The main federal government agency responsible for health care is the **Centers for Medicare and Medicaid Services,** known as **CMS** (formerly the Health Care Financing Administration, or HCFA). An agency of the Department of Health and Human Services (HHS), CMS administers the Medicare and Medicaid programs to more than 90 million Americans. CMS implements annual federal budget acts and laws such as the Medicare Prescription Drug, Improvement, and Modernization Act that has created help in paying for drugs and for annual physical examinations for Medicare beneficiaries.

CMS also performs activities to ensure the quality of health care, such as:

• Regulating all laboratory testing other than research performed on humans

- Preventing discrimination based on health status for people buying health insurance
- Researching the effectiveness of various methods of health care management, treatment, and financing
- Evaluating the quality of health care facilities and services

CMS policy is often the model for the health care industry. When a change is made in a Medicare rule, for example, private payers often adopt a similar rule. When federal laws regarding Americans' rights to health care are enacted, CMS often has a key role in developing and implementing them.

The most important recent legislation is called the **Health Insurance Portability and Accountability Act (HIPAA) of 1996.** This law is designed to:

- Protect peoples' private health information
- Ensure health insurance coverage for workers and their families when they change or lose their jobs
- Uncover fraud and abuse

State Regulation

States are also major regulators of the health care industry. Operating an insurance company without a license is illegal in all states. State commissioners of insurance investigate consumer complaints about the quality and financial aspects of health care. State laws ensure the solvency of insurance companies and managed care organizations so that they will be able to pay enrollees' claims. States may also restrict price increases on premiums and other charges to patients, require that policies include guaranteed renewal provisions, and control the situations in which an insurer can cancel a patient's coverage.

Tech Check

What is the main federal government agency responsible for health care?

What legislative act is designed to protect peoples' private health information and uncover fraud and abuse?

Pharmacy Records

Patients' **medical records** that are stored in the pharmacy practice—their medication files and other clinical materials—are legal documents that belong to the pharmacy that created them. But the pharmacy cannot withhold the information in a record from the patient unless providing it would be detrimental to the patient's health. The information belongs to the patient.

Patients control the amount and type of information that is released, except for the use of data to treat them or to conduct the normal business transactions of the practice. Only patients or their legally appointed representatives have the authority to authorize the release of information to anyone not directly involved in their care.

Billing Tip

State-Mandated Benefits

States may require benefits that are not mandated in federal regulations. For example, fifteen states mandate coverage of infertility treatments for women.

Health Insurance Portability and Accountability Act (HIPAA) of 1996 law designed to protect people's private health information, ensure health coverage for workers and their families when they change or lose jobs, and uncover fraud and abuse

medical records patient's medication files and other clinical materials that are legal documents belonging to the pharmacy that created them

Compliance Guideline

Staying Current with HIPAA

HIPAA laws undergo a lengthy review process before being released as final rules. Future changes are expected. Pharmacy technician insurance specialists need to stay current with HIPAA regulations that affect their areas of responsibility.

Internet Resource

CMS HIPAA Home Page

www.cms.hhs.gov/ hipaageninfo/

Pharmacy technician insurance specialists handle issues such as requests for information from patients' pharmacy records. They need to know what information can be released about a patient's conditions and treatments, what information can be legally shared with other providers and health plans, and what information the patient must specifically authorize to be released. The answers to these questions are based on the HIPAA Administrative Simplification provisions.

Congress passed the Administrative Simplification provisions partly because of rising health care costs. A significant portion of every health care dollar is spent on administrative and financial tasks. These costs can be controlled if the business transactions of health care are standardized and handled electronically.

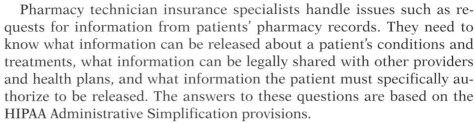

There are three parts to HIPAA's Administrative Simplification provisions:

1. *HIPAA Privacy Rule:* The privacy requirements cover patients' health information.
2. *HIPAA Security Rule:* The security requirements state the administrative, technical, and physical safeguards that are required to protect patients' health information.
3. *HIPAA Electronic Health Care Transactions and Code Sets standards:* These standards require every provider that does business electronically to use the same health care transactions, code sets, and identifiers.

Complying with HIPAA

Health care organizations that are required by law to obey the HIPAA regulations are called **covered entities.** A covered entity is an organization that electronically transmits any information that is protected under HIPAA. Other organizations that work for the covered entities must also agree to follow the HIPAA rules.

covered entities organizations that electronically transmit any information that is protected under HIPAA

Covered Entities

Under HIPAA, three types of covered entities must follow the regulations:

1. *Health plans:* The individual or group plan that provides or pays for medical care and pharmacy benefits.
2. *Health care **clearinghouses:*** Companies that help providers handle such electronic transactions such as pharmacy claims.
3. *Health care providers:* People or organizations that furnish, bill, or are paid for health care in the normal course of business, such as doctors, hospitals, and pharmacy practices, are included under HIPAA. The only excepted entities are those that do not send any claims (or other HIPAA transactions) electronically *and* do not employ any other firm to send electronic claims for them.

Business Associates

HIPAA also affects many others in the health care field. For instance, outside billing services are not covered entities; they are not themselves required to comply with the law. However, they must follow HIPAA's rules in order to do business with covered entities. In HIPAA terms, they are **business associates,** a category that includes law firms, accountants, information technology (IT) contractors, transcription companies, compliance consultants, and collection agencies. Through agreements with their business associates, covered entities make sure that they will perform their work as required by HIPAA.

clearinghouses companies that help providers handle electronic transactions such as pharmacy claims

business associates in HIPAA terms, agencies that must comply with the law in order to do business with covered entities

---

✳ Tech Check

Patients' medication files and other clinical materials are known as what?

Under HIPAA, what are the three types of covered entities that must follow the regulations?

HIPAA Privacy Rule

The HIPAA Standards for Privacy of Individually Identifiable Health Information rule is known as the **HIPAA Privacy Rule.** It was the first comprehensive federal protection for the privacy of health information. Its national standards protect individuals' medical records and other personal health information. Before the HIPAA Privacy Rule became law, the personal information stored in hospitals, physician practices, pharmacies, and health plans was governed by a patchwork of federal and state laws. Some state laws were strict, but others were not.

The Privacy Rule says that covered entities must:

- Have a set of privacy practices that are appropriate for its health care services
- Notify patients about their privacy rights and how their information can be used or disclosed
- Train employees so that they understand the privacy practices

HIPAA Privacy Rule the first comprehensive federal protection for the privacy of health information

🔒 HIPAA Tip

45 CFR Parts 160 and 164

The HIPAA Privacy Rule is also often referred to by its number in the *Federal Register*, which is 45 CFR Parts 160 and 164.

protected health information (PHI) individually identifiable health information that is transmitted or maintained by electronic media

HIPAA Exemptions

Certain benefits are always exempt from HIPAA, including coverage for accident only, disability income coverage, liability insurance, workers' compensation, automobile pharmacy payment and liability insurance, credit-only insurance (such as mortgage insurance), and coverage for on-site provider clinics.

PHI and Release of Information Document

A patient release of information document is not needed when PHI is shared for TPO under HIPAA. However, state law may require authorization to release data, so many providers continue to ask patients to sign releases.

treatment, payment, and health care operations (TPO) term referring to providing and coordinating a patient's medical care, the exchange of information with health plans, and general business management functions

minimum necessary standard precautions a covered entity must take to limit the usage of protected health information by taking reasonable safeguards to protect it from incidental disclosure

- Appoint a privacy official responsible for seeing that the privacy practices are adopted and followed
- Safeguard patients' records

The HIPAA rules do not replace state regulations or other laws that may grant even greater privacy protections. Pharmacies are also free to retain or adopt practices and policies that are more stringent than those required by HIPAA.

Protected Health Information

The HIPAA Privacy Rule covers the use and disclosure of patients' **protected health information (PHI).** PHI is defined as individually identifiable health information that is transmitted or maintained by electronic media, such as over the Internet, by computer modem, or on magnetic tape or compact disks. This information includes a person's:

- Name
- Address (including street address, city, county, and ZIP code)
- Names of relatives and employers
- Birth date
- Telephone numbers
- Fax number
- E-mail address
- Social Security number
- Medical and/or pharmacy record number
- Health plan beneficiary number
- Account number
- Certificate or license number
- Serial number of any vehicle or other device
- Website address
- Fingerprints or voiceprints
- Photographic images

Disclosure for Treatment, Payment, and Health Care Operations

Under HIPAA, patients' PHI can be used and disclosed by providers for treatment, payment, and health care operations. *Use of PHI* means sharing or analysis *within* the entity that holds the information. *Disclosure of PHI* means the release, transfer, provision of access to, or divulging of PHI *outside* the entity holding the information.

Both use and disclosure of PHI are necessary and permitted for **treatment, payment, and health care operations (TPO).** *Treatment* means providing and coordinating the patient's medical care; *payment* refers to the exchange of information with health plans; and *health care operations* are general business management functions.

Minimum Necessary Standard When using or disclosing protected health information, a covered entity must try to limit the information to the minimum amount of PHI necessary for the intended purpose. The **minimum necessary standard** means taking reasonable safeguards to protect PHI from incidental disclosure.

Here are examples of complying with HIPAA:

- A pharmacy technician insurance specialist does not disclose a patient's history of cancer on a workers' compensation claim for pain medication for a sprained ankle. Only the information the recipient needs to know is given.
- A physician's assistant faxes appropriate patient cardiology test results before scheduled surgery.
- A physician sends an e-mail message to another physician requesting a consultation on a patient's case.
- A patient's family member picks up pharmacy supplies and a prescription.

Designated Record Set A covered entity must disclose individuals' PHI to them (or to their personal representatives) when they request access to, or an accounting of disclosures of, it. Patients' rights apply to a **designated record set (DRS).** For a pharmacy, the designated record set means the medication and billing records the pharmacy maintains. For a health plan, the designated record set includes enrollment, payment, claim decisions, and management systems of the plan.

Within the designated record set, patients have the right to:

- Access, copy, and inspect their PHI
- Request amendments to their health information

Compliance Guideline

Health Care Providers and the Minimum Necessary Standard

The minimum necessary standard does not apply to any type of disclosure—oral, written, phone, fax, e-mail, or other—among providers for treatment purposes.

designated record set (DRS) medication and billing records a pharmacy maintains

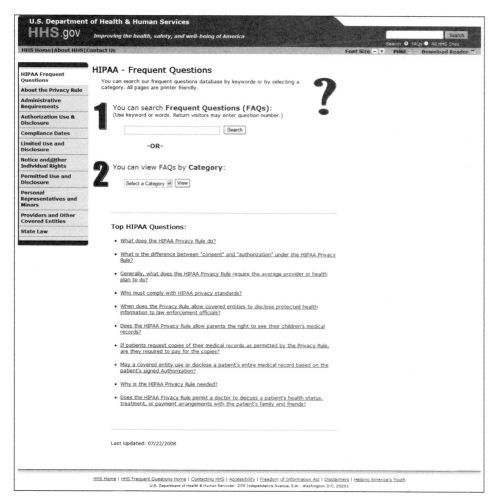

Internet Resource

Questions and Answers on HIPAA Privacy Policies

http://www.hhs.gov/hipaafaq/

Compliance Guideline

Patient Complaints

Patients who observe privacy problems in retail pharmacies can complain either to the practice or to the Office for Civil Rights of the Department of Health and Human Services (HHS). Complaints must be put in writing, either on paper or electronically, and sent to OCR within 180 days.

Compliance Guideline

PHI and Pharmacy Office Staff

Be careful not to discuss patients' cases with anyone outside the practice, including family and friends. Avoid talking about cases, too, in the pharmacy's public areas where other patients might hear. Position computer screens so that only the person working with a file can view it.

Notice of Privacy Practices (NPP) document explaining how patients' protected health information may be used and describing their rights

- Obtain accounting of most disclosures of their health information
- Receive communications from pharmacies via other means, such as in Braille or in foreign languages
- Complain about alleged violations of the regulations and the pharmacy's own information policies

Notice of Privacy Practices Covered entities must give each patient a notice of privacy practices at the first contact or encounter. To meet this requirement, a pharmacy gives patients its **Notice of Privacy Practices (NPP)** (see Figure 2.1) and must clearly post the document in a prominent location. The notice explains how patients' PHI may be used and describes their rights.

Figure 2.1 Notice of Privacy Practices

Notice of Privacy Practices

THIS NOTICE DESCRIBES HOW MEDICAL INFORMATION ABOUT YOU MAY BE USED AND DISCLOSED AND HOW YOU CAN GET ACCESS TO THIS INFORMATION. PLEASE REVIEW IT CAREFULLY.

Roberts Pharmacy Co., including its subsidiaries, is required by law to maintain the privacy of Protected Health Information ("PHI") and to provide you with notice of our legal duties and privacy practices with respect to PHI. PHI is information that may identify you and that relates to your past, present, or future physical or mental health or condition and related health care services. This Notice of Privacy Practices ("Notice") describes how we may use and disclose PHI to carry out treatment, payment, or health care operations and for other specified purposes that are permitted or required by law. The Notice also describes your rights with respect to your PHI. We are required to provide this notice to you by the Health Insurance Portability and Accountability Act ("HIPAA").

Roberts is required to follow the terms of this Notice. We will not use or disclose your PHI without your written authorization, except as described or otherwise permitted by this Notice. We reserve the right to change our practices and this Notice and to make the new Notice effective for all PHI we maintain. Upon request, we will provide any revised Notice to you.

Examples of How We Use and Disclose Protected Health Information About You

The following categories describe different ways that we use and disclose your protected health information. We have provided you with examples in certain categories; however, not every use or disclosure in a category will be listed.

Treatment. We may use your health information to provide and coordinate the treatment, medications, and services you receive. For example, we may contact you regarding medications, equipment, supplies, compliance programs such as drug recommendations, therapeutic substitution, refill reminders, other product or service recommendations such as specialty and infusion therapies, counseling and drug utilization review (DUR), product recalls, or disease state management.

Payment. We may use your health information for various payment-related functions. Example: We may contact your insurer, pharmacy benefit manager, or other health care payer to determine whether it will pay for your medications, equipment, and supplies and the amount of your copayment. We will bill you or a third-party payer for the cost of medications, equipment, and supplies dispensed to you. The information on or accompanying the bill may include information that identifies you, as well as the medications you are taking.

Health Care Operations. We may use your health information for certain operational, administrative, and quality assurance activities. Example: We may use information in your health record to monitor the performance of the staff and pharmacists providing treatment to you. This information will be used in an effort to continually improve the quality and effectiveness of the health care and service we provide. We may disclose health information to business associates if they need to receive this information to provide a service to us, and will agree to abide by specific HIPAA rules relating to the protection of health information.

We may also use your health information to provide you with information about benefits available to you and, in limited situations, about health-related products or services that may be of interest to you. If you register your e-mail address on Roberts.com, or any of our other websites, you may elect to receive this information via e-mail.

We are permitted to use or disclose your PHI for the following purposes. However, Roberts may never have reason to make some of these disclosures.

To Communicate with Individuals Involved in Your Care or Payment for Your Care. We may disclose to a family member, other relative, close personal friend, or any other person you identify PHI directly relevant to that person's involvement in your care or payment related to your care.

Figure 2.1 Notice of Privacy Practices (*cont.*)

Food and Drug Administration (FDA). We may disclose to the FDA, or persons under the jurisdiction of the FDA, PHI relative to adverse events with respect to drugs, foods, supplements, products, and product defects, or post-marketing surveillance information to enable product recalls, repairs, or replacement.

Workers' Compensation. We may disclose your PHI to the extent authorized by and to the extent necessary to comply with laws relating to workers' compensation or other similar programs established by law.

Public Health. As required by law, we may disclose your PHI to public health or legal authorities charged with preventing or controlling disease, injury, or disability.

Law Enforcement. We may disclose your PHI for law enforcement purposes as required by law or in response to a subpoena or court order.

As Required by Law. We will disclose your PHI when required to do so by federal, state, or local law.

Health Oversight Activities. We may disclose your PHI to an oversight agency for activities authorized by law. These oversight activities include audits, investigations, inspections, and credentialing, as necessary for licensure and for the government to monitor the health care system, government programs, and compliance with civil rights laws.

Judicial and Administrative Proceedings. If you are involved in a lawsuit or a dispute, we may disclose your PHI in response to a court or administrative order. We may also disclose health information about you in response to a subpoena, discovery request, or other lawful process instituted by someone else involved in the dispute, but only if efforts have been made, either by the requesting party or us, to tell you about the request or to obtain an order protecting the information requested.

Research. We may disclose your PHI to researchers when their research has been approved by an institutional review board or privacy board that has reviewed the research proposal and established protocols to ensure the privacy of your information.

Coroners, Medical Examiners, and Funeral Directors. We may release your PHI to a coroner or medical examiner. This may be necessary, for example, to identify a deceased person or determine the cause of death. We may also disclose PHI to funeral directors consistent with applicable law to enable them to carry out their duties.

Organ or Tissue Procurement Organizations. Consistent with applicable law, we may disclose your PHI to organ procurement organizations or other entities engaged in the procurement, banking, or transplantation of organs for the purpose of tissue donation and transplant.

Notification. We may use or disclose your PHI to notify or assist in notifying a family member, personal representative, or another person responsible for your care, regarding your location and general condition.

Fundraising. We may contact you as part of a fundraising effort.

Correctional Institution. If you are or become an inmate of a correctional institution, we may disclose to the institution or its agents PHI necessary for your health and the health and safety of other individuals.

To Avert a Serious Threat to Health or Safety. We may use and disclose your PHI when necessary to prevent a serious threat to your health and safety or the health and safety of the public or another person.

Military and Veterans. If you are a member of the armed forces, we may release PHI about you as required by military command authorities. We may also release PHI about foreign military personnel to the appropriate foreign military authority.

National Security, Intelligence Activities, and Protective Services for the President and Others. We may release PHI about you to federal officials for intelligence, counterintelligence, protection to the President, and other national security activities authorized by law.

Victims of Abuse or Neglect. We may disclose PHI about you to a government authority if we reasonably believe you are a victim of abuse or neglect. We will only disclose this type of information to the extent required by law, if you agree to the disclosure, or if the disclosure is allowed by law and we believe it is necessary to prevent serious harm to you or someone else.

Other Uses and Disclosures of PHI

We will obtain your written authorization before using or disclosing your PHI for purposes other than those provided for above (or as otherwise permitted or required by law). You may revoke an authorization in writing at any time. Upon receipt of the written revocation, we will stop using or disclosing your PHI, except to the extent that we have already taken action in reliance on the authorization.

Figure 2.1 Notice of Privacy Practices (*cont.*)

Your Health Information Rights

Obtain a Paper Copy of the Notice upon Request. You may request a copy of our current Notice at any time. Even if you have agreed to receive the Notice electronically, you are still entitled to a paper copy. You may obtain a paper copy from a pharmacy, home care facility, mail service location, or the Privacy Office.

Request a Restriction on Certain Uses and Disclosures of PHI. You have the right to request additional restrictions on our use or disclosure of your PHI by sending a written request to the Privacy Office. We are not required to agree to those restrictions. We cannot agree to restrictions on uses or disclosures that are legally required, or which are necessary to administer our business.

Inspect and Obtain a Copy of PHI. In most cases, you have the right to access and copy the PHI that we maintain about you. To inspect or copy your PHI, you must send a written request to the Privacy Office. We may charge you a fee for the costs of copying, mailing, and supplies that are necessary to fulfill your request. We may deny your request to inspect and copy in certain limited circumstances.

Request an Amendment of PHI. If you feel that PHI we maintain about you is incomplete or incorrect, you may request that we amend it. To request an amendment, you must send a written request to the Privacy Office. You must include a reason that supports your request. In certain cases, we may deny your request for amendment.

Receive an Accounting of Disclosures of PHI. You have the right to receive an accounting of the disclosures we have made of your PHI after April 14, 2003, for most purposes other than treatment, payment, or health care operations. The right to receive an accounting is subject to certain exceptions, restrictions, and limitations. To request an accounting, you must submit a request in writing to the Privacy Office. Your request must specify the time period. The time period may not be longer than six years and may not include dates before April 14, 2003.

Request Communications of PHI by Alternative Means or at Alternative Locations. For instance, you may request that we contact you at a different residence or post office box. To request confidential communication of your PHI, you must submit a request in writing to the Privacy Office. Your request must tell us how or where you would like to be contacted. We will accommodate all reasonable requests.

Where to Obtain Forms for Submitting Written Requests. You may obtain forms for submitting written requests from any Roberts store, home care facility, mail service location, or by contacting the Privacy Officer at Roberts Co. Privacy Office, 321 Main St., Venice, Fl 34285. You can also visit **www.Roberts.com** to obtain these forms.

Incidental Disclosures

Roberts will make reasonable efforts to avoid incidental disclosures of protected health information. An example of an incidental disclosure is conversations that may be overheard between the pharmacy staff and the patient at the drive-thru, as a result of the speaker system. To reduce the likelihood of this happening, we recommend that you go inside the store to the pharmacy for any consultations.

Minors

If you are a minor who has lawfully provided consent for treatment and you wish for Roberts to treat you as an adult for purposes of access to and disclosure of records related to such treatment, please notify a staff member, pharmacist, or the Privacy Office.

For More Information or to Report a Problem

If you have questions or would like additional information about Roberts' privacy practices, you may contact our Privacy Officer at 321 Main St., Venice, Fl 34285. If you believe your privacy rights have been violated, you can file a complaint with the **Privacy Officer** or with the Secretary of Health and Human Services. You can also file a complaint through **www.Roberts.com,** and we will route your complaint to the Privacy Office. There will be no retaliation for filing a complaint.

Effective Date

This Notice is effective as of April 13, 2003.

PHI and Accounting for Disclosures Patients have the right to an accounting of disclosures of their PHI other than for TPO. When a patient's PHI is accidentally disclosed, the disclosure should be documented in the individual's pharmacy record, since the individual did not authorize it and it was not a permitted disclosure. An example is faxing a discharge summary to the wrong physician office.

Authorizations

For use or disclosure other than for TPO, the covered entity must have the patient sign an **authorization** to release the information. Information about substance (alcohol and drug) abuse, sexually transmitted diseases (STDs) or human immunodeficiency virus (HIV), and behavioral or mental health services may not be released without a specific authorization from the patient. The authorization document must be in plain language and must include the following:

- A description of the information to be used or disclosed
- The name or other specific identification of the person(s) authorized to use or disclose the information
- The name of the person(s) or group of people to whom the covered entity may make the use or disclosure
- A description of each purpose of the requested use or disclosure
- An expiration date
- The signature of the individual (or authorized representative) and the date

    In addition, the rule states that a valid authorization must include:

- A statement of the individual's right to revoke the authorization in writing
- A statement about whether the covered entity is able to base treatment, payment, enrollment, or eligibility for benefits on the authorization
- A statement that information used or disclosed after the authorization may be disclosed again by the recipient and may no longer be protected by the rule

A sample authorization form is shown in Figure 2.2.

Uses or disclosures for which the covered entity has received specific authorization from the patient do not have to follow the minimum necessary standard. Incidental use and disclosure are also allowed. For example, the pharmacy practice may use pharmacy logs at the point of sale area.

Requests for Information Other Than for TPO

There are a number of exceptions to the usual rules for release:

- Court orders
- Workers' compensation cases
- Statutory reports
- Research

All these types of disclosures must be logged, and the release information must be available to the patient who requests it.

Charging for Copying

Practices may charge patients a fee for supplying copies of their records but cannot hold records "hostage" while awaiting payment.

authorization document a patient must sign for a covered entity to use or disclose information other than for TPO

PHI and Authorization to Release

To legally release PHI for purposes other than treatment, payment, or health care operations, a signed authorization document is required.

PHI and Practice Policy

The release of protected health information must follow the pharmacy practice's policies and procedures. For example, employees are trained in procedures to verify the identity and authority of a person requesting PHI.

Figure 2.2 Sample Authorization to Use or Disclose Health Information

Patient Name: _____

Health Record Number: _____

Date of Birth: _____

1. I authorize the use or disclosure of the above named individual's health information as described below.

2. The following individual(s) or organization(s) are authorized to make the disclosure: _____

What specific information can be released

3. The type of information to be used or disclosed is as follows (check the appropriate boxes and include other information where indicated)

☐ problem list
☐ medication list
☐ list of allergies
☐ immunization records
☐ most recent history
☐ most recent discharge summary
☐ lab results (please describe the dates or types of lab tests you would like disclosed): _____
☐ x-ray and imaging reports (please describe the dates or types of x-rays or images you would like disclosed): _____
☐ consultation reports from (please supply doctors' names): _____
☐ entire record
☐ other (please describe): _____

4. I understand that the information in my health record may include information relating to sexually transmitted disease, acquired immunodeficiency syndrome (AIDS), or human immunodeficiency virus (HIV). It may also include information about behavioral or mental health services, and treatment for alcohol and drug abuse.

5. The information identified above may be used by or disclosed to the following individuals or organization(s):

Name: _____

Address: _____

To whom

Name: _____

Address: _____

For what purpose

6. This information for which I'm authorizing disclosure will be used for the following purpose:
☐ my personal records
☐ sharing with other health care providers as needed/other (please describe): _____

7. I understand that I have a right to revoke this authorization at any time. I understand that if I revoke this authorization, I must do so in writing and present my written revocation to the health information management department. I understand that the revocation will not apply to information that has already been released in response to this authorization. I understand that the revocation will not apply to my insurance company when the law provides my insurer with the right to contest a claim under my policy.

8. This authorization will expire (insert date or event): _____

If I fail to specify an expiration date or event, this authorization will expire six months from the date on which it was signed.

9. I understand that once the above information is disclosed, it may be redisclosed by the recipient and the information may not be protected by federal privacy laws or regulations.

10. I understand authorizing the use or disclosure of the information identified above is voluntary. I need not sign this form to ensure health care treatment.

Signature of patient or legal representative: _____ Date: _____

If signed by legal representative, relationship to patient

Signature of witness: _____ Date: _____

Distribution of copies: Original to provider; copy to patient; copy to accompany use or disclosure

Note: This sample form was developed by the American Health Information Management Association for discussion purposes. It should not be used without review by the issuing organization's legal counsel to ensure compliance with other federal and state laws and regulations.

Release Under Court Order If the patient's PHI is required as evidence by a court of law, the pharmacy may release it without the patient's approval if a judicial order is received. In the case of a lawsuit, a court sometimes decides that a pharmacist or pharmacy practice staff member must provide testimony. The court issues a **subpoena,** an order of the court directing a party to appear and testify. If the court requires the witness to bring certain evidence, such as a patient pharmacy record, it issues a **subpoena *duces tecum,*** which directs the party to appear, to testify, and to bring specified documents or items.

subpoena order of the court directing a party to appear and testify

subpoena *duces tecum* order of the court directing a party to appear, testify, and bring specified documents or items

Workers' Compensation Cases State law may provide for release of records to employers in workers' compensation cases (see Chapter 5). The law may also authorize release to the state workers' compensation administration board and to the insurance company that handles these claims for the state.

Statutory Reports Some specific types of information are required by state law to be released to state health or social services departments. For example, physicians must make statutory reports for patients' births and deaths and for cases of abuse. Because of the danger of harm to patients or others, communicable diseases such as tuberculosis, hepatitis, and rabies must usually be reported.

A special category of communicable disease control is applied to patients with diagnoses of human immunodeficiency virus (HIV) infection and acquired immunodeficiency syndrome (AIDS). Every state requires AIDS cases to be reported. Most states also require reporting of the HIV infection that causes the syndrome. However, state law varies concerning whether just the fact of a case is to be reported or if the patient's name must also be reported. The practice guidelines reflect the state laws and must be strictly observed, as all these regulations should be, to protect patients' privacy and to comply with the regulations.

Research Data PHI may be made available to researchers who are approved by the practice. When the researcher issues reports or studies based on the information, specific patients' names may not be identified.

De-Identified Health Information

de-identified health information health information that neither identifies nor provides a reasonable basis to identify an individual

There are no restrictions on the use or disclosure of **de-identified health information** that neither identifies nor provides a reasonable basis to identify an individual. For example, these identifiers must be removed: names, record numbers, health plan beneficiary numbers, and biometric identifiers such as fingerprints and voiceprints.

State Statutes

Some state statutes are more stringent than HIPAA specifications. Areas in which state statutes may differ from HIPAA include the following:

- Designated record set
- Psychotherapy notes
- Rights of inmates
- Information complied for civil, criminal, or administrative court cases

Compliance Guideline

PHI and Answering Machines

If possible, ask patients whether staff members may leave messages on answering machines or with friends or family. If this is not done, messages should follow the minimum necessary standard; the staff member should leave a phone number and a request for the patient to call back. For example: "This is the pharmacy with a message for Mr. Warner. Please call us at 203-123-4567."

Each practice's privacy official reviews state laws and develops policies and procedures for compliance with the HIPAA Privacy Rule. The tougher rules are implemented.

Tech Check

What is the name of the first comprehensive federal protection for the privacy of health information?

Under HIPAA, what does PHI stand for?

What term describes taking reasonable safeguards to guard protected health information from incidental disclosure?

What order will a court give to direct a party to appear and testify?

HIPAA Security Rule

HIPAA Security Rule rule that requires covered entities to establish safeguards to protect a patient's protected health information

The **HIPAA Security Rule** requires covered entities to establish safeguards to protect PHI. The rule specifies how to guard data on computers and PC networks, the Internet, and storage disks.

Encryption Is Requried

encryption process of encoding information in such a way that only the person or computer with the key can decode it

Information security is needed when computers exchange data over the Internet. Security measures rely on **encryption,** the process of encoding information in such a way that only the person (or computer) with the key can decode it. Pharmacy management (PM) systems encrypt data traveling between the pharmacy and the Internet, such as patients' Social Security numbers, so that the information is secure.

Security Measures

A number of other security measures help enforce the HIPAA Security Rule. These include:

- Access control, passwords, and log files to keep intruders out
- Backups to replace items after damage
- Security policies to handle violations that do occur

Access Control, Passwords, and Log Files

Billing Tip

Internet Security Symbol

On the Internet, when an item is secure, a small padlock appears in the status bar at the bottom of the browser window.

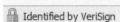

The padlock symbol shows that encryption is being used.

password key to information for individuals who have been granted access rights

Most covered entities use *role-based access*, meaning that only people who need information can see it. Once access rights have been assigned, each user is given a key to the designated databases. Users must enter a user ID and a **password** (the key) to see files to which they have been granted access rights. Passwords prevent unauthorized users from gaining access to information on a computer or network. The PM system also creates activity logs showing who has accessed—or has tried to access—information.

Backups

Backing up is the activity of copying files to another medium so that they will be preserved in case the originals are no longer available. A successful backup plan is critical in recovering from either a minor or major security incident that jeopardizes critical data.

Security Policy

Pharmacies have security policies that inform employees about their responsibilities for protecting electronically stored information. Procedures may include regular periods of time for changing passwords, scheduled backups, and similar guidelines. Often employees must sign confidentiality agreements that prohibit them from disclosing their user names and passwords to others and that require them to inform their manager if they believe that someone has attempted unauthorized access through violations of security measures.

 Tech Check

What does the process of encryption ensure?

What term refers to the activity of copying files to another medium so that they will be preserved in case the originals are no longer available?

 **Compliance Guideline**

Selecting Good Passwords

- Always use a combination of at least six letters and numbers that are not real words and also are not obvious (such as a number string like 123456 or a birth date).

- Do not use a user ID (logon, sign-on) as a password. Even if an ID has both numbers and letters, it is not secret.

- Select a mixture of uppercase and lowercase letters if the system permits, and include special characters such as @, $, or &, if possible.

- Change passwords periodically, but not too often. Forcing frequent changes can make security worse because users are more likely to write down passwords.

HIPAA Electronic Health Care Transactions and Code Sets

The **HIPAA Electronic Health Care Transactions and Code Sets (TCS)** standards make it possible for providers and health plans to exchange electronic data using a standard format and standard code sets.

Standard Transactions

The HIPAA **transactions** standards apply to the electronic data that are regularly sent back and forth between providers, health plans, and employers. Each standard is labeled with both a number and a name. Either the number (such as "the 837") or the name (such as the "HIPAA Claim") may be used to refer to the particular electronic document format.

HIPAA Electronic Health Care Transactions and Code Sets (TCS) code sets that make it possible for providers and health plans to exchange data using a standard format and standard code sets

transactions electronic data that are regularly sent back and forth between providers, health plans, and employers

NUMBER	OFFICIAL NAME
X12 837	Health Care Claims or Equivalent Encounter Information/Coordination of Benefits ("coordination of benefits" refers to an exchange of information between payers when a patient has more than one health plan)
X12 276/277	Health Care Claim Status Inquiry/Response
X12 270/271	Eligibility for a Health Plan Inquiry/Response
X12 278	Referral Authorization Inquiry/Response
X12 835	Health Care Payment and Remittance Advice
X12 820	Health Plan Premium Payments
X12 834	Health Plan Enrollment and Disenrollment
NCPDP Version 1	Batch Standard 1.1

 Billing Tip

The NCPDP is the approved format to submit retail pharmacy *drug* claims. Claims for other services and supplies, and claims from nonretail pharmacies, must use the X12 827 format.

Table 2.1 HIPAA Standard Code Sets

Purpose	Standard
Codes for diseases, injuries, impairments, and other health-related problems	International Classification of Diseases, Ninth Revision, Clinical Modification (ICD-9-CM), Volumes 1 and 2
Codes for procedures or other actions taken to prevent, diagnose, treat, or manage diseases, injuries, and impairments	Physicians' and pharmacists' services: Current Procedural Terminology (CPT) Inpatient hospital services: International Classification of Diseases, Ninth Revision, Clinical Modification, Volume 3: Procedures
Codes for dental services	Current Dental Terminology (CDT-4)
Codes for medications	National Drug Code (NDC)
Codes for other supplies and services	Healthcare Common Procedures Coding System (HCPCS)

Standard Code Sets

code set any group of codes used for encoding data elements

Under HIPAA, a **code set** is any group of codes used for encoding data elements, such as tables of terms and diagnosis codes. Code sets used in the health care industry include coding systems for diseases, treatments, and procedures and for supplies or other items used to perform these actions.

Pharmacy technician insurance specialists encounter several code sets regularly and need to recognize them. The diagnosis codes to describe patients' symptoms and conditions used in the United States are based on the International Classification of Diseases (ICD). The U.S. version of the ninth edition, published in 1979, is known as the ICD-9's Clinical Modification, or **ICD-9-CM,** and is the mandated code set for diagnoses under the HIPAA TCS standards. Physicians also use a code set to report the medical, surgical, and diagnostic services they provide. These codes are selected from the **Current Procedural Terminology (CPT)** data set, which is the mandated code set for physician procedures and services under TCS. Another class of codes under CPT, which is known as the **Healthcare Common Procedure Coding System (HCPCS),** was created to be the mandated code set for reporting supplies, orthotic and prosthetic devices, and durable medical equipment. Standard code sets are listed in Table 2.1.

ICD-9-CM mandated code set for diagnoses under TCS

Current Procedural Terminology (CPT) mandated code set for physician procedures and services under TCS

Healthcare Common Procedure Coding System (HCPCS) mandated code set for reporting supplies, orthotic and prosthetic devices, and durable medical equipment under TCS

EXAMPLE

CODING EXAMPLE: ICD-9-CM

The coding system in ICD-9-CM contains three-digit categories for diseases, injuries, and symptoms. Almost all these three-digit categories are divided into four-digit code groups called subcategories. Many are further divided into five-digit codes called subclassifications. The fourth and fifth digits are separated from the first three by a period. The purpose of the fourth- and fifth-level diagnosis codes is to permit reporting the most specific diagnoses possible. The following is an example of how disorders of the ear would be reported with increasing specificity in ICD-9-CM.

380	Disorders of external ear	
	380.0	Perichondritis of pinna
	380.00	Perichondritis of pinna, unspecified
	380.01	Acute perichondritis of pinna
	380.02	Chronic perichondritis of pinna

CODING EXAMPLE: CPT

EXAMPLE

CPT Category I codes, which are most of the codes in CPT, are five-digit numbers. They are organized into six sections:

Section	Range of Codes
Evaluation and Management	99201–99499
Anesthesia	00100–01999
Surgery	10021–69990
Radiology	70010–79999
Pathology and Laboratory	80048–89356
Medicine	90281–99602

Procedure codes are located by starting with the CPT's index and alphabetical list of procedures, organs, and conditions. The six primary section of the CPT are divided into subsections, which are further divided into headings according to the type of test, service, or body system. The following examples shows how a main term and its subsections and headings appear in the CPT's index:

Tonsils
  Abscess
    Incision and Drainage   **42700**
  Excision   **42825–42826**
    with Adenoids   **42820–42821**
    Lingual   **42870**
    Radical   **42842, 42844–42845**
    Tag   **42860**
  Lingual
    Destruction   **42870**
  Unlisted Services and Procedures   **42999**

CODING EXAMPLE: HCPCS

EXAMPLE

HCPCS was developed by CMS for use in coding services for Medicare patients. The HCPCS coding system has two levels. Level I codes duplicate those from CPT. Level II codes are issued by CMS in the *Medicare*

Carrier Manual. They are called national codes and cover many supplies, such as sterile trays, drugs, and durable medical equipment, as well as other services and procedures not included in CPT. Level II HCPCS codes have five characters, either numbers or letters or a combination of the two. The following example demonstrates some Level II codes and their description.

Code Number	Description
E0607	Home blood glucose monitor
G0168	Wound closure using tissue adhesive(s) only
V5008	Hearing screening

HCPCS modifiers, either two letters or a letter with a number, are also available for use. These modifiers are different from the CPT modifiers.

The Drug Listing Act of 1972 requires registered drug establishments to provide the Food and Drug Administration (FDA) with a current list of all drugs manufactured, prepared, propagated, compounded, or processed by them for commercial distribution. (See Section 510 of the Federal Food, Drug, and Cosmetic Act [Act] [21 U.S.C. § 360]). Each drug product is identified and reported using a unique three-segment number, called the National Drug Code (NDC), which is a universal product identifier for human drugs.

The FDA inputs the full NDC number and the information submitted as part of the listing process into a database known as the Drug Registration and Listing System (DRLS). Several times a year, the FDA extracts some of the information from the DRLS database (currently, properly listed marketed prescription drug products and insulin) and publishes that information in the NDC Directory, which is available online at www.fda.gov/cder/ndc/.

HIPAA National Identifiers

HIPAA National Identifiers
numbers of predetermined length
and structure used for identification
purposes

HIPAA National Identifiers are used to identify:

- Employers
- Health care providers
- Health plans
- Patients

An *identifier* is a unique number of predetermined length and structure, such as a person's Social Security number, that is important because it can be used in electronic transactions. The HIPAA National Identifiers can replace many of the numbers that are currently used.

Employer Identification Number (EIN)

The employer identifier is used when employers enroll or disenroll employees in health plans (X12 834) or make premium payments to plans on behalf of their employees (X12 820). The Employer Identification Number (EIN) issued by the Internal Revenue Service is the HIPAA standard.

National Provider Identifier (NPI)

The **National Provider Identifier (NPI)** is the HIPAA standard for the identification of providers when filing claims and other transactions. The NPI replaces many other identifying numbers that have been in use (called *legacy numbers)*, such as those assigned by each payer to the pharmacy.

However, the NPI does not replace the **NCPDP Provider Identification Number** (NCPDP Provider ID), formerly known as the NABP number, which was developed over twenty-five years ago to provide pharmacies with unique national identifiers that would assist them in interactions with pharmacy payers and claim processors. NCPDP Provider IDs are seven-digit numbers that are assigned to every licensed pharmacy and qualified non-pharmacy dispensing site (NPDS) in the United States. NCPDP currently maintains and updates information on the NCPDP Pharmacy Database, which contains over seventy thousand pharmacies.

An NPI has nine numbers and a check digit, for a total of ten numbers. The federal government assigns NPI numbers to individual providers, such as physicians and nurses, and also to organizations such as hospitals, pharmacies, and clinics. Once assigned, the NPI does not change; it remains with the entity regardless of job or location changes.

All providers that transmit health information electronically must obtain NPIs, even if they use business associates to prepare the transactions. A pharmacy must have both an NPI and an NCPDP Provider ID.

National Provider Identifier (NPI) standard for the identification of providers when filing claims and other transactions

NCPDP Provider Identification Number provides pharmacies with a unique national identifier for use in interactions with payers and claim processors

---

 $ Billing Tip

NPPES Online Database

All NPIs that are issued are stored on the NPPES (National Plan and Provider Enumeration System) and can be accessed to check for accurate NPIs for ordering physicians.

 Tech Check

What standards make it possible for providers and health plans to exchange electronic data using a standard format and standard code sets?

What are HIPAA National Identifiers used for?

Other Legislation Affecting Pharmacy

Pharmacy insurance technician specialists must have a solid understanding of the legislative acts that affect their work. In addition to knowing relevant past legislation, they follow ongoing changes in the industry as they occur.

Medicare Prescription Drug Improvement and Modernization Act of 2003 (MMA)

Among the recent legislative actions that pharmacy insurance technician specialists make themselves familiar with is the Medicare Prescription

Drug, Improvement, and Modernization Act of 2003 (MMA). This legislation provided seniors and individuals with disabilities access to prescription drug plans with more choices and better benefits under Medicare.

E-Prescribing

Electronic prescribing, or e-prescribing, enables physicians to submit prescriptions to pharmacies electronically in the interest of decreasing prescribing errors and increasing efficiency. E-prescribing enables the sending of accurate, error-free, and understandable prescriptions. This feature was included in the MMA and is currently voluntary for physicians and pharmacies.

Electronic Health Record (EHR)

The electronic health record (EHR) is a computer-based record of patient health information that is generated by one or more encounters in any medical care delivery setting. The information includes patient demographics, progress notes, problems, medications, vital signs, past medical history, immunizations, laboratory data, and radiology reports. The EHR can automatically generate a complete record of patient encounters, simplifying and uniting the work for physicians all across health care, to create a reliable and readily available electronic record.

Freedom of Choice

The Freedom of Choice law is a pharmacy law that focuses on the plan member and the pharmacy or pharmacist. It allows the member to select a pharmacy of choice, even if the pharmacy is a nonparticipating pharmacy. The prescription plan cannot deny the nonparticipating pharmacy the right to provide benefits to the member as long as the pharmacy agrees to the terms of the reimbursement and the other terms and conditions of the plan. The patient cannot be financially penalized for obtaining benefits at a nonparticipating provider.

Prescription Drug Equity Act

The federal Prescription Equity Act of 1997 prohibits a prescription drug plan from providing mail-order coverage without also providing non-mail-order prescription benefits. This legislation allows the patient to obtain benefits from a participating community pharmacy as opposed to being able to get benefits only through mail order. State laws may prohibit financial incentives—such as lower copays—to use a mail-order pharmacy rather than a community pharmacy.

Antitrust/Exclusive Pharmacy Contracts

Antitrust laws prohibit trade restraints that prevent competition. An exclusive contract exists when a pharmacy in a particular area contracts with a

---

$ Billing Tip

Savings from E-Prescribing

E-prescribing systems that permit physicians to select lower cost or generic medications can save $845,000 per 100,000 patients annually—and perhaps even more, according to a study funded by the Department of Health and Human Services' Agency for Healthcare Research and Quality (AHRQ)

benefit plan to be the only provider for plan members. Exclusive contracts are legal but may be in violation of antitrust laws.

 Tech Check

What process enables physicians to submit their prescriptions to pharmacies electronically?

What types of laws prohibit trade restraints that prevent competition?

Fraud and Abuse Regulations

Almost everyone involved in the delivery of health care is trustworthy and is devoted to patients' welfare. However, some people are not. Health care fraud and abuse laws help control cheating in the health care system. Are they really necessary? The evidence says that they are. For example, during 2006, the federal government recovered an estimated $2.2 billion in fraud-related judgments and settlements with companies and individuals.

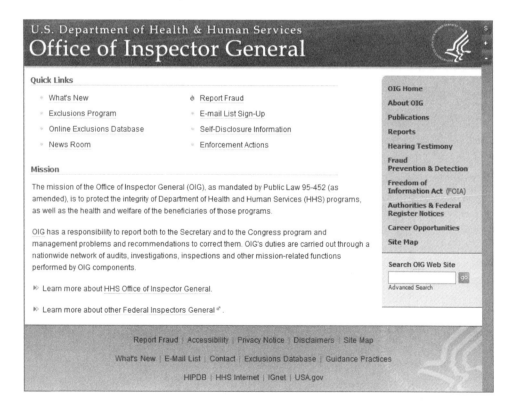

Internet Resource

Office of the Inspector General (OIG) Home Page
http://oig.hhs.gov

The Health Care Fraud and Abuse Control Program

HIPAA created the **Health Care Fraud and Abuse Control Program** to uncover and prosecute fraud and abuse. The HHS **Office of the Inspector General (OIG)** has the task of detecting health care fraud and

Health Care Fraud and Abuse Control Program program created to uncover and prosecute fraud and abuse

Office of the Inspector General (OIG) detects health care fraud and abuse and enforces all laws relating to them

Extending Laws to Private Payers

HIPAA extended existing laws governing fraud in the Medicare and Medicaid programs to all health plans.

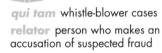

qui tam whistle-blower cases
relator person who makes an accusation of suspected fraud

abuse and enforcing all related laws. The OIG works with the U.S. Department of Justice (DOJ)—the federal department directed by the U.S. Attorney General that houses the Federal Bureau of Investigation (FBI)—to prosecute people suspected of pharmacy fraud and abuse. In 2005, the OIG reported nearly 4,000 fraud and abuse exclusions, 537 criminal actions against individuals and facilities, and 262 civil actions. Two large settlements were a $325 million-plus fraud settlement with HealthSouth Corporation related to Medicare fraud and a $532 million refund from New York State related to Medicaid audits.

Federal False Claims Act

The federal False Claims Act (FCA, 31 USC § 3729), a related law, prohibits submitting a fraudulent claim or making a false statement or representation in connection with a claim. It also encourages reporting suspected fraud and abuse against the government by protecting and rewarding people involved in *qui tam,* or whistle-blower, cases. The person who makes the accusation of suspected fraud is called the **relator.** Under the law, the relator is protected against employer retaliation. If the lawsuit results in a fine paid to the federal government, the whistle-blower may be entitled to 15 to 25 percent of the amount paid. People who blow the whistle are current or former employees of insurance companies or pharmacy practices, program beneficiaries, and independent contractors.

Additional Laws

Additional laws relating to health care fraud and abuse control include:

- An *antikickback statute* (42 USC § 1320a-7b[b]) that makes it illegal to knowingly offer incentives to induce referrals for services that are paid by government health care programs. Many financial actions are considered to be incentives, including illegal direct payments to other physicians and routine waivers of coinsurance and deductibles.
- *Self-referral prohibitions* (called Stark rules) that make it illegal for physicians (or members of their immediate families) to have financial relationships with clinics to which they refer their patients, such as radiology service clinics and clinical laboratory services. (Note, however, that there are many legal exceptions to this prohibition under various business structures.)
- The *Sarbanes-Oxley Act* of 2002 that requires publicly traded corporations to attest that their financial management is sound. These provisions apply to for-profit health care companies. The act includes whistle-blower protection so that employees can report wrongdoing without fear of retaliation.
- *State laws.* Twenty states have their own versions of the federal False Claims Act. For example, a private individual in New Jersey can bring an action alone or by working with the state attorney general against any person who knowingly causes the state to pay a false claim. The bill provides for civil penalties between $5,000 and $10,000 for each verified count of a false claim and imposes damages of up to three times the cost of any losses sustained because of the false claim.

OIG Enforcement Actions for Fraud, Kickbacks, and Theft

Fraud, kickbacks, and theft were the center of three enforcement actions recently announced by the OIG:

- In South Carolina, a physical therapist was sentenced to nineteen months in prison and was fined $400,000 for health care fraud. The therapist billed Medicare as a private insurer for three to five hours of therapy, but performed only one hour.
- In Florida, a durable medical equipment company owner was sentenced to prison for antikickback violations after he received kickbacks from the owner of a pharmacy in exchange for referring patients in need of aerosol medications. The company owner was sentenced to five months in prison and five months of home detention. He was also fined $15,000.
- In Maryland, a former National Institutes of Health purchasing agent was fined $2,400 after she pled guilty to theft of government property. The woman used her government credit card to secure rental cars for personal use.

CASE

Definition of Fraud and Abuse

Fraud is an act of deception used to take advantage of another person. For example, misrepresenting professional credentials and forging another person's signature on a check are fraudulent. Dispensing medications without a valid license is also fraudulent. Fraudulent acts are intentional; the individual expects an illegal or unauthorized benefit to result.

Claim fraud occurs when pharmacies or others falsely report charges to payers. A pharmacy may bill for services that were not performed, overcharge for services, or fail to provide complete services. A patient may exaggerate an injury to get a settlement from an insurance company or may ask a pharmacy insurance specialist to change a date on a script so that it is covered by a health plan.

In federal law, **abuse** means an action that misuses money that the government has allocated, such as Medicare funds. Abuse is illegal because taxpayers' dollars are misspent. An example of abuse is an ambulance service that billed Medicare for transporting a patient to the hospital when the patient did not need ambulance service. This abuse—billing for services that were not medically necessary—resulted in improper payment to the ambulance company. Abuse is not necessarily intentional; it may be the result of ignorance of or not understanding a rule.

fraud act of deception used to take advantage of another person

$ Billing Tip

Fraud Versus Abuse

To bill when the task was not done is fraud; to bill when it was not necessary is abuse.

abuse action that misuses money that the government has allocated

Examples of Fraudulent and Abusive Acts

One aspect of fraud concerns patients who present forged or altered prescriptions. The law holds the pharmacist responsible for knowingly dispensing a prescription that was not issued in the usual course of professional treatment. These are examples of such acts:

- Prescription pads are stolen from physician offices, and prescriptions are written for fictitious patients.

CASE

CVS Caremark was recently involved in a dispute in which it paid $36.7 million to settle allegations of fraud. The money was paid to settle claims that it increased Medicare reimbursement by improperly switching patients to the more expensive form of Ranitidine. Between 2000 and 2006, CVS Caremark allegedly dispensed Ranitidine capsules instead of tablets, netting the company as much as $62 per prescription. Medicaid sets maximum reimbursement prices for the tablet form only, which is less expensive and more frequently prescribed by doctors.

In 2003, a licensed pharmacist filed a whistle-blower lawsuit calling attention to this practice. As a result of the settlement, twenty-three states and the District of Columbia have received money. CVS Caremark also entered into a five-year **corporate integrity agreement** with the OIG, which is a compliance action under which a provider's Medicare billing is monitored by the OIG.

- In an effort to obtain additional amounts of legitimately prescribed drugs, some patients alter physicians' prescriptions.
- Some drug abusers have prescription pads of a legitimate doctor printed with a different call-back number that is answered by an accomplice to verify the prescription.
- Some drug abusers call in their own prescriptions and give their own telephone numbers for call-back confirmation.
- Computers are often used to create prescriptions for nonexistent doctors or to copy legitimate doctors' prescriptions.

Another aspect is fraudulent or abusive claims generated by the pharmacy. Investigators reviewing pharmacy billing work look for patterns like these:

- Intentionally billing for services that were not performed or documented
  Example: A pharmacy bills Medicare for two scripts when only one was filled.
- Reporting services at a higher level than was carried out
  Example: A pharmacy bills a payer for a specialty drug when a generic was dispensed.
- Performing and billing for procedures that are not related to the patient's condition and therefore are not medically necessary
  Example: A pharmacy reports a customer's prescription for a topical cream for acne as medically necessary when the drug has been prescribed as an anti-aging skin treatment.

Enforcement and Penalties

HIPAA privacy regulations are enforced by the **Office for Civil Rights (OCR).** When OCR investigates a complaint, the covered entity must cooperate and provide access to its facilities, books, records, and systems, including relevant protected health information. People who do not comply with HIPAA may be fined. Civil penalties for HIPAA violations—for covered entities, not for business associates—can be up to $100 for each offense, with an annual cap of $25,000 for repeated violations of the same requirement. Criminal penalties, which also apply to the covered entity but not necessarily to staff or business associates, include larger fees and/or prison sentences. Providers can also lose their contracts with payers and can be excluded from participation as providers in all government health care programs.

The Office of the Inspector General enforces rules relating to fraud and abuse. Most billing-related accusations under the False Claims Act are based on the guideline that pharmacies that *knew or should have known* that a claim for service was false can be held liable. The intent to commit fraud does not have to be proved by the accuser in order for the pharmacy to be found guilty. Actions that might be viewed as errors or occasional slips might also be seen as establishing a pattern of violations, which constitutes the knowledge meant by the phrase "knew or should have known."

OIG has the authority to investigate suspected fraud cases and to **audit** the records of providers and payers. In an audit, which is a methodical examination, investigators review selected pharmacy records to see if they match the billing. The accounting records are often reviewed as well. When problems are found, the investigation proceeds and may result in charges of fraud or abuse against the pharmacy.

In some situations, the FBI is brought in, as the following case illustrates:

audit methodical examination of selected pharmacy records

CASE

Operation Goldpill—investigated by seventeen different FBI field offices over a three-year period—targeted pharmacy fraud. In the end, fake prescriptions, false Medicaid billings, unnecessary medical testing, and the illegal sale of prescription drugs to street vendors and corrupt pharmacists were uncovered. Over two hundred pharmacists and others were arrested and convicted before the case was closed.

State agencies, as indicated by the following case, may also be involved in uncovering fraud:

New York Pharmacy Owner Receives Jail in Medicaid Fraud

On November 30, 2005, Maher Ishak, owner of Woodbury Pharmacy, was sentenced by Orange County Court Judge Jeffrey G. Berry to a term of ninety days in jail and five years' probation following his May 5, 2005, guilty plea to grand larceny in the third degree. At his plea, Ishak admitted having stolen $257,000 from the Medicaid program in a fraudulent scheme that spanned nearly six years, from January 9, 1998, through November 10, 2003. During that time, Ishak submitted hundreds of false reimbursement claims for medications that he never dispensed and, in some instances, that had never been prescribed.

Before his sentencing, Ishak repaid the $257,000 that he stole. At his sentencing, he also agreed to repay the Medicaid program an additional $843,455 to resolve civil allegations that he and his pharmacy were overpaid. To date, Ishak has repaid approximately $395,000 of this civil liability. Woodbury Pharmacy, Inc., which had also previously been convicted of grand larceny in the third degree, was ordered by Judge Berry to be jointly liable with Ishak to make full restitution and, in addition, to pay a criminal fine of $5,000.

In total, Ishak will pay $1.1 million to resolve civil and criminal liability.

Compliance Plans

Because of the risk of fraud and abuse liability, pharmacy practices must be sure that all staff members follow billing rules. In addition to responsibility for their own actions, physicians and other medical professionals are liable for the professional actions of employees they supervise. This responsibility is a result of the law of ***respondeat superior,*** which states that an employer is responsible for an employee's actions. Pharmacists are held to this doctrine, so they can be charged for the fraudulent behavior of any staff member.

A wise slogan is that "the best defense is a good offense." To avoid risking liability, pharmacy practices write and implement **compliance plans**

respondeat superior law stating that an employer is responsible for employees' actions

compliance plans plans a pharmacy practice writes and implements to uncover compliance problems and correct them to avoid risking liability

to uncover compliance problems and correct them. A compliance plan is a process for finding, correcting, and preventing illegal pharmacy office practices. It is a written document prepared by a compliance officer and committee that sets up the steps needed to (1) audit and monitor compliance with government regulations, especially in coding and billing, (2) have policies and procedures that are consistent, (3) provide for ongoing staff training and communication, and (4) respond to and correct errors.

Ongoing Compliance Education

Pharmacy staff members receive ongoing training and education in current rules so that they can avoid even the appearance of fraud.

Goals

The goals of the compliance plan are to:

- Prevent fraud and abuse through a formal process to identify, investigate, fix, and prevent repeat violations relating to reimbursement for health care services
- Ensure compliance with applicable federal, state, and local laws, including employment and environmental laws as well as antifraud laws
- Help defend the practice if it is investigated or prosecuted for fraud by substantiating the desire to behave compliantly and to thus reduce any fines or criminal prosecution

Having a compliance plan demonstrates to outside investigators that the practice has made honest ongoing attempts to find and fix weak areas.

Components

Generally, according to the OIG, voluntary plans should contain seven elements:

1. Consistent written policies and procedures
2. Appointment of a compliance officer and committee
3. Training
4. Communication
5. Disciplinary systems
6. Auditing and monitoring
7. Responding to and correcting errors

Following the OIG's guidance can help in the defense against a false claim accusation. Having a plan in place shows that efforts are made to understand the rules and correct errors. This indicates to the OIG that the problems may not add up to a pattern or practice of abuse, but may simply be errors.

 Tech Check

What entity is responsible for detecting health care fraud and abuse and enforcing all laws relating to them?

In federal law, what does the term *abuse* refer to?

Pharmacy practices write and implement compliance plans for what purpose?

Pharmacy Questions and Answers

Pharmacy technician insurance specialists regularly work with patients' PHI and need to be aware of the applicable laws and guidelines to follow under HIPAA and their state, as well as of any rules specific to their pharmacy. Table 2.2 contains questions and answers to situations that may arise in the pharmacy.

Table 2.2 Common Pharmacy Questions and Answers

Question	Answer
1. Can patients have friends or family members pick up their prescriptions for them?	Yes. Pharmacists may use their professional judgment and experience to allow a person other than the patient to pick up a prescription. The patient does not have to provide a list of people eligible to pick up a prescription in advance.
2. Must pharmacies give an NPP to anyone who requests a copy?	Yes. Pharmacies must make this notice available to any person who asks for it and must post it on any website they maintain where information about customer services or benefits can be found.
3. Under HIPAA, is it illegal for a pharmacy to be paid to send a patient a prescription refill reminder without prior authorization?	No. It is not considered marketing for pharmacists to send prescription refill reminders, even if a third party pays for the communications. A prescription refill reminder is considered treatment.
4. Can pharmacists use PHI to fill prescriptions phoned in by the physician of a new patient without consent?	Yes. Under HIPAA, the pharmacist is not required to obtain the patient's consent prior to using or disclosing PHI when it is for TPO.
5. Are pharmacists restricted from giving advice about over-the-counter medicines?	No. Under the HIPAA Privacy Rule, a pharmacist may provide advice to customers about over-the-counter medication.
6. May pharmacies use signing the log book as acknowledgement of the NPP by patients?	Yes. If the patient is clearly informed that signing the log book is also an acknowledgement of the pharmacy's notice, and if the signature is not used as a waiver or permission for anything else in the log book, this is a valid practice.
7. Should pharmacies avoid leaving answering machine or personal messages at a patient's home?	No. It is acceptable for a pharmacy to leave a message on an answering machine or with a family member to tell a patient that a prescription is ready. However, the amount of information disclosed should be limited.
8. Can pharmacists discuss patient matters even if they may be overheard?	Yes. A pharmacist may discuss a prescription at the pharmacy counter or over the phone with a patient or physician, but should do so with sensitivity.

Pharmacy Dialogues

The following dialogues are examples of conversations that may occur at the pharmacy between a pharmacy technician insurance specialist and a patient or customer. These dialogues are based on scenarios described in the questions and answers in Table 2.2. The dialogues correspond with the question numbers in Table 2.2.

Sample Dialogue for Question 1

Customer: I am here to pick up a prescription for my friend.

Technician: Who will you be picking up the prescription for, and does the person want you to pick it up?

Customer: Yes, my friend James Smith asked me to pick it up for him because he has been sick at home for the past few days.

Technician: OK, we will give you the prescription to deliver to Mr. Smith.

Sample Dialogue for Question 2

Patient: Although I am not currently enrolled in your pharmacy, I am wondering if I can receive a copy of your Notice of Privacy Practices.

Technician: Yes, you may have a copy of our notice. I will give you a physical copy, and the information is also available on our website.

Sample Dialogue for Question 6

Patient: Hello, my name is Sarah Jones, and I am here to pick up a new prescription at the pharmacy.

Technician: Here is your prescription, Ms. Jones, along with a copy of our pharmacy's Notice of Privacy Practices.

Patient: Thank you.

Technician: Please sign this log book to indicate that you have picked up your prescription and to verify that you have been given our notice.

Sample Dialogue for Question 7

Technician: Hello, this call is from Mr. Thompson of the Neighborhood Pharmacy. Is Mr. Edwards available?

Customer: No, Mr. Edwards is not here right now. May I take a message?

Technician: Yes, will you please inform Mr. Edwards that his prescription is ready for pickup at our pharmacy?

Customer: OK, I will tell him. Is there anything else he should know about the prescription?

Technician: No, if you tell him it is ready to be picked up, that will be sufficient. Thank you.

Tech Check

Do pharmacies need a list of people eligible to pick up a prescription for a patient in advance?

What information should the pharmacy release when leaving a message for a patient about a prescription?

Chapter Summary

1. Federal and state governments pass laws to protect the privacy of patients' health information that limit how and when this information can be shared. Specifically, the HIPAA Privacy Rule set national standards to protect individuals' medical records and other personal health information. This law replaced a patchwork of state and federal laws that had governed the handling of such information.

2. Three types of covered entities must follow the regulations set by HIPAA. Health plans, health care clearinghouses, and health care providers are all directly subject to these regulations. Business associates, which may include law firms, accountants, information technology (IT) contractors, transcription companies, compliance consultants, and collection agencies, are all required to comply with HIPAA when doing business with covered entities.

3. Covered by the HIPAA Privacy Rule, patients' protected health information (PHI) is defined as individually identifiable health information that is transmitted or maintained by electronic media, such as over the Internet, by computer modem, or on magnetic tape or compact disks. PHI includes demographic information that may be used to identify patients.

4. Under HIPAA, patients' PHI can be used and disclosed by providers for treatment, payment, and health care operations. Covered entities must follow the minimum necessary standard when disclosing PHI, meaning that they must take reasonable safeguards to protect the information from incidental disclosure. Patients have the right to obtain their PHI from the pharmacy's designated record set upon request. PHI may sometimes be released for court orders, workers' compensation cases, statutory reports, and research, when appropriate.

5. Under the HIPAA Security Rule, covered entities are required to establish safeguards to protect PHI. The Security Rule specifies how to guard data on computers and PC networks, the Internet, and storage disks. Security measures rely on encryption, the use of good passwords for access and control, the implementation of a security policy, and the backing up of important information.

6. The HIPAA Electronic Health Care Transactions and Code Sets (TCS) standards enable providers and health plans to exchange electronic data using a standard format and standard code sets. The code sets are a group of codes used for encoding data elements that are used in the health care industry for diseases, treatments, and procedures and for supplies or other items used to perform these actions. HIPAA National Identifiers are used by employers, health care providers, health plans, and patients as unique numbers for identification purposes.

7. Legislative acts continue to affect the pharmacy industry. One of the most recent actions is the Medicare Prescription Drug, Improvement, and Modernization Act of 2003 (MMA). The implementation of e-prescribing options and patients' electronic health records (EHRs) are modernizing the industry. The Freedom of Choice law, the Prescription Equity Act of 1997, and antitrust laws are among the actions with ongoing affects on pharmacy.

8. The Health Care Fraud and Abuse Control Program was created by HIPAA to uncover and prosecute fraud and abuse. The HHS Office of the Inspector General (OIG) is in charge of detecting health care fraud and abuse and enforcing the relevant laws. The Office for Civil Rights (OCR) enforces the HIPAA privacy regulations and investigates complaints against covered entities. Pharmacy practices often create and implement compliance plans to protect against the risks of compliance problems and liability.

Chapter Review

Multiple Choice

Read the question and select the best response.

1. The use and disclosure of patients' protected health information is acceptable for all of these reasons *except* which one?
   - A. education
   - B. payment
   - C. treatment
   - D. health care operations

2. When is it acceptable for a covered entity to release de-identified health information?
   - A. under court order
   - B. for research
   - C. for payment purposes
   - D. at all times

3. What does a covered entity need to have a patient sign to release information for use other than TPO?
   - A. minimum necessary standard
   - B. designated record set
   - C. authorization
   - D. Notice of Privacy Practices

4. Which legislation prohibits a prescription drug plan from providing mail-order coverage without also providing non-mail-order prescription benefits?
   - A. the Freedom of Choice Law
   - B. the Prescription Equity Act of 1997
   - C. Health Insurance Portability and Accountability Act (HIPAA) of 1996
   - D. Medicare Prescription Drug, Improvement, and Modernization Act of 2003

5. When should a pharmacy give a patient its Notice of Privacy Practices?
   - A. at the first contact or encounter
   - B. when the patient asks for it
   - C. after the patient has become a repeat customer
   - D. It is not necessary for a pharmacy to give it to a patient if it is posted

6. Which of the following is not one of the three parts of HIPAA's Administrative Simplification provisions?
   - A. HIPAA Security Rule
   - B. HIPAA Transaction Rule
   - C. HIPAA Privacy Rule
   - D. HIPAA Electronic Health Care Transactions and Code Sets standards

7. The term referring to taking reasonable safeguards to protect PHI from incidental disclosure is known by what name?
   - A. treatment, payment, and health care operations
   - B. authorization
   - C. Current Procedural Terminology
   - D. minimum necessary standard

8. Which actions are performed by CMS to ensure the quality of health care?
   - A. preventing discrimination based on health status for people buying health insurance
   - B. evaluating the quality of health care facilities and services
   - C. regulating all laboratory testing other than research performed on humans
   - D. all of the above

9. According to the OIG, which component does not necessarily need to be included in a voluntary compliance plan?
   - A. employee payment plan
   - B. communication
   - C. consistent written policies and procedures
   - D. auditing and monitoring

10. The first comprehensive federal protection for the privacy of health information is known by what name?
    - A. HIPAA Security Rule
    - B. HIPAA Transaction Rule
    - C. HIPAA Privacy Rule
    - D. HIPAA Electronic Health Care Transactions and Code Sets standards

11. Which legislation requires covered entities to establish safeguards to protect PHI?
    - A. HIPAA Security Rule
    - B. HIPAA Transaction Rule
    - C. HIPAA Privacy Rule
    - D. HIPAA Electronic Health Care Transactions and Code Sets standards

12. The Health Insurance Portability and Accountability Act (HIPAA) of 1996 was designed to do all of the following *except*
    - A. uncover fraud and abuse
    - B. protect peoples' private health information
    - C. enable physicians to use electronic prescribing
    - D. ensure health insurance coverage for workers and their families when they change or lose their jobs

47

13. Which of the following would be the strongest password?

A. Bobjones

B. 7hZ#1m

C. 02468

D. Jimmy1998

14. Which of the following information would you *not* expect to see on a patient's protected health information?

A. employment history

B. e-mail address

C. Social Security number

D. photographic images

15. Which of these is the HIPAA code set used for documenting diagnoses?

A. ICD-9-CM

B. Current Procedural Terminology

C. Healthcare Common Procedure Coding System

D. National Drug Code

16. Which of these is the HIPAA code set used for reporting supplies, orthotic and prosthetic devices, and durable medical equipment?

A. ICD-9-CM

B. Current Procedural Terminology

C. Healthcare Common Procedure Coding System

D. National Drug Code

17. What is the name of the main federal government agency responsible for health care?

A. Office for Civil Rights

B. Centers for Medicare and Medicaid Services

C. Office of the Inspector General

D. Covered Entity

18. Which term is used to describe whistle-blower cases?

A. *respondeat superior*

B. *qui tam*

C. subpoena

D. subpoena *duces tecum*

19. Under HIPAA, which of these is *not* defined as a covered entity that must follow the regulations?

A. health plan

B. health care provider

C. compliance consultant

D. health care clearinghouse

20. What is the name of a court order that directs the party to appear, to testify, and to bring specified documents or items?

A. *respondeat superior*

B. *qui tam*

C. subpoena

D. subpoena *duces tecum*

....

Matching

Match the key term with the appropriate definition.

_____ 1. Act of deception used to take advantage of another person

_____ 2. Requires covered entities to establish safeguards to protect a patient's protected health information

_____ 3. An outside agency that must comply with the law in order to do business with covered entities

_____ 4. An organization that electronically transmits information that is protected under HIPAA

_____ 5. A methodical examination of selected pharmacy records

_____ 6. Individually identifiable health information that is transmitted or maintained by electronic media

_____ 7. The first comprehensive federal protection for the privacy of health information

A. HIPAA Privacy Rule

B. HIPAA Security Rule

C. abuse

D. designated record set

E. Notice of Privacy Practices

F. covered entity

G. business associate

H. fraud

I. audit

J. protected health information

____ 8. Document explaining how patients' protected health information may be used and describing their rights

____ 9. Medication and billing records a pharmacy maintains

____ 10. Action that misuses money that the government has allocated

True/False

Indicate whether the following statements are true or false.

____ 1. The first comprehensive federal protection for the privacy of health information is known as the HIPAA Security Rule.

____ 2. There are no restrictions on the use or disclosure of de-identified health information.

____ 3. Information in a patient's medical records belongs to the pharmacy only.

____ 4. E-prescribing enables sending of accurate, error-free, and understandable prescriptions.

____ 5. Protected health information may sometimes be released for reasons other than patients' treatment, payment, and health care operations.

____ 6. Accountants and collection agencies may be business associates, in HIPAA terms.

____ 7. The most important recent legislation in the health care industry is called the Health Insurance Portability and Accountability Act (HIPAA) of 1996.

____ 8. ICD-9-CM is the mandated code set for physician procedures and services under the HIPAA TCS standards.

____ 9. Covered entities do not have to give patients a Notice of Privacy Practices at the first contact or encounter.

____ 10. The Office for Civil Rights is responsible for assigning compliance plans for pharmacies to follow.

Short Answer

Think carefully about the following questions, and write your answers in the space provided.

1. Imagine that you are employed as a pharmacy technician insurance specialist for Nationwide Pharmacy. Make up a password to use to keep your files secure. Why did you choose this password?

_____

_____

2. As an employee, how would you respond to another staff member who asked to see your latest claim files in order to see how you handled a particular situation?

_____

_____

3. Examine the sample Notice of Privacy Practices in Figure 2.1. Do any components surprise you? Are there any that you had not considered? If so, why do you think these components are necessary?

_____

_____

_____

Internet Activities

1. Using a search engine such as Google, search for information on some of the unique state statutes on protected health information in your area.

2. Use a search engine to look for examples in the news of abuse and fraud in the medical field. Observe and consider the consequences for such violations and the corresponding need for pharmacies to protect themselves.

Private Insurance Payers and Plans

3

 Learning Outcomes

After completing this chapter, you will be able to define the key terms and:

3-1. Compare and contrast employer-based and individual plans.

3-2. Discuss the major types of health plans.

3-3. Describe patients' financial responsibilities under various types of pharmacy benefit plans.

3-4. Compare and contrast the three types of formularies.

3-5. Explain the concept of a tier.

3-6. Calculate patients' payments due for pharmacy benefits under tiered private plans.

 Chapter Outline

Private Insurance

Types of Health Plans

Pharmacy Plan Benefits

Pharmacy Benefit Management Techniques

Calculating Charges

Key Terms

any willing provider

capitation

closed formulary

compounded medications

consumer-driven health plan (CDHP)

covered expenses

disease management (DM) programs

drug utilization review

family deductible

group health plan (GHP)

health maintenance organization (HMO)

individual deductible

individual health plan (IHP)

member pharmacy network

open enrollment period

open formulary

out-of-network

out-of-pocket expenses

pharmacy benefit manager (PBM)

preferred provider organization (PPO)

prescription drug deductible amount

prescription legend drug

prior authorization (preauthorization)

restricted formulary

specialty drug

therapeutic interchange

tier

Private Insurance

People who are not covered by entitlement programs such as government-sponsored health insurance are usually covered by private insurance. Many employers offer their employees the opportunity to become covered under employee health care benefit plans. Sponsorship of medical insurance is an important benefit to employees, and it gives employers federal income tax advantages. Self-employed people may buy individual health coverage.

Employer-Sponsored Medical Insurance

group health plan (GHP)
medical insurance coverage that employers buy from insurance companies for their employees

Many employees have medical insurance coverage under **group health plans (GHP)** that their employers buy from insurance companies. Human resource departments manage these health care benefits, negotiating with health plans and then selecting products to offer employees. Both basic plans and riders are offered. *Riders*, also called options, may be purchased by employees to add coverage such as vision and dental services. A popular rider is for complementary health care, covering treatments such as chiropractic/manual manipulation, acupuncture, massage therapy, dietetic counseling, and vitamins and minerals.

Employers may *carve out* certain benefits—that is, change standard coverage or providers—during negotiations to reduce the price. An employer may:

pharmacy benefit manager (PBM) third-party administrator of prescription drug programs that processes and pays prescription drug claims

- Omit a specific benefit, such as coverage of prescription drugs.
- Use a different network of providers for a certain type of care, such as negotiating with a local practice network for mental health coverage.
- Hire (either directly or through the health plan) a **pharmacy benefit manager (PBM)** to operate the prescription drug benefit more inexpensively. Because PBMs do this work for many employers, they represent a large group of buyers and can negotiate favorable prices with pharmaceutical companies.

> ### (fyi) Pharmacy Benefit Managers
>
> A PBM is a third-party administrator of prescription drug programs that processes and pays prescription drug claims. It also is responsible for developing and maintaining the formulary for the plan, contracting with pharmacies, providing cards to beneficiaries, and negotiating discounts and rebates with drug manufacturers.
>
> The aim of a PBM is to better manage the pharmacy benefit for the plan beneficiaries. A pharmacy benefit manager may, for example, choose a mail-order option for filling prescriptions as part of a corporate health insurance plan. When used with member cost-sharing like copayments, the PBM can help employers ensure employee satisfaction, convenience, and access to affordable drug therapies.
>
> Many PBMs earn profits by keeping the money saved by paying manufacturers wholesale prices and charging health plans higher prices. Others generate profits by charging flat, per claim, or per member administrative fees.
>
> Some PBMs are under exclusive contracts with single large organizational pharmacies or buyers, such as PharmaCare (part of CVS) and Walgreens Health Initiatives (part of Walgreens), or managed care organizations, such as Prescription Solutions, a subsidiary of UnitedHealth Group. Others are independent entities, such as Medco Health Solutions and Express Scripts. Many PBMs own their own mail-order pharmacies. This service is supported by access to a pharmacist when a patient needs specific guidance about a medication.

Figure 3.1 Example of Selecting Benefits During Open Enrollment

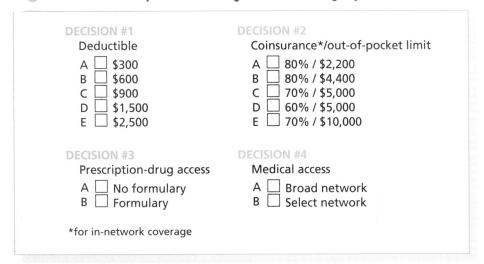

The group health plan specifies the rules for eligibility and the process of enrolling and disenrolling members. Rules cover employment status, such as full-time, part-time, disabled, and laid-off or terminated employees, as well as the conditions for enrolling dependents. Many plans have a *waiting period*, an amount of time that must pass before a newly hired employee or a dependent is eligible to enroll. The waiting period is the time between the date of hire and the date the insurance becomes effective.

During specified periods (usually once a year) called **open enrollment periods,** the employee chooses a particular set of benefits for the coming benefit period (see Figure 3.1). The employer provides tools (often Internet-based) and information to help employees match their personal and family needs with the best-priced plans. Employees can customize the policies by choosing to accept various levels of premiums, deductibles, and other costs.

The plan may impose different eligibility rules on a *late enrollee*, an individual who enrolls in a plan at a time other than the earliest possible enrollment date or a special enrollment date. For example, special enrollment may occur when a person becomes a new dependent through marriage.

Federal Employees Health Benefits Program

The largest employer-sponsored health program in the United States is the *Federal Employees Health Benefits (FEHB) program*, which covers more than 8 million federal employees, retirees, and their families through more than 250 health plans from a number of carriers. FEHB is administered by the federal government's Office of Personnel Management (OPM), which receives and deposits premiums and remits payments to the carriers. Each carrier is responsible for furnishing identification cards and benefits brochures to enrollees, adjudicating claims, and maintaining records.

Self-Funded Health Plans

To save money, some large employers cover the costs of employee medical benefits themselves rather than buying insurance from other companies. They create self-funded (or self-insured) health plans that do not pay premiums to an insurance carrier or a managed care organization. Instead, self-funded

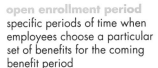

open enrollment period
specific periods of time when employees choose a particular set of benefits for the coming benefit period

HIPAA Tip

Group Health Plan Regulation

Employer-sponsored group health plans must follow federal and state laws that mandate coverage of specific benefits or treatments and access to care. When a state law is more restrictive than the related federal law, the state law is followed.

Internet Resource

State Departments of Insurance
http://www. healthinsurance.com/ insurance_departments. html

health plans "insure themselves" and assume the risk of paying directly for medical services, setting aside funds with which to do so. The employer establishes the benefit levels and the plan types offered to employees. Self-funded health plans may set up their own provider networks or, more often, lease a managed care organization's networks. They may also buy other types of insurance—like a vision package—instead of insuring the benefit themselves.

In contrast to employer-sponsored "fully insured plans," which are regulated by state laws, self-funded health plans are regulated by the federal Employee Retirement Income Security Act of 1974 (ERISA), which is run by the Employee Benefits Security Administration (EBSA) of the federal Department of Labor.

Individual Health Plans

individual health plan (IHP) medical insurance plan purchased by an individual

Individual health plans (IHP) can be purchased. Almost 10 percent of people with private health insurance have individual plans. People often elect to enroll in individual plans, although coverage is expensive, in order to continue their health insurance between jobs. Purchasers also include self-employed entrepreneurs, students, recent college graduates, and early retirees. Individual insurance plans usually have basic benefits without the riders or additional features associated with group health plans.

$ Billing Tip

Timely Payments

Group health plans must follow the state's Clean Claims Act and/or Prompt Payment Act and pay claims they accept for processing on a timely basis. ERISA (self-funded) plans are obligated by the federal Department of Labor to follow similar rules.

❋ Tech Check

What job do employers hire pharmacy benefit managers to perform?

What is the largest employer-sponsored health program in the United States?

In what type of insurance do people often enroll in order to continue their health insurance between jobs?

Types of Health Plans

Group health plans and individual plans are structured into a number of plan types. Most insured patients have medical coverage under a managed care plan, while a few have fee-for-service plans. Pharmacy technician insurance specialists need to become familiar with patients' health plans because the type of health plan affects the payments that patients must make for pharmacy benefits.

The major types of health insurance plans are summarized in Table 3.1 and described in the following section.

Preferred Provider Organizations

preferred provider organization (PPO) most popular type of managed care organization that combines flexibility in patients' choice of physicians with reduced costs for medical services

network group of participating providers, including physicians, hospitals, and pharmacies, created by a managed care organization for its policyholders

The **preferred provider organization (PPO)** is the most popular type of managed care organization. PPOs have the largest membership because patients like the way they combine flexibility in the choice of physicians with reduced costs for medical services.

A PPO is a managed care organization that creates a **network** of physicians, hospitals, and pharmacies for its policyholders. These providers sign participation contracts with the PPO under which they agree to accept

Table 3.1 Comparison of Major Health Plan Types

Plan Type	Provider Options	Cost Containment	Features
Preferred provider organization (PPO)	Network or out-of-network providers	• Referral not required for specialists • Fees are discounted • Preauthorization for some procedures	• Higher cost for out-of-network providers • Preventive care coverage varies
Health maintenance organization (HMO)	Network only	• Primary care physician paid by employment contract or capitation • Specialists paid according to a contractual arrangement • No payment for out-of-network nonemergency services	• Only network provider visits covered • Covers preventive care
Point-of-service (POS)	Network providers or out-of-network providers	• Within network, primary care physician manages care	• Lower copayments for network providers • Higher costs for out-of-network providers • Covers preventive care
Indemnity	Any provider	• Little or none • Preauthorization required for some procedures	• Higher costs • Deductibles • Coinsurance • Preventive care not usually covered
Consumer-driven health plan	Usually similar to PPO	• Increases patient awareness of health care costs • Patient pays directly until high deductible is met	• High deductible • Low premium

reduced fees in exchange for access to a large pool of potential patients who may choose to use their services.

Patients who belong to a PPO are encouraged, but not required, to see providers that are in the network, such as a **member pharmacy.** If patients receive services from **out-of-network** providers, the plan pays lower benefits. For example, a larger copayment is usually required if the member fills a prescription at a nonmember pharmacy.

Health Maintenance Organizations

In **health maintenance organizations (HMOs),** another popular type of managed care organization, patients enroll by paying fixed premiums and very small (or no) copayments when they need services. HMOs have been popular because of their low costs, although in exchange for paying less, patients give up the flexibility of choosing their own physicians. Instead, they must use health care providers from the plan's network in order to have medical services covered.

member pharmacy pharmacy that falls within the network created by a managed care organization

out-of-network term for physicians, hospitals, and pharmacies that are not part of the network created by a managed care organization for its policyholders

health maintenance organization (HMO) type of managed care organization where patients pay fixed premiums and very small (or no) copayments when they need services

In some plans, a primary care physician (PCP), also known as a gate-keeper, is assigned to each patient. This physician, usually a family or internal medicine doctor, directs all aspects of the patient's care. The plan may require the PCP to authorize visits to specialists.

HMOs have various contractual arrangements with providers. In some cases, physicians are employees of the HMO and work full-time seeing patients who are members of the plan. In other structures, physicians are self-employed members of the HMO's network and see both HMO policyholders and nonmember patients in their practice. In this type of structure, physicians receive a fixed payment from the HMO for each member patient, rather than reimbursement for the services provided. For each patient there is a single fee, usually paid to the PCP monthly, regardless of the number of times the patient visits the physician. This way of paying is called **capitation.**

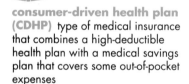

capitation fee usually paid monthly by a patient to the primary care physician regardless of the number of times the patient visits the physician

Point-of-Service Plans

Because many HMO patients do not wish to accept services from only network providers, some HMOs have become *point-of-service (POS) plans*. Patients who choose this option do not have to use only the HMO's physicians. However, if they choose to see physicians outside the HMO's network, they must pay more, such as by making larger copayments. This option makes the HMO more like a PPO in terms of choices available to the patients.

Indemnity Plans

Under traditional indemnity (fee-for-service) plans, the payments physicians receive are based on their regular charges for services, and patients owe coinsurance based on those fees. Currently, though, in many plans, the payer negotiates a discount for its members from the physician, just as in a PPO or POS plan. In fact, there is a great deal of overlap among the features of the various types of plans as payers attempt to control costs. Figure 3.2 provides an overview of the range of plans that might be offered by one payer. It shows the trade-offs for patients between the lowest price and the highest flexibility. It also lists the insurance options, such as prescription drug coverage, that patients can buy from this payer.

Consumer-Driven Health Plans

consumer-driven health plan (CDHP) type of medical insurance that combines a high-deductible health plan with a medical savings plan that covers some out-of-pocket expenses

Because of the growing costs of providing health care coverage to employees, employers search for ways to control this expense. One way is to require employees to pay more of the costs themselves, such as by increasing annual premiums and copayments. Another way is to offer **consumer-driven health plans (CDHP).** These plans were first made possible by federal laws that allow employees to avoid paying taxes on the cost of the plan on their federal income taxes, just as a federal law created individual retirement accounts (IRAs) to encourage people to save for retirement by not taxing the money saved in these accounts until it is withdrawn.

> **fyi**
>
> Some of the names of the various types of CDHPs are health savings account (HSA), flexible spending account (FSA), and health reimbursement arrangement (HRA).

Figure 3.2 Medical Group Plans Offered by Payer

	Maximum Provider Choice	◄──────────────────────►		Maximum Control of Cost and Quality
	Indemnity	In Network or Out of Network		In Network Only
	Managed Indemnity	**PPO/Open Access**	**Point-of-Service**	**HMO/Exclusive Provider**
Network	None; use any provider	220,000 physicians 4,300 hospitals	150,000 physicians 2,000 hospitals	150,000 physicians 2,000 hospitals
Care Managed by Primary Care Physicians (PCP)	No	No	Yes: Open access OB/GYN, behavioral, vision	Yes: Open access OB/GYN, behavioral, vision
Access to Providers	May use any provider	Use any PPO network provider; may use out-of-network providers at a higher cost	Use network providers; may use out-of-network providers at a higher cost	Must use network providers
Provider Compensation	Fee-for-service, reasonable and customary rate	**In Network:** Discounted fee-for-service **Out of Network:** Fee-for-service, reasonable and customary rate	**In Network:** Capitation and discounted fee-for-service **Out of Network:** Fee-for-service, reasonable and customary rate	Capitation and discounted fee-for-service
Options	**Prescription Drug Coverage Behavioral Care Dental Care Vision Care Medicare HMO Life and Disability Expectant Mother**			

Consumer-driven health plans combine two elements. The first element is a health plan, usually a PPO, that has a high deductible (such as $1,000) and low premiums. The second element is a special "savings account" that is used to pay medical bills before the deductible has been met. The savings account, similar to an individual retirement account, lets people put aside untaxed wages that they can use to cover their out-of-pocket medical expenses. This account may be managed by the employer or by an outside institution, like a bank. Some employers contribute to employees' accounts as a benefit, while others require employees to fund them alone.

Cost control in consumer-driven health plans begins with the fact that the patient is paying for health care services directly. Both insurance companies and employers believe that paying for medical services causes patients to be careful consumers of health care. The other controls typical of a PPO, such as in-network savings, are also in effect.

 Tech Check

What are the five major types of health plans?

Which is the most popular type of managed care organization?

Pharmacy Plan Benefits

The pharmacy benefits that a beneficiary receives vary according to the type of health plan in which they are enrolled. Specifically, patients' payments and medical coverage depend on their health insurance. For these reasons, pharmacy technician insurance specialists need to be familiar with patients' health plans.

Covered and Noncovered Expenses

Covered expenses for outpatient prescription drugs are limited to charges from a licensed pharmacy for:

prescription legend drug medication whose label is required to bear the legend "Caution: federal law prohibits dispensing without a prescription"

- A **prescription legend drug**—any medication whose label is required to bear the legend "Caution: federal law prohibits dispensing without a prescription"
- A compounded medication of which at least one ingredient is a prescription legend drug
- Injectable insulin dispensed at the written prescription of a doctor
- Any drug that, under the applicable state law, may be dispensed only upon the written prescription of a doctor
- Hypodermic needles or syringes prescribed by a doctor for the purpose of administering medications covered under the policy

covered expenses expenses incurred by or on behalf of a covered person for supplies that are ordered by a doctor, are medically necessary, and are not excluded by any provision of the policy

The term **covered expenses** means expenses actually incurred by or on behalf of a covered person for supplies that are ordered by a doctor and medically necessary (provided because of an injury or illness) and not excluded by any provision of the policy. *Noncovered expenses* are those the policy does not cover that must be paid by the insured.

Exceptions to Coverage

Pharmacy benefits do not include the following:

- In many policies, expenses that are higher than the cost of a generic drug when the insured's physician authorizes the use of a generic equivalent but the insured elects to buy the brand-name drug
- Immunization agents, biological sera, blood, or blood plasma
- Medication received while the covered person is a patient at an institution that has a facility for dispensing pharmaceuticals (such as during a hospital stay)

- A refill dispensed more than one year from the date of a doctor's order
- Medication that is to be taken by the covered person, in whole or in part, at the place where it is dispensed

 Tech Check

On what do patients' payments and medical coverage depend?

Expenses that a policy does not cover and must be paid by the insured are known by what name?

Pharmacy Benefit Management Techniques

To control costs, employers—primarily through their PBMs—have a number of techniques, including:

- Pharmacy network management
- Formulary management
- Drug utilization management
- Mail service
- Disease management programs

Employers must balance cost-containment efforts with employee satisfaction, convenience, and access to affordable drugs. Pharmacy network sizes vary, and the majority of states have **"any willing provider"** laws requiring PBMs to contract with any pharmacies willing to accept their reimbursement rates. Formularies range greatly in their restrictiveness and the generic drugs they offer, and the drugs prescribed to patients are reviewed to ensure that safe and appropriate practices are followed. Obtaining drugs from mail-order pharmacies is cost-effective and is encouraged by employers, who offer discounts to participating employees.

any willing provider state laws requiring pharmacy benefit managers to contract with any pharmacy willing to accept their reimbursement rates

Network Requirements

PBMs offer a range of broad to narrow retail pharmacy networks. A narrower network gives the PBM more purchasing power by limiting the pharmacies at which members are covered, so that greater discounts can be negotiated. Beneficiaries must fill prescriptions at member pharmacies for the best price, except in certain cases involving:

- Emergency situations
- Medications that are needed while the beneficiary is traveling and unable to use a member pharmacy
- Inability of member pharmacies to fill a particular prescription in a timely manner

 Compliance Guideline

Over half of the states have "any willing provider" laws requiring PBMs to contract with any pharmacies willing to accept their reimbursement rates.

Formulary

The formulary is a fundamental tool for the PBM. It is a list of the plan's preferred drugs within each therapeutic class. Formulary options range from the least restrictive **open formulary** to the most restrictive **closed formulary.** An open formulary will sometimes cover medications that are not listed in the formulary, while a closed formulary will not provide coverage

 open formulary least restrictive type of formulary, which will sometimes cover medications that are not listed

closed formulary type of formulary that will not provide coverage for unlisted drugs without an authorized medical exception from a physician

restricted formulary type of formulary that limits the drugs listed to generics or limited medications within a drug class

tier specific list of drugs within a formulary

compounded medications medications containing one or more ingredients that are prepared on-site by a pharmacist

specialty drug category of medication including biotech and other drugs that are designed to treat serious diseases such as cancer, multiple sclerosis, and rheumatoid arthritis and other inflammatory maladies

for these drugs unless a physician authorizes a medical exception. A **restricted formulary** limits the drugs listed in the formulary to generics only or to limited medications within a drug class.

Certain medications in the formulary have notations, such as *N* (for "notification"), *QL* (for "quantity limitations"), *QD* (for "quantity duration"), and *DS* (for "diabetic supplies").

The Concept of Tiers

Formularies are managed by the PBM into **tiers.** A tier is a specific list of drugs. Plans may have several tiers, and each represents a different cost to the beneficiary. The insured's copayment depends on which tier the particular drug is listed in. For example, a first-tier drug might have a copay of $5, while a third-tier drug might require cost-sharing of $25. A two-tier structure is usually divided into generics versus brand-name medications. Three-tier and four-tier cost-sharing structures are popular because they allow for open formularies that provide beneficiaries with many different choices while requiring higher member contributions for nonpreferred drugs. Here is an example of a three-tier formulary:

1. *Generic drugs:* The first tier is the lowest cost option. For the lowest out-of-pocket expense, the insured should always consider tier 1 medications if the insured and the doctor decide they are appropriate for the treatment.
2. *Midrange cost option, preferred brand medications:* The second tier is the middle cost option. It is used if the insured and the doctor decide that a tier 2 medication is the most appropriate to treat the condition.
3. *The highest cost option, nonpreferred brand medications:* Tier 3 is the highest cost option. Sometimes there are alternatives available in tier 1 or tier 2. If the insured is currently taking a medication in tier 3, the doctor may determine that there are tier 1 or tier 2 alternatives that are appropriate for the treatment.

Figure 3.3 shows one plan's tier structure.

Compounded medications, medications containing one or more ingredients that are prepared on-site by a pharmacist, are classified at the tier 3 level, provided that the individual ingredients used in compounding are covered under the pharmacy benefit.

The PBM may update the tiers on which medications appear. Additionally, when a brand-name medication becomes available as a generic, the tier status of the brand-name medication and its corresponding generic are evaluated. When a medication changes tiers, the insured may be required to pay more or less for it. These changes may occur without prior notice to the insured. The cost information is available by phone or on the website of the PBM.

Specialty Drugs

Specialty drugs are a separate category of medications, including biotech and other drugs designed to treat serious diseases such as cancer, multiple sclerosis, and rheumatoid arthritis and other inflammatory maladies. The demand for this category of drugs is growing at an accelerated rate in the United States, causing health plans and PBMs to consider options for

Figure 3.3 Sample Tier Structure of a Health Plan

HealthPlanRx

2008 Three-Tier Prescription Drug List Reference Guide

Tier One
Acebutolol
Acetaminophen with Caffeine
    and Butalbital
Acetaminophen with Codeine **QLL/QD**
Acetaminophen with Codeine, Caffeine
    and Butalbital **QLL/QD**
Acetaminophen with Hydrocodone

Betamethasone Dipropionate Cream,
    Lotion, Ointment, Gel
Betamethasone Valerate
Betamethasone with Clotrimazole
Bisoprolol
Bisoprolol with Hydrochlorothiazide
Bromocriptine
Bumetanide
Bupropion **QLL**

Clotrimazole with Betamethasone
Colestipol
Cromolyn
Cryselle
Cyclobenzaprine
Cyproheptadine
Desipramine
Desmopressin
Desonide

Tier Two
Aceon
Aciphex **QLL/QD**
Activella
Actonel **QLL**
Actonel with Calcium **QLL**
Actoplus Met **QLL**
Actos **QLL**
Adderall XR **QLL**
Adoxa (Dosepack= Tier 3)
Advicor
Aldara
Alesse

Cozaar **QLL/QD**
Crestor **QLL/QD**
Dapsone
Depakote
Depakote ER
Depakote Sprinkle
Dilantin
Diovan **QLL/QD**
Diovan HCT **QLL/QD**
Dovonex **QLL**
Duetact **QLL**
Effexor XR **QLL**
Elestat

Micardis HCT **QLL/QD**
Mirapex
Nasonex **QLL**
Neoral
Neupogen
Niaspan
Norditropin **QLL/QD, N**
Novolin Pens/Cartridges
Novolog Pens/Cartridges
Nutropin **QLL/QD, N**
Nuvaring
Optivar
Oxycontin **QLL/QD**

Tier Three
Abilify **QLL**
Accolate **QLL**
Accu-Chek Test Strips **QLL, DS**
Aclovate
Acular
Advair Diskus **QLL**
Advair HFA **QLL**
Aggrenox
Allegra ODT **QLL/QD**
Allegra Suspension **QLL/QD**
Allegra-D **QLL/QD**
Alocril
ALo

Covera-HS
Cutivate
Cyclessa
Cymbalta **QLL/QD**
Cytomel
Daytrana **QLL**
Denavir
Derma-Smoothe/FS
Desogen
Detrol
Datrol LA **QLL**
Differin **QLL, N**
Diprolene

Lialda
Locoid
Loestrin
Loestrin FE
Loprox
Lotemax
Lovaza **QLL**
Lunesta **QLL/QD**
Luxiq
Lybrel
Lyrica **QLL/QD**
Maxair Autohaler **QLL**
Menest

Some medications are noted with N, QD, QLL, or DS. The definitions for these symbols are listed below. Your benefit plan determines how these medications may be covered for you.

N   = Notification. There are a few medications that your doctor must notify us of to make sure their use is covered within your benefit.
QD   = Quantity Duration. Some medications have a limited amount that can be covered for a specific period of time.
QLL = Quantity Level Limit. Some medications have a limited amount that can be covered at one time.
DS   = Diabetic Supplies. Diabetic supplies may be covered by your benefit plan.

Health Plan Rx 3-Tier 3/08

controlling costs, including recommending making biotech drugs available as generic drugs, or *biogenerics*.

Drug Utilization Review

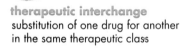

drug utilization review tool used to ensure safety, improve care quality, and promote compliance with the formulary

prior authorization (preauthorization) review required to be conducted by a plan before medications are dispensed and, ideally, before they are prescribed

Another tool used to control costs is the **drug utilization review,** which is used to ensure safety, improve care quality, and promote compliance with the formulary. One type of review is the requirement for **prior authorization** (also known as **preauthorization**) by the plan before medications are dispensed and, ideally, before they are prescribed. Prior authorization programs target specific drugs and require special authorization at the pharmacy for coverage by the plan. Most often, the programs apply to drugs that are expensive and have potential for being misused.

The pharmacy also does drug utilization reviews electronically before medications are dispensed. The prescription is checked against the formulary as well as the member's eligibility, against the prescription record for drug interactions and drug-disease interactions (when available), and for appropriate dosage and other factors. The pharmacist may receive one of two types of alerts (or edits) regarding the transaction. The first does not allow the transaction to proceed. The second allows the transaction to be processed and provides information to the pharmacist. Based on the information, the pharmacist may contact the prescribing physician before proceeding or after the transaction is processed.

Plans may also review doctors' prescribing patterns to see if they follow best medical practice. Often, physicians who frequently prescribe drugs that are not on the formulary are contacted in writing.

Generic Substitution and Drug Interchange

therapeutic interchange substitution of one drug for another in the same therapeutic class

Substitution of generic drugs for their brand-name equivalents is a common cost-saving measure. Although this practice is under scrutiny, health plans may offer financial incentives to physicians to prescribe cheaper generic medicines. **Therapeutic interchange** is the substitution of one drug for another in the same therapeutic class, such as the replacement of one statin by another. The technique encourages formulary compliance. However, physician permission and compliance with state pharmacy law to interchange drugs is required due to differences in drug chemical compounds.

Internet and Mail-Order Services

Dispensing medications by the Internet and mail order is cost-effective for maintenance drugs because of discounts negotiated with wholesalers and manufacturers and the absence of retail pharmacy overhead. Member communications and a range of benefit design options are used to encourage members to use mail service when appropriate. Some PBMs own and operate their own mail-order pharmacies, while others outsource the service. Many PBMs allow members to order maintenance medications via an Internet option.

Disease Management

disease management (DM) programs programs that are often provided by pharmacy benefit managers for common and potentially high-cost conditions such as asthma, diabetes, heart disease, and depression

Many PBMs provide **disease management (DM) programs** for common and potentially high-cost conditions such as asthma, diabetes, heart disease, and depression. Often education and disease-specific information are available to members, and members may be encouraged to comply with their treatment regimens and to take an active role in the management of their conditions.

 Tech Check

What type of formulary is the least restrictive?

What term is used to describe a specific list of drugs in a formulary?

What is the object of drug utilization reviews?

For what purpose do many pharmacy benefit managers offer disease management programs?

Calculating Charges

Insured individuals have a variety of financial responsibilities under their health plans. Usually, a periodic premium payment is required. Patients may also be obligated to make five other types of payments: deductibles, copayments, coinsurance, noncovered (excluded) and over-limit services, and balance billing. The amounts that a patient pays are referred to as the insured's **out-of-pocket expenses.**

Deductibles

Most payers require policyholders to pay their deductibles before the insurance benefits begin. For example, a plan may require a patient to pay the first $200 of physician charges each year. Payments for noncovered (excluded) services—those that the policy does not cover—do not count toward the deductible. Some plans require an **individual deductible** that must be met for each individual—whether the policyholder or a covered dependent—who has an encounter with a provider. In other cases, there is a **family deductible** that can be met by combined payments to providers for any covered members of the insured's family. For prescription benefit plans, the deductible is referred to as the **prescription drug deductible amount.**

INDIVIDUAL DEDUCTIBLE

Mr. Butler is arriving at the pharmacy to pick up his prescription. So far this year, Mr. Butler has made total payments of $95.00 for other prescriptions. The charge for this prescription will be $30.00. Under his health insurance, Mr. Butler has a yearly individual deductible of $100.00 for pharmacy benefits.

out-of-pocket expenses amounts that a patient pays for medical expenses

individual deductible deductible that must be met for each individual—whether the policyholder or a covered dependent—who has an encounter

family deductible deductible that can be met by the combined payments to providers for any covered members of the insured's family

prescription drug deductible amount term used to refer to a deductible in prescription benefit plans

EXAMPLE

Calculating the Payment

Total individual deductible	$100.00
Previous payments	$95.00
Amount owed to fulfill deductible requirement ($100.00 − $95.00)	$5.00
Amount insurance owes for this appointment ($30.00 − $5.00)	$25.00

In this situation, Mr. Butler is required to pay only $5.00 of the pharmacy charge of $30.00 for this prescription. Once he has paid that amount, he will have met his yearly deductible. The insurance company is now responsible for paying the outstanding $25.00.

Consumer-driven health plans have the highest deductibles of any plan type. Because these plans are growing in popularity, pharmacy technician insurance specialists must be aware of and prepare for collecting payments from patients enrolled in CDHPs at the time of service.

Copayments

Many health care plans require patient copayments (copays). Copayments are always due and collected at the time of service. They may be different for various types of services. Usually, a copay is stated as a dollar amount, such as $15 for an office visit or $10 for a prescription drug. After checking with the health plan, many offices have a policy of telling patients who are scheduling visits what copays they will owe at the time of service so that they are prepared to pay.

Coinsurance

Many payers require coinsurance. Noncapitated health care plans such as PPOs usually require patients to pay a greater percentage of the charges of out-of-network providers than of plan providers. For example, a patient may owe 20 percent of the charge when using a network member but 40 percent of the charge of a physician who is not in the network.

Noncovered (Excluded) and Over-Limit Services

All payers require patients to pay for noncovered (excluded) services. Providers generally can charge their usual fees for these services. Likewise, in managed care plans that set limits on the annual (or other period) usage of covered services, patients are responsible for usage beyond the allowed number. For example, if one preventive physical examination is permitted annually, additional preventive examinations are paid for by the patient.

Pharmacy Charges

Pharmacy technician insurance specialists need to know when to charge patients for their medications and how to determine the appropriate charges based on patients' insurance. As explained in the ten-step pharmacy billing cycle in Chapter 1, the point-of-sale patient payment and follow-up payment balancing and processing are critically important.

When a patient presents a medical insurance ID card, the pharmacy technician insurance specialist needs to know how to examine it and find the relevant information. Insurance cards contain most of the information

Figure 3.4 Sample Medical Insurance ID Card

HealthPlan

RxBin: 610014
RxGrp: UGRI6104
Issuer: Medco
ID Number: 111 222 333
Primary Insured:
Vijay Singh

Effective Date: Illness: 03/29/07
Injury: 03/15/07
Group Number: 765432

03096293

Notification is required for hospital stays that exceed 3 days.
Call 1-800-555-5555. Notification does not guarantee payment.
(Not required for CO, KY, MO or TX residents.)

Send medical claims to: Customer Service: (222) 333-4444
HealthPlan
7000 Woods Drive   To find network providers:
Indianapolis, IN 46278-1720   www.healthplan.net
Electronic Submission: 37602 (877) 999-8888

Pharmacists: Submit claims via the Telepaid System. Pharmacy Service
Help Desk: 1-800-666-6666 or www.healthplanrx.net.

To find a pharmacy, call Member Services at 1-877-123-4567 or go to
www.healthplan.net. Mail Pharmacy claims to:
HealthPlanRx Solutions, Inc.

necessary to fill a patient's prescription and accurately process payments, including the patient's name, group and identification numbers, the health insurance issuer's name, and ways to contact the health insurance company.

Sample ID Card Analysis

Using the sample ID card in Figure 3.4, find answers to the following questions:

- What company issued the card?
- What is the patient's ID number?
- When is the card valid?
- Who is the primary insured person?
- Based on the information on the card, how can the patient find a pharmacy?

Payment Examples

The following examples illustrate situations that pharmacy technician insurance specialists will encounter on a regular basis and demonstrate the decisions and calculations needed to fill a prescription. The expenses patients may encounter when filling a prescription come from the HealthCareRx Prescription Drug List Reference Guide in Figure 3.3, for locating the sample drugs' tiers, and from the hypothetical payment system presented in Table 3.2.

Table 3.2 Hypothetical Tier Chart

Tier	Deductible	Copayment	Coinsurance
Tier 1	$0.00	$5.00	0%
Tier 2	$200.00	$10.00	10%
Tier 3	$500.00	$20.00	20%

EXAMPLE 1

Mrs. Davidson arrives at the pharmacy to fill a prescription for Advair Diskus for her asthma. Over the course of the year, Mrs. Davidson has already paid a total of $700.00 toward tier 3 prescription drugs. Assuming this prescription costs $200.00 and falls under the category of coinsurance only, how much will she owe?

Calculating the Payment

Total cost of the prescription	$200.00
Amount owed by the patient as coinsurance ($200.00 × 20%)	$40.00

You determine that Mrs. Davidson owes $40.00 because her yearly deductible has already been met and the drug is listed under tier 3. Table 3.2 shows that she owes 20% of the cost as coinsurance.

EXAMPLE 2

Mr. Smithers has been prescribed acetaminophen with codeine by his physician. He has received $100.00 worth of benefits so far during the year. By determining that the drug is located in tier 1, you find that Mr. Smithers owes only a $5.00 copayment in order to fill this prescription, as no deductible or coinsurance is required.

EXAMPLE 3

Ms. Wang comes to the pharmacy to fill a prescription for the drug Depakote. In the present year, she has paid $180.00 in out-of-pocket expenses toward tier 2 drug prescriptions. She has a $200.00 deductible. Looking up the cost of the prescription, you determine that the drug costs $80.00 and will require a coinsurance payment, but no copayment. How much will Ms. Wang owe in order to fill the prescription?

Calculating the Payment

Amount owed to meet the deductible ($200.00 − $180.00)	$20.00
Amount still owed after meeting deductible ($80.00 − $20.00)	$60.00
Amount owed as coinsurance ($60.00 × 10%)	$6.00
Total amount owed by Ms. Wang ($20.00 + $6.00)	$26.00

Ms. Wang owes a total of $26.00 for this prescription. After her deductible has been met, the coinsurance for this tier 2 drug activates, and she owes that payment on the outstanding balance.

 Tech Check

What is the term for the money that patients pay under their health plans?

What is the name given to a deductible for a prescription benefit plan?

Chapter Summary

1. Health insurance is available to people through their employers and through individual plans. Many employers offer group health plans and utilize their human resource departments and pharmacy benefit managers to operate the company program and the prescription drug plan, respectively. Federal employees have unique health plan options, and many large companies offer their own self-funded health plans, rather than buying insurance from an outside company. Individual health plans are available to people who do not have access to other plans and those who prefer to select their own independent coverage.

2. Several types of group and individual health plan choices offer people medical coverage. Preferred provider organizations (PPOs) are the most popular type of managed care organization as they combine flexibility in patients' choice of physicians and reduced costs for medical services. Health maintenance organizations (HMOs) offer patients fixed premiums and very small copayments for services. Point-of-service plans (POS) exist within HMOs to allow patients to see physicians outside the network for a higher cost. Under indemnity (fee-for-service) plans, physicians receive payments based on their regular charges for services, with patients owing coinsurance based on those fees. Consumer-driven health plans (CDHPs) offer alternative methods for employers seeking to control health care costs.

3. Patients' payments and medical coverage depend on their health insurance. Patients and pharmacy technician insurance specialists need to be aware of the expenses they can incur. Covered expenses are incurred by or on behalf of an insured person for supplies that are ordered by a doctor, are medically necessary, and are not excluded by any provision of the policy. Noncovered expenses are those the policy does not cover that must be paid by the insured person.

4. Formularies, which are lists of plans' preferred drugs within each therapeutic class, are divided into three types. Open formularies are the least restrictive and sometimes cover medication that is not on the drug list. A closed formulary will not offer coverage for such drugs without a physician-authorized medical exception. Restricted formularies limit the drugs listed in the formulary to generics only or limited medications within a drug class.

5. Pharmacy benefit managers organize formularies into tiers, which are specific lists of drugs. Plans may have several tiers, with the insured's payment depending on which tier a particular drug is listed in. A two-tier structure usually classifies drugs by whether they are generics or brand-name medications, while three- and four-tier cost-sharing structures allow for a more open formulary. Multiple tier systems may be divided into categories, such as generic drugs, preferred brand-name medications, and nonpreferred brand-name medications.

6. Insured individuals have financial responsibilities under their health plans. Periodic premium payments are typically required, and patients may also need to pay deductibles, copayments, coinsurance, fees for noncovered and over-limit services, and other charges. These patient payments are known as out-of-pocket expenses. Pharmacy technician insurance specialists need to be aware of all these features and analyze a plan's regulations when calculating patient payments.

Chapter Review

Multiple Choice

Read the question and select the best response.

1. Which of these techniques is used by employers—primarily through their PBMs—to control costs?
   A. mail service
   B. drug utilization management
   C. pharmacy network management
   D. all of the above

2. What name is given to medication required to bear the message "Caution: federal law prohibits dispensing without a prescription"?
   A. prescription legend drug
   B. specialty drug
   C. compounded medication
   D. none of the above

3. Which tool is used to control costs by ensuring safety, improving care quality, and promoting compliance with a formulary?
   A. family deductible
   B. drug utilization review
   C. capitation
   D. out-of-pocket expense

4. Which of these tasks is *not* a common function of pharmacy benefit managers?
   A. contracting with pharmacies
   B. negotiating discounts and rebates with drug manufacturers
   C. choosing a particular set of benefits for the employees
   D. providing cards to beneficiaries

5. Which of the following features is *not* common to the disease management programs offered by many pharmacy benefit managers?
   A. Education and disease-specific information are often available to members
   B. They offer assistance for high-cost conditions such as asthma, diabetes, heart disease, and depression
   C. Members may be encouraged to take an active role in the management of their conditions
   D. They provide a unique network for beneficiaries to use

6. Which term describes the laws in over half the states that require pharmacy benefit managers to contract with any pharmacies willing to accept their reimbursement rates?
   A. any willing provider laws
   B. therapeutic interchange laws
   C. preauthorization laws
   D. member pharmacy laws

7. What is the substitution of one drug for another in the same therapeutic class called?
   A. therapeutic replacement
   B. therapeutic substitution
   C. therapeutic interchange
   D. none of the above

8. Approximately what percentage of people with private health insurance have individual plans?
   A. 0 percent
   B. 10 percent
   C. 50 percent
   D. 75 percent

9. Which of these health plans allows beneficiaries to see providers in the network only?
   A. preferred provider organization (PPO)
   B. health maintenance organization (HMO)
   C. point-of-service plan (POS)
   D. consumer-driven health plan (CDHP)

10. Which of these health plans has a high deductible and low premium?
    A. preferred provider organization (PPO)
    B. health maintenance organization (HMO)
    C. point-of-service plan (POS)
    D. consumer-driven health plan (CDHP)

11. Which of these health plans generally has the largest membership?
    A. preferred provider organization (PPO)
    B. health maintenance organization (HMO)
    C. point-of-service plan (POS)
    D. consumer-driven health plan (CDHP)

12. Which of these health plans does not allow beneficiaries to see providers outside of their program's network at a higher cost?
    A. preferred provider organization (PPO)
    B. health maintenance organization (HMO)
    C. point-of-service plan (POS)
    D. consumer-driven health plan (CDHP)

13. Which of these types of formularies will *not* provide coverage for drugs not listed on the formulary without a physician authorizing a medical exception?
    A. open formulary
    B. closed formulary
    C. restricted formulary
    D. all of the above

14. Which financial features can employers choose to customize the health plan options they offer their employees?
    A. deductibles
    B. premiums
    C. other associated costs
    D. all of the above

15. What is the name of a deductible that may be met by the combined payments to providers for any covered members of the insured's family?
    A. family deductible
    B. prescription drug deductible
    C. individual deductible
    D. pharmacy deductible

Matching

Match the key term with the appropriate definition.

_E_ 1. Specific periods of time when employees choose a particular set of benefits for the coming benefit period

_G_ 2. Category of medications including biotech and other drugs that are designed to treat serious diseases such as cancer, multiple sclerosis, rheumatoid arthritis, and other inflammatory maladies

_A_ 3. Tool used to ensure safety, improve care quality, and promote compliance with the formulary

_I_ 4. A pharmacy that falls within the network created by a managed care organization

_B_ 5. Type of formulary that limits the drugs listed to generics or limited medications within a drug class only

_J_ 6. Medications containing one or more ingredients that are prepared on-site by a pharmacist

_H_ 7. The substitution of one drug for another in the same therapeutic class

_D_ 8. A group of participating providers, including physicians, hospitals, and pharmacies, created by a managed care organization for its policyholders

_C_ 9. A third-party administrator of prescription drug programs that processes and pays prescription drug claims

_F_ 10. Expenses incurred by or on behalf of a covered person for supplies that are ordered by a doctor, are medically necessary, and are not excluded by any provision of the policy

A. drug utilization review

B. restricted formulary

C. pharmacy benefit manager

D. network

E. open enrollment period

F. covered expense

G. specialty drug

H. therapeutic interchange

I. member pharmacy

J. compounded medications

True/False

Indicate whether the following statements are true or false.

_____ 1. Specialty drugs may include biotech and other drugs that are designed to treat serious diseases.

_____ 2. Almost 50 percent of people with private health insurance have individual plans.

_____ 3. A consumer-driven health plan combines a health plan that has a high deductible and low premiums with a special savings account that is used to pay medical bills before the deductible has been met.

_____ 4. Therapeutic interchange encourages formulary compliance.

_____ 5. Payers do not require patients to pay for non-covered (excluded) services.

_____ 6. Health maintenance organizations are the most popular type of managed care organization.

_____ 7. Many employees have medical insurance coverage under group health plans that their employers buy from insurance companies.

_____ 8. The most restrictive type of formulary is known as a restricted formulary.

_____ 9. A deductible that must be met by each individual in a plan who has an encounter—whether the policyholder or a covered dependent—is called a family deductible.

_____ 10. Noncovered expenses are defined as those the policy does not cover that must be paid by the insured.

....

Short Answer

Think carefully about the following questions, and write your answers in the space provided.

1. Take another look at the descriptions of the common types of health plans in Table 3.1. Which plans do you think would appeal to people of various financial backgrounds and types of employment? Why do you think all these types of plans are necessary options?

_____

_____

_____

....

Internet Activities

1. Visit the website of the Blue Cross and Blue Shield Association at **http://www.bcbs.com/.** Examine the different types of health care coverage offered by the company.

2. Using an Internet search engine such as Google, locate some other health plans' tiered drug formularies and compare them to the formulary of HealthPlanRx in Figure 3.3. Determine what differences exist in the various formularies.

Medicare

 Learning Outcomes

After completing this chapter, you will be able to define the key terms and:

4-1. Identify four parts of Medicare coverage.

4-2. Discuss the fees that Medicare participating and nonparticipating physicians are allowed to charge.

4-3. Explain the difference between an excluded service and a medically unnecessary service.

4-4. Compare and contrast the pharmacy benefit provided by the Original Medicare Plan and the Medicare Advantage plan.

4-5. Calculate payments due from Medicare patients for their prescriptions.

 Chapter Outline

Medicare Overview
Medicare Part B Plans
Who Pays First?
Medicare Part D

Key Terms

advance beneficiary notice (ABN) of noncoverage

coverage gap

crossover claim

diagnostic services

hospice

initial preventive physical examination (IPPE)

limiting charge

medical savings account (MSA)

Medicare

Medicare administrative contractors (MACs)

Medicare Advantage

Medicare beneficiary

Medicare Fee Schedule (MFS)

Medicare Part A

Medicare Part B

Medicare Part C

Medicare Part D

Medicare Remittance Notice (MRN)

Medicare Summary Notice (MSN)

medication therapy management (MTM)

Medigap insurance

Medi-Medi beneficiary

Original Medicare Plan

Prescription Drug Plan (PDP)

Quality Improvement Organization (QIO)

screening service

special needs plans (SNP)

TrOOP Facilitator

Medicare Overview

Medicare federal health insurance program for people who are sixty-five and older and some people with disabilities and end-stage renal disease (ESRD)

Medicare beneficiary person covered by Medicare

The federal health insurance program for people who are sixty-five and older is known as **Medicare.** Medicare also provides benefits to people with some disabilities and end-stage renal disease, which is permanent kidney failure. A person covered by Medicare is called a **Medicare beneficiary.** Some beneficiaries qualify through the Social Security Administration. Others are eligible through the Railroad Retirement System. Medicare has two major parts, one for care given by institutions and the other for services by physicians.

To receive benefits, individuals must be eligible under one of six beneficiary categories:

1. *Individuals age sixty-five and older:* Persons age sixty-five and older who have paid FICA taxes or railroad retirement taxes for at least forty calendar quarters.
2. *Disabled adults:* Individuals who have been receiving Social Security disability benefits or Railroad Retirement Board disability benefits for more than two years. Coverage begins five months after the two years of entitlement.
3. *Individuals disabled before age eighteen:* Individuals under age eighteen who meet the disability criteria of the Social Security Act.
4. *Spouses of entitled individuals:* Spouses of deceased, disabled, or retired individuals who are (or were) entitled to Medicare benefits.
5. *Retired federal employees enrolled in the Civil Service Retirement System (CSRS):* Retired CSRS employees and their spouses.
6. *Individuals with end-stage renal disease (ESRD):* Individuals of any age who receive dialysis or a renal transplant for ESRD. Coverage typically begins on the first day of the month following the start of dialysis treatments. In the case of a transplant, entitlement begins the month the individual is hospitalized for the transplant (the transplant must be completed within two months). The donor is covered for services related to the donation of the organ only.

The federal government does not pay Medicare claims directly. Instead, it contracts with insurance organizations known as **Medicare administrative contractors (MACs)** to process claims on its behalf.

Medicare Part A

Medicare administrative contractors (MACs) insurance organizations the federal government contracts with to pay Medicare claims on its behalf

Medicare Part A program that helps pay for inpatient hospital services, care in skilled nursing facilities, home health care, and hospice care

hospice public or private organization that provides services for terminally ill patients and their families

Medicare Part A helps pay for inpatient hospital services, care in a skilled nursing facility, home health care, and hospice care. A **hospice** is a public or private organization that provides services for terminally ill patients and their families. Hospice care extends beyond medical services to include psychological and spiritual care.

Fees paid by Medicare Part A for inpatient hospital services are based on groupings of diagnoses. Hospital cases across the country have been analyzed to arrive at the fixed fees Medicare pays for hospital services. The payment is based on the principal diagnosis.

People who are eligible for Social Security benefits are automatically enrolled in Medicare Part A. They do not have to pay insurance premiums. People age sixty-five and older who do not qualify for Social Security

Table 4.1 Medicare Part A Coverage

Coverage	Description
Inpatient hospital stays	Semiprivate room, meals, general nursing, and other hospital services and supplies, including blood.
Stays at a skilled nursing facility (SNF) following a related, covered three-day hospital stay	At an SNF, skilled nursing and rehabilitation care are provided, in contrast to a nursing home that provides custodial care. Coverage includes semiprivate room, meals, skilled nursing and rehabilitative services, and other services and supplies, including blood.
Home health care	Intermittent skilled nursing care, physical therapy, occupational therapy, speech-language pathology, home health aide services, durable medical equipment, but not prescription drugs.
Psychiatric inpatient care	Similar coverage as inpatient hospital stay except a facility must accept Medicare assignments on all claims and the lifetime benefit is limited to 190 days of inpatient psychiatric care.
Hospice care	Pain and symptom relief and supportive services.
Benefits periods	Medicare Part A coverage is tied to a benefit period of 60 days for a spell of illness. A spell of illness benefit period commences on the first day of the patient's stay in a hospital or in a skilled nursing facility and continues until 60 consecutive days have lapsed and the patient has received no skilled care. Medicare does not cover care that is or becomes primarily custodial, such as assistance with bathing and eating.
	The patient benefit period with Medicare, the spell of illness, does not end until 60 days after discharge from the hospital or the skilled nursing facility. Therefore, if the patient is readmitted within those 60 days, the patient is considered to be in the same benefit period and is not subject to another deductible. A new spell of illness begins if the patient is readmitted more than 60 days after discharge. There is no limit on the number of spells of illness Medicare will cover in a patient's lifetime.
Patient's responsibility	For the first 60 days, the patient's responsibility is the annual deductible (the amount changes each year). For days 61–90, there is a per-day copayment, with another per-day copayment for days 91–150. Beyond 150 days, Medicare Part A does not make any payment.

benefits have the option of enrolling in Part A, but they must pay premiums to get benefits.

Details of Part A coverage are provided in Table 4.1.

Medicare Part B

Medicare Part B helps pay for physician services, outpatient hospital services, durable medical equipment, and other services and supplies. All Medicare providers must file claims on behalf of patients at no cost to the patients. Part B coverage is optional. Everyone who is eligible for

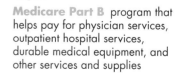

Medicare Part B program that helps pay for physician services, outpatient hospital services, durable medical equipment, and other services and supplies

Table 4.2 Medicare Part B Coverage

Covered Services	Patient Payment (PAR Provider)
Medical services: Physicians' services, including inpatient and outpatient medical and surgical services and supplies; physical, occupational, and speech therapy; diagnostic tests; and durable medical equipment (DME)	• Annual deductible • 20 percent coinsurance of approved amount after the deductible, except in the outpatient setting • 50 percent coinsurance for most outpatient mental health services
Clinical laboratory services: Blood tests, urinalysis, and so forth	Covered fully by Medicare
Home health care: Intermittent skilled care, home health aide services, DME	• Services fully covered by Medicare • 20 percent coinsurance for DME
Outpatient hospital services: Services for diagnoses or treatment of an illness or injury	Coinsurance or copayment that varies according to the service
Blood: As an outpatient or as part of a Part B covered service	For the first three pints plus 20 percent of the approved amount for additional pints (after the deductible)

Part A may choose to enroll in Part B by paying monthly premiums (usually deducted automatically from Social Security retirement benefit payments). Therefore, the medical insurance specialist should check the patient's Medicare identification card for coverage information at each visit, since coverage may be renewed monthly in some states and might expire between office visits.

Medicare Part B benefits include both regular services and preventive services, as listed in Table 4.2.

Part B also covers the following:

- Ambulance services when other transportation would endanger the patient's health
- Artificial eyes
- Artificial limbs that are prosthetic devices and their replacement parts
- Braces
- Chiropractic services (limited)
- Emergency care
- Eyeglasses—one pair of glasses or contact lenses after cataract surgery (if an intraocular lens has been inserted)
- Immunosuppressive drug therapy for transplant patients under certain conditions
- Kidney dialysis
- Medical nutrition therapy (MNT) services for people with diabetes or kidney disease
- Medical supplies
- Outpatient prescription drugs (such as oral drugs for cancer)—very limited
- Prosthetic devices

- Second surgical opinion by a physician
- Services of practitioners such as clinical social workers, physician's assistants, and nurse-practitioners
- Telemedicine services in rural areas
- Therapeutic shoes for diabetes patients
- Transplants (some)
- X-rays, MRIs, CT scans, ECGs, and some other purchased tests

Preventive Services

Certain preventive services for qualified individuals are covered:

- Bone mass measurements
- Cardiovascular screening blood tests
- Colorectal cancer screening
- Diabetes screening tests (for certain at-risk patients), services, and supplies
- Glaucoma screening
- **Initial preventive physical examination (IPPE),** a once-in-a-lifetime benefit that must be received in the first six months after the date of enrollment
- Mammogram screening
- Pap test and pelvic examination (includes clinical breast examination)
- Prostate cancer screening
- Vaccinations

A **screening service** is performed for a patient who does not have symptoms, abnormal findings, or any past history of the disease. The purpose is to detect an undiagnosed disease so that medical treatment can begin to prevent harm. The Medicare policy may limit screening services or their frequency according to the health status of the patient. Screenings are different from **diagnostic services,** which are done to treat a patient who has been diagnosed with a condition or with a high probability for it.

Medicare Part C

In 1997, **Medicare Part C** (originally called Medicare + Choice) became available to individuals who are eligible for Part A and enrolled in Part B. Under Part C, private health insurance companies can contract with the Centers for Medicare and Medicaid Services (CMS) to offer Medicare benefits through their own policies.

In 2003, under the Medicare Modernization Act (MMA; see Chapter 2), **Medicare Advantage** became the new name for Medicare + Choice plans, and certain rules were changed to give Part C enrollees better benefits and lower costs.

Medicare Part D

Medicare Part D, authorized under the MMA, provides voluntary Medicare prescription drug plans that are open to people who are eligible for Medicare. All Medicare prescription drug plans are private insurance plans, and most participants pay monthly premiums to access discounted prices.

initial preventive physical examination (IPPE) once-in-a-lifetime benefit under Medicare Part B that must be received in the first six months after the date of enrollment

$ **Billing Tip**

Preventive Services and Deductibles

Under Medicare Part B, some preventive services are subject to deductibles, and some are not. The Medicare plan summary grid should note these requirements.

screening service treatment for a patient who does not have symptoms, abnormal findings, or any past history of a disease

diagnostic services treatment for a patient who has been diagnosed with a condition or with a high probability for it

Medicare Part C program that enables private health insurance companies to contract with CMS to offer Medicare benefits through their own policies

Medicare Advantage new name for Medicare + Choice plans, with some changed rules to give Part C enrollees better benefits and lower costs

Medicare Part D program that provides voluntary Medicare prescription drug plans to people who are eligible for Medicare

Figure 4.1 Sample Medicare Patient Identification Card

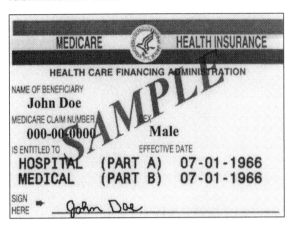

Medicare Insurance Card

Each Medicare enrollee receives a health insurance card (see Figure 4.1) that lists the beneficiary's name, sex, and Medicare number and the effective dates for Part A and Part B coverage. The Medicare number is assigned by CMS and usually consists of the Social Security number followed by a numeric or alphanumeric ending. The letter at the end provides additional information about the patient. For example, *A* stands for wage earner, *B* for spouse's number, and *D* for widow or widower.

 Tech Check

In order to receive Medicare benefits, individuals must be eligible under at least one of what six beneficiary categories?

What types of benefits are included under Medicare Part B services?

Medicare Part B Plans

Medicare beneficiaries can choose from among a number of insurance plans. Medicare beneficiaries who enroll in the Medicare fee-for-service plan (referred to by Medicare as the **Original Medicare Plan**) can choose any licensed physician certified by Medicare. They must pay the premium, the coinsurance (which is 20 percent), and the annual deductible specified each year by the Medicare law, which is voted on by Congress. The amount of a patient's medical bill that has been applied to the annual deductible is shown on the **Medicare Remittance Notice (MRN)** that the office receives and also on the **Medicare Summary Notice (MSN)** that the patient receives. Each time a beneficiary receives services, a fee is billable. Most offices bill the patient for any balance due after the MRN is received, rather than at the time of the appointment.

Original Medicare Plan term used by Medicare to refer to its fee-for-service plan

Medicare Remittance Notice (MRN) notice sent to an office to show the amount of a patient's medical bills that has been applied to the annual deductible

Medicare Summary Notice (MSN) notice sent to a patient to show the amount of his or her medical bills that has been applied to the annual deductible

Medicare also offers Medicare Advantage plans. A beneficiary can choose to enroll in one of the following types of plans instead of in the Original Medicare Plan:

- Medicare managed care plan
- Medicare preferred provider organization plan
- Medicare private fee-for-service plan
- Medical savings account

The Original Medicare Plan is administered by the Center for Medicare Management, a department of CMS.

Medicare Managed Care Plans

Some beneficiaries choose to join managed care plans such as HMOs. Most managed care plans charge monthly premiums and small copayments for office visits, but not deductibles. Medicare managed care plans, like other managed care plans, often require patients to use a specific network of physicians, hospitals, and facilities. Some plans offer patients the option of seeing providers outside the network for a higher fee. On the other hand, they offer coverage for services not reimbursed in fee-for-service plans, such as routine physical examinations and additional days in the hospital.

Managed care plans offer beneficiaries a number of advantages:

- Low copayment when receiving treatment
- Minimal paperwork
- Coverage for additional services
- No need for a supplemental Medigap policy (covered below)

Disadvantages of Medicare managed care plans include the following:

- Physician choices limited to those in the particular plan
- Prior approval from the primary care physician (PCP) typically needed before seeing a specialist, undergoing elective surgery, or receiving other services

Preferred Provider Organization

In the Medicare preferred provider organization plan (PPO), patients are given a financial incentive to use doctors within a network, but they may choose to go outside the network. A PPO contracts with a certain group of providers to offer health care services to patients. Visits outside this network of providers incur additional costs, which may include higher copayments or higher coinsurance. Unlike HMOs, many PPOs do not require patients to select PCPs.

Private Fee-for-Service (PFFS)

Under a private fee-for-service plan, patients receive services from any Medicare-approved providers or facilities they choose. The plan is operated by a private insurance company that contracts with Medicare to provide services to beneficiaries. The plan sets its own rates for services, and physicians are allowed to bill patients the amount of the charge not covered by the plan as long as it does not exceed 15 percent of the charge. A copayment may or may not be required. Under a private fee-for-service plan, patients may pay rates that are higher or lower than the rates on the Medicare Fee Schedule, but they cannot be billed for the difference if the rate is higher.

medical savings account (MSA) program that combines a high-deductible fee-for-service plan with a tax-exempt trust to pay for qualified medical expenses

Compliance Guideline

The Medicare Advantage program is administered by the Center for Beneficiary Choices, a department of CMS.

HIPAA Tip

A National Provider Identifier (NPI) is used to identify the Medicare provider as well as the practice, if applicable.

Medicare Fee Schedule (MFS) basis for payments for all Original Medicare Plan services

EXAMPLE

Medical Savings Accounts

The Medicare Modernization Act created a new plan for Medicare called a **medical savings account (MSA).** Similar to private medical savings accounts, this plan combines a high-deductible fee-for-service plan with a tax-exempt trust to pay for qualified medical expenses. CMS pays premiums for the insurance policies and makes a contribution to the MSA. The only beneficiary premium is for supplemental benefits that may be offered by the plan. Beneficiaries use the money in their MSAs to pay for their health care before the high deductible is reached. At that point, the Medicare Advantage plan offering the MSA pays for all expenses for covered services. The maximum annual deductible is set by federal law.

Medicare Charges Under Part B

The **Medicare Fee Schedule (MFS)** is the basis for payments for all Original Medicare Plan services. This national system is based on the resource-based relative value scale (RBRVS) system, using cost factors that represent the physician's time and how much it costs to run a practice (see Chapter 6).

Participation

Annually, providers choose whether they want to participate in the Medicare program. Participating physicians agree to accept assignment for all Medicare claims and to accept Medicare's allowed charge according to the Medicare Fee Schedule as payment in full for services. A PAR provider may bill the patient for coinsurance and deductibles but may not collect amounts higher than the Medicare amount allowed by the fee schedule. Medicare is responsible for paying 80 percent of this allowed charge (after patients have met their annual deductibles). Patients are responsible for the other 20 percent. The provider may bill the patient for services not covered by Medicare.

A Medicare PAR provider has a usual charge of $200 for a certain prescription drug, and the Medicare allowed charge is $84. The provider must write off the difference between the two charges. The patient is responsible for 20 percent of the allowed charge, not of the provider's usual charge:

Provider's usual fee:	$200.00
Medicare allowed charge:	$84.00
Medicare pays 80 percent	$67.20
Patient pays 20 percent	$16.80

The total the provider can collect is $84. The provider must write off the $116 difference between the usual fee and the allowed charge.

Nonparticipation

Nonparticipating providers decide whether to accept assignment on a claim-by-claim basis. Providers who elect not to participate in the Medicare program but who accept assignment on a claim are paid 5 percent less for their services than are PAR providers. For example, if the Medicare allowed amount for a service is $100, the PAR provider receives $80 (80 percent of $100), and the nonPAR provider receives $76 ($80 minus 5 percent). NonPAR providers who do not accept assignment are subject to Medicare's charge limits. They may not charge a Medicare patient more than 115 percent of the amount listed in the Medicare nonparticipating fee schedule. This amount—115 percent of the fee listed in the nonPAR MFS—is called the **limiting charge.**

For a claim that is not assigned, the provider can collect the full payment of the limiting charge from the patient at the time of the visit. The claim is then submitted to Medicare. If approved, Medicare will pay 80 percent of the allowed amount on the nonPAR fee schedule—not the limiting amount. Medicare sends this payment directly to the patient, since the provider has already been paid.

limiting charge maximum amount a nonPar provider can charge a Medicare patient based on the Medicare nonparticipating fee schedule

The following example illustrates the different fee structures for PARs, nonPARs who accept assignment, and nonPARs who do not accept assignment:

EXAMPLE

Participating Provider

Provider's standard fee	$120.00
Medicare fee	$60.00
Medicare pays 80% ($60.00 × 80%)	$48.00
Patient or supplemental plan pays 20% ($60.00 × 20%)	$12.00
Provider adjustment (write-off) ($120.00 − $60.00)	$60.00

Nonparticipating Provider (Accepts Assignment)

Provider's standard fee	$120.00
Medicare nonPAR fee ($60.00 − 5%)	$57.00
Medicare pays 80% ($57.00 × 80%)	$45.60
Patient or supplemental plan pays 20% ($57.00 × 20%)	$11.40
Provider adjustment (write-off) ($120.00 − $57.00)	$63.00

Nonparticipating Provider (Does Not Accept Assignment)

Provider's standard fee	$120.00
Medicare nonPAR fee ($60.00 − 5%)	$57.00
Limiting charge (115% × $57.00)	$65.55
Patient billed	$65.55
Medicare pays patient (80% × $57.00)	$45.60
Total provider can collect	$65.55
Patient out-of-pocket expense ($65.55 − $45.60)	$19.95

✳ Compliance Guideline

Physicians must accept assignment for clinical diagnostic laboratory services (generally, procedures with CPT codes in the 80000s). A physician may not bill Medicare patients for these services. If the physician does not accept Medicare assignment for them, the right to bill the patient is forfeited. The physician may accept assignment for laboratory services only and refuse to accept assignment for other services. In this case, two separate claims are filed. One claim accepts assignment for laboratory services, and the other refuses assignment for other services.

Excluded and Not Medically Necessary Services

Medicare is a defined benefits program, meaning that to be covered, an item or service must be in a benefit category established by law and not otherwise excluded. Payment will be denied for services that are excluded by Medicare and for services not considered reasonable and necessary for the patient.

Excluded Services

Excluded services are those that are not covered under any circumstances, such as routine physical examinations and many screening tests. These services change from year to year. Providers are not required to warn patients that the services are excluded, but it is good practice to do so. Before the excluded service is provided, the patient may be given written notification that Medicare does not pay for it and an estimate of how much they may have to pay.

Medically Unnecessary Services

Services that the Medicare program does not consider generally medically necessary are not covered unless certain conditions are met, such as the relation of the procedure, treatment, or service to the diagnosis. For example, a vitamin B_{12} injection is a covered service only for patients with certain diagnoses, such as pernicious anemia. To be considered medically necessary, a treatment must be:

- Appropriate for the symptoms or diagnoses of the illness or injury
- Not elective
- Not an experimental or investigational procedure
- An essential treatment, not one performed for the patient's convenience
- Delivered at the most appropriate level that can safely and effectively be administered to the patient

Several common categories of medical necessity denials include:

- *Improper linkage between the diagnosis and the service:* The diagnosis does not justify the procedures performed. The denial may result from a clerical error (for example, a fifth digit was missing from an ICD-9-CM code). In many of such instances, the claim can be corrected and will eventually be paid. In other situations, the diagnosis is not specific enough to justify the treatment.
- *Too many services in a brief period of time:* Examples of these denials include more than one office visit in a day or too many visits for treatment of a minor problem.
- *Level of service denials:* Claims in this category are either denied or reduced because the services provided were in excess of what was required to adequately diagnose and/or treat the problem.

The Advance Beneficiary Notice (ABN) of Noncoverage

A provider who thinks that a procedure will not be covered by Medicare because it will be deemed not reasonable and necessary, or is excluded must notify the patient before the treatment, using a standard **advance beneficiary notice (ABN) of noncoverage** from CMS (see Figure 4.2). The ABN form is designed to:

- Identify the service or item that Medicare is unlikely to pay for
- State the reason Medicare is unlikely to pay
- Estimate how much the service or item will cost the beneficiary if Medicare does not pay

The ABN includes a mandatory field for cost estimates of the items/services at issue.

advance beneficiary notice (ABN) of noncoverage form given to a patient before treatment when a provider thinks that Medicare will deem a procedure not reasonable and necessary and will not cover it

Figure 4.2 Advance Beneficiary Notice (ABN) of Noncoverage

Patient's Name: _____   Medicare # (HICN): _____

ADVANCE BENEFICIARY NOTICE (ABN)

NOTE: You need to make a choice about receiving these health care items or services.

We expect that Medicare will not pay for the item(s) or service(s) that are described below. Medicare does not pay for all of your health care costs. Medicare only pays for covered items and services when Medicare rules are met. The fact that Medicare may not pay for a particular item or service does not mean that you should not receive it. There may be a good reason your doctor recommended it. Right now, in your case, **Medicare probably will not pay for –**

Items or Services:

Because:

The purpose of this form is to help you make an informed choice about whether or not you want to receive these items or services, knowing that you might have to pay for them yourself. Before you make a decision about your options, you should **read this entire notice carefully.**
- Ask us to explain, if you don't understand why Medicare probably won't pay.
- Ask us how much these items or services will cost you (**Estimated Cost: $_____**), in case you have to pay for them yourself or through other insurance.

PLEASE CHOOSE **ONE** OPTION. CHECK **ONE** BOX.   **SIGN & DATE** YOUR CHOICE.

☐ **Option 1. YES.** **I want to receive these items or services.**

I understand that Medicare will not decide whether to pay unless I receive these items or services. Please submit my claim to Medicare. I understand that you may bill me for items or services and that I may have to pay the bill while Medicare is making its decision. If Medicare does pay, you will refund to me any payments I made to you that are due to me. If Medicare denies payment, I agree to be personally and fully responsible for payment. That is, I will pay personally, either out of pocket or through any other insurance that I have. I understand I can appeal Medicare's decision.

☐ **Option 2. NO.** **I have decided not to receive these items or services.**

I will not receive these items or services. I understand that you will not be able to submit a claim to Medicare and that I will not be able to appeal your opinion that Medicare won't pay.

_____   _____
Date   Signature of patient or person acting on patient's behalf

NOTE: **Your health information will be kept confidential.** Any information that we collect about you on this form will be kept confidential in our offices. If a claim is submitted to Medicare, your health information on this form may be shared with Medicare. Your health information which Medicare sees will be kept confidential by Medicare.

OMB Approval No. 0938-0566   Form No. CMS-R-131-G   (June 2002)

It also includes an option for beneficiaries to choose to receive an item/service and pay for it out of pocket, rather than have a Medicare claim submitted.

When provided, the ABN must be verbally reviewed with the beneficiary or his/her representative and questions posed during that discussion must be answered before the form is signed. The form must be provided in advance to allow the beneficiary or representative time to consider options and make an informed choice. The ABN may be delivered by employees or subcontractors of the provider, and is not required in an emergency situation. After the form has been completely filled in and the form is signed, a copy is given to the beneficiary or his or her representative. In all cases, the provider must retain the original notice on file.

The CMS website contains a Medicare coverage home page (http://medicare.gov) that informs the public about coverage issues and about how coverage decisions are made. The page contains links to the coverage database and to issues about how national coverage is determined.

Tech Check

What four types of Medicare Advantage plans may beneficiaries choose to enroll in instead of the Original Medicare Plan?

What is the basis for payments for all Original Medicare Plan services?

What terms are used to describe services that may not be covered under Medicare?

Who Pays First?

Medigap insurance policies from federally approved private insurance carriers to fill gaps in Medicare coverage

Many beneficiaries choose to buy **Medigap insurance** policies from federally approved private insurance carriers to fill gaps in Medicare coverage. Generally, the plan pays the beneficiary's deductibles and coinsurance. Some policies also cover services that Medicare does not cover. Medicare beneficiaries enrolled in managed care plans usually do not need Medigap insurance. Their plans have the same benefits that Medigap policies offer without an additional premium.

Medi-Medi beneficiary individuals who are eligible for both Medicaid and Medicare

crossover claim claims submitted first to Medicare and then to Medicaid

If a beneficiary has Medigap insurance, Medicare is the primary payer. That means that Medicare pays first, and then the Medigap carrier determines its obligations. File the claim with Medicare first. Some individuals are eligible for both Medicaid and Medicare (**Medi-Medi beneficiary**). Claims for these patients are first submitted to Medicare. Then they are sent to Medicaid along with the Medicare Remittance Notice. Most Medicare carriers automatically transmit these **crossover claims** to the state Medicaid payer.

In some situations, Medicare is the secondary payer. Generally, these situations are related to accidents or job-related illnesses or injuries. Medicare is a secondary payer when:

- The patient is covered through an employer's group health plan or the spouse's employer's group health plan.
- The services are for treatment of a work-related illness or injury covered by workers' compensation or federal black lung benefits.
- No-fault insurance or liability insurance covers the services, such as those for illness or injury resulting from an automobile accident.
- A patient with end-stage renal disease is covered by an employer's group health plan. In this case, Medicare is the secondary payer for the first eighteen months.

Medicare Part D

Upon the passage of the Medicare prescription benefit in 2006, beneficiaries quickly took advantage of the savings. People who used to forgo or cut back on medicine had the means to fill more prescriptions. For example, in 2006, spending on prescription drugs increased 8.5 percent nationally, compared to a 5.8 percent increase in 2005. Of the current Medicare population of more than 44 million people, over 25 million are already enrolled in Medicare Advantage plans with drug benefits or in independent prescription drug plans.

Nearly all retail pharmacies participate in at least one prescription drug plan, and more than two-thirds offer beneficiaries the choice of all available plans in their region. Clearly, pharmacy technician insurance specialists handle a tremendous number of Medicare prescriptions. The ability to understand the various types of plans, coverage, and benefits and the accompanying regulations is vital to handling these cases successfully.

The Plans

Medicare offers two basic options for prescription drug coverage. In the first option, under the Original Medicare Plan, participants can choose and join a Medicare **Prescription Drug Plan (PDP).** The second option is to select a Medicare Advantage Plan (such as an HMO or a PPO) that includes drug coverage. The different plans vary by cost, coverage, and convenience, and patients elect the most suitable plans based on these criteria.

Prescription Drug Plan (PDP)
basic option for offering prescription drug coverage

Medicare Prescription Drug Plans

Medicare Prescription Drug Plans are run by insurance companies and other private companies that have been approved by Medicare. PDPs provide coverage for prescription drugs only and may be used with the Original Medicare Plan, medical savings accounts, and with Medicare Cost Plans, a type of HMO. They may be used with some PFFS plans that do not include the Medicare prescription drug benefit.

This example illustrates the payment a beneficiary would be required to make under a specific Medicare Prescription Drug Plan. The beneficiary has a deductible of $200.00, and the plan pays 75% of the remaining cost of the drugs, leaving the beneficiary to pay 25% as coinsurance.

EXAMPLE

Beneficiary Prescription Drug Expenses

Total amount owed for the prescription drugs	$500.00
Amount left to be paid after the deductible ($500.00 − $200.00)	$300.00
Amount plan pays after deductible ($300.00 × 75%)	$225.00
Amount beneficiary pays after deductible ($300.00 × 25%)	$75.00
Total amount paid by the beneficiary ($200.00 + $75.00)	$275.00

In this situation, the pharmacy technician would need to tell the beneficiary that the deductible had not yet been met and the beneficiary owed 25% of the remaining cost as coinsurance, for a total out-of-pocket expense of $275.00 for the prescription drugs.

Medicare Advantage Drug Plans

Medicare Advantage plans are an alternative method for getting Medicare benefits. These plans combine coverage for doctor and hospital benefits (from Medicare Parts A and B) with coverage for prescription drugs under Part D in one plan provided through a private insurance company. Both HMO and PPO plans may fall under this category.

Medicare Special Needs Plans (SNPs)

special needs plans (SNP)
prescription drug coverage offered by Medicare to some patients with specific needs

A third type of plan that some patients with specific needs have is the Medicare **special needs plan (SNP).** SNPs also provide Medicare prescription drug coverage, but only some people are eligible. SNPs serve people who:

- Live in certain institutions (such as nursing homes) or who require nursing care at home
- Are eligible under both Medicare and Medicaid
- Have at least one specific chronic or disabling condition (including diabetes, congestive heart failure, mental illness, or HIV/AIDS)

Sponsoring Companies

Many different health care companies compete to offer Medicare prescription drug coverage through different methods (private fee-for-service, Medicare Advantage, and so on). These sponsors contract with pharmacies to create pharmacy networks that provide covered drugs to beneficiaries enrolled in their plans. The companies are located in different regions and offer different benefits, exclusions, limitations, and conditions of coverage. The plans vary on a number of points, such as:

- Service area (availability of different companies varies by region, state, and/or city, while many types are available nationwide)
- Monthly premium and copayments
- Yearly deductible for drug coverage
- Amount required to pay for each prescription
- Whether there is coverage during a gap in service

Available coverage varies by region and/or state. Some companies are national and offer varying services in different locations, while others are regional, and some may operate within only one state. At least two plans offered by different sponsors are required to be available in every region.

> EXAMPLE

AARP is a well-known national company that offers three Medicare Prescription Drug Plans: AARP MedicareRX Plan, AARP MedicareRX Plan-Enhanced, and AARP MedicareRX Plan-Saver. The plans vary in the amounts of their copays, which can be as low as $6, and their annual deductibles—only one of the three plans has one. AARP MedicareRX Plan-Enhanced offers tier 1 generic drug coverage through the gap and a bonus drug list.

Beneficiary Eligibility and Enrollment

All people who are enrolled in Medicare are eligible for coverage under Medicare Part D. Drug plans are available from private collaborating companies. Those who wish to be enrolled must select and join a plan between November 15 and December 31 each year, with coverage beginning on January 1 of the following year. An enrolled patient can switch health and drug coverage to a new plan during that same time period each year. Enrollment generally lasts for a full calendar year, and patients may be subject to auto-enrollment in their current plans if new ones are not selected. Late enrollment may result in a penalty; people who join when first eligible will pay lower monthly premiums.

Once a person has selected the appropriate drug plan, he or she will need to join by one of the following methods:

- *Paper application:* The company offering the plan can provide an application to be completed and returned via mail or fax.
- *Online registration:* Some Medicare drug plan companies allow people to join through their websites.
- *Over the phone:* It may be possible to call the company offering the drug plan to enroll.
- *Online through Medicare:* Some Medicare drug plans allow registration through Medicare's online enrollment center.
- *Over the phone with Medicare:* People can call Medicare at 1-800-MEDICARE to enroll by giving the name of the Medicare drug plan they wish to join.

The following information is required for someone to enroll in a Medicare drug plan:

- Personal identification information (such as name, birth date, and the like)
- Permanent street address
- The information found on the person's Medicare card

Benefit Structure

The benefits patients receive through Medicare vary depending on the plans selected. In general, the patient and the plan each pay part of the costs for the prescription drug coverage. The plans also generally have monthly premiums that patients pay and a set deductible that must be paid prior to the start of cost-sharing with the drug plan. Once the deductible has been met, the beneficiary makes a copayment or coinsurance payment at the time he or she receives a prescription. There may be different tiers with different costs, and payments may vary based on whether the drugs are brand name or generics. Some plans increase the patient's cost for prescription drugs once they reach a certain limit.

Another benefit factor is the **coverage gap** or "doughnut hole." A coverage gap occurs when a patient and the Medicare drug plan have spent a

Compliance Guideline

Companies that offer Medicare drug plans to patients must follow certain rules and regulations in the way they conduct their business and contact prospective enrollees.

coverage gap point where a patient and the Medicare drug plan have spent a predetermined amount of money for covered drugs and the patient is responsible for the entire cost of the drugs

predetermined amount of money for covered drugs and the patient is responsible for all costs of the drugs. While in a coverage gap, patients are still required to pay monthly premiums. Even when a coverage gap exists, the most a patient would ever have to pay out-of-pocket before leaving the coverage gap is $3,850 (in 2007). Every state offers at least one Medicare drug plan with some sort of coverage during a gap. Additionally, many plans cover generic drugs during the coverage gap, allowing people to get the medications they need.

EXAMPLE

The following example shows the payments a beneficiary might be required to make when entering into a coverage gap. In this example, the coverage gap begins after the beneficiary spends $2,400 during a calendar year. Beneficiaries can calculate what they would expect to spend out-of-pocket by estimating their monthly prescription drug expenses.

Beneficiary Coverage Gap Expenses

Amount of coverage at which coverage gap initiates	$2,400.00
Beneficiary's monthly prescription drug expenses	$300.00
Beneficiary's yearly expenses (12 × $300.00)	$3,600.00
Amount paid by beneficiary ($3,600.00 − $2,400.00)	$1,200.00

In this situation the beneficiary would have to pay $300.00 out-of-pocket monthly for a total of four months ($1,200.00 / $300.00 = 4), or from September through December.

Sample Dialogue

The following is a sample conversation, using figures from the example above, between a pharmacy technician and a beneficiary who is confused by the situation.

Technician: Here is your medication. You owe $300.00 for your order today.

Beneficiary: I have Medicare coverage for my drugs; they pay for my medication.

Technician: Under your Medicare prescription drug plan, you have coverage for up to $2,400 per year for your expenses. With your order last month, you reached that mark, and you are now required to pay out-of-pocket.

Beneficiary: For how long will I have to pay for the medication?

Technician: At the end of the year, your drug plan will renew, and you will once again be covered until you reach the predetermined amount of expenses.

Formulary Administration

As discussed in Chapter 3, a formulary is a list of a plan's preferred drugs within each therapeutic class. Medicare Part D also has a formulary, which is selected with the help of a team of health care providers and includes both brand-name and generic drugs. The formulary is required to include at least two drugs in each category, although the plan can choose the specific drugs to cover.

A Medicare Part D drug plan often divides its formulary into different tiers that vary in terms of the patient's payment and the coverage. Here is an example of a tiered system:

- *Tier 1:* Lowest copayment; coverage for most generic prescription drugs
- *Tier 2:* Medium copayment; coverage for less expensive brand-name prescription drugs (determined by the plan to be less costly but as effective)
- *Tier 3:* Higher copayment; coverage for typical brand-name prescription drugs
- *Specialty tier:* Highest copayment or coinsurance; coverage for unique, very high-cost drugs

An exception can sometimes be made if a patient's doctor believes that a specific drug from a higher tier is necessary. A complete list of drugs covered under Medicare formularies by state is available online at the Medicare website.

Covered Drugs

Medicare Part D drug plans typically cover all the drugs listed in their formularies as long as all the coverage rules are followed and the drugs are medically necessary. The drug plans are required to cover almost all drugs that fall in the following six classes:

1. Antipsychotics
2. Antidepressants
3. Anticonvulsants
4. Immunosuppressants
5. Cancer drugs
6. HIV/AIDS drugs

Medicare drug plans are not required to cover certain types of drugs such as benzodiazepines, barbiturates, drugs for weight loss or gain, and drugs for erectile dysfunction. Plans usually do not cover over-the-counter drugs either.

Since not all drugs are covered under Medicare drug plans, patients have the right to select generic versions of prescription drugs or different drugs that are safe and effective for the same purposes. Patients also have the right to ask Medicare to make an exception to cover a drug and to pay out-of-pocket for the drug and request reimbursement from the plan.

Electronic Prescribing

In April 2008, the Centers for Medicare and Medicaid Services issued a final rule establishing additional electronic prescribing standards for Medicare Part D. Prescribers, dispensers, and other providers are not required to implement e-prescribing, but those who do must comply with the new standards for Part D covered drugs effective April 1, 2009. The final rule sets new standards for four types of information:

1. *Formulary and benefits:* Doctors and prescribers will be able to communicate with Part D sponsors about which prescription drugs are covered under a beneficiary's plan and which generic drugs may be less expensive.
2. *Medication history:* Doctors will be able to communicate among themselves about the prescribed medications a patient is taking or has taken.

3. *Fill status notification:* A pharmacy will be able to send an e-mail notice to a doctor about whether a patient's prescription has been picked up or has been partially filled.
4. *Provider identifier:* Providers, dispensers, and sponsors will be required to use the NPI to identify individual health care providers in Part D e-prescribing transactions.

Pharmacy Enrollment

When a patient enrolls in a Medicare drug plan and presents prescriptions at the pharmacy, specified procedures are followed to verify the patient's information. The technician should first request the patient's Medicare Part D plan ID card. A patient who does not have an ID card may have a plan enrollment "acknowledgement letter" or "confirmation letter" that should contain the following four prescription (Rx) data:

1. Bank identification number (BIN)
2. Processor control number (PCN)
3. Group ID for the patient's specific plan (GROUP)
4. Member ID information

TrOOP Facilitator Medicare online eligibility and enrollment system

If an individual has no proof of enrollment, the plan's billing information may be available through the Medicare Part D online eligibility and enrollment system, known as the **TrOOP Facilitator.** Once the information is processed, the patient's plan will verify that the patient is or is not covered by means of a computer message. Some individuals are dually eligible under both Medicare and Medicaid and may require different treatment (see Chapter 5).

Some Medicare beneficiaries will also be issued Rx cards (see Figure 4.3) by their prescription drug plans. These cards contain information about prescription drug discounts available to the cardholders.

Quality Improvement Organizations

Quality Improvement Organization (QIO) group of practicing doctors and other health care experts paid by the federal government to check and improve the care given to people with Medicare

A **Quality Improvement Organization (QIO)** is a group of practicing doctors and other health care experts paid by the federal government to check and improve the care given to Medicare beneficiaries. There are many local branches of these organizations, and they can be contacted with complaints about the quality of care, such as about the incorrect dosage of a drug. The Part D plan is required to cooperate with the QIO in order to resolve the

Figure 4.3 Medicare Rx Card

SeniorCare

A Medicare Prescription Drug Plan

ID: R97382672-01   Effective 2009
Name: SMITH, JANE S.   HN Group ID: 123456B

Rx Claims Processor: Caremark
RxBIN: 004212
RXPCN: AVD
RxGrp: RX5792   MedicareR$_x$
                             Prescription Drug Coverage

Material ID: S5678_2007_85 CMS Approved 09/07
CMS_S5678 XXX

Member questions call 1-800-555-5555
(TTY/TTD: 1-800-666-6666

For Provider Inquiries, Call 1-888-999-9999

For Pharmacist Inquiries, Call 1-888-777-7777

Submit Part D Prescription Drug Claims to:
Claims Net
10965 Rancho Cordova Dr., Ste. 210
San Diego, CA 92143

complaints. Quality of care complaints must be filed in writing, and quality of care grievances do not have to be filed within a specific time period.

Retiree Prescription Drug Coverage

Retired patients must consider how existing drug coverage from their previous employer works in conjunction with Medicare Part D. Medicare helps employers and labor unions continue to provide retiree drug coverage that meets its standards, although employers do have choices about how to work with Medicare. Former employers and unions may use some of these methods to offer retirees drug plans:

- Ask retirees to join a Medicare drug plan, and then provide additional coverage to supplement that plan
- Make special arrangements with a particular Medicare drug plan
- Get financial support from Medicare to help to continue to provide retirees with high-quality coverage

When electing whether to enroll in Medicare Part D, retirees examine whether it is beneficial, since the prescription drug coverage offered by their former employer or union may be better.

Medication Therapy Management (MTM)

At least 1.5 million American are sickened, injured, or killed each year by errors in prescribing, dispensing, and taking medications. **Medication therapy management (MTM)** is a provision of the Medicare Modernization Act of 2003 designed to address the growing problem of medication mismanagement in the United States, which is currently estimated as the fourth leading cause of death among the elderly. MTM offers pharmacists free education to improve medication use and reduce the number of adverse drug events and also pays pharmacists for their expert services. MMA Part D allows pharmacists to enter into contracts with Medicare patients' prescription drug plans to provide reimbursable health evaluation and to review eligible patients' profiles.

medication therapy management (MTM) provision of the Medicare Part D prescription drug plan that offers pharmacists free education to improve medication use and reduce the number of adverse drug events

MTM Objectives

MTM is a service or group of services that increases the likelihood of positive therapeutic outcomes for patients. The primary goals of MTM are to:

- Optimize therapeutic outcomes through quality medication use
- Reduce the risk of adverse drug events
- Improve health outcomes and cost reduction
- Offer eligibility to enroll in MTM

MTM Eligibility

Not all Medicare members covered by Medicare Part D are eligible for MTM. Medicare members are eligible for MTM if they:

- Are referred for MTM services by a health care provider
- Receive medications from more than one prescriber
- Are taking four or more medications for chronic conditions
- Have at least one chronic disease (for example, congestive heart failure or diabetes)

- Have laboratory values outside the normal range that could improve with medication therapy
- Do not demonstrate adherence to their medication regimen for more than three months
- Have limited health literacy or cultural differences, so that intensive communication is needed to maximize care
- Spend at least $4,000 annually for prescription drugs covered by Part D
- Have been discharged from a hospital or skilled nursing facility where they were prescribed a new medication regimen within fourteen days of being admitted

MTM Services

Licensed health care professionals, such as nurses, pharmacists, and physicians, provide the MTM services. Each Medicare prescription drug plan selects its method of communication. Some Medicare agents refer a beneficiary to a special counseling session with a pharmacist; some mail educational materials directly to beneficiaries; some send medication information with recommendations to physicians; and others have nurses or pharmacists consult with patients over the phone.

All MTM services document information relating to medication therapy reviews, personal medication records, medication action plans, interventions and referrals, and follow-up visits. The documentation of these MTM services includes the following:

- Referral for MTM services by a health care provider
- Patient demographics
- Patient allergies, diseases, or conditions
- All medications, including prescription, nonprescription, herbal, and other dietary supplement products
- Assessment of medication therapy problems and plans for resolution
- Performance of therapeutic monitoring
- Interventions or referrals
- Education
- Scheduling and planning of follow-up appointments
- Recording of amount of time spent with patient
- Feedback to providers or patients
- Coding and billing

Starting in 2005, pharmacists began adopting CPT codes for billing MTM services, removing a major barrier that once prevented delivering quality MTM programs.

 Tech Check

What benefit became available with the implementation of Medicare Part D in 2006?

Which people enrolled in Medicare are eligible for participation in Medicare Part D?

Who pays for prescription drug benefits when a patient has entered the coverage gap?

What is the name of the provision of the Medicare Part D prescription drug plan that offers pharmacists free education to improve medication use and reduce the number of adverse drug events?

Chapter Summary

1. Medicare, the federal health insurance program for people who are sixty-five and older, is divided into four parts. Medicare Part A helps pay for inpatient hospital services, care in a skilled nursing facility, home health care, and hospice care. Medicare Part B helps pay for physician services, outpatient hospital services, durable medical equipment, and other services and supplies. Medicare Part C allows private health insurance companies to contract with CMS to offer Medicare benefits through their own policies. Medicare Part D provides voluntary Medicare prescription drug plans to eligible members through private insurance plans.

2. Providers annually choose whether to participate in the Medicare program, and participating physicians agree to accept the Medicare terms and fee schedule. PAR providers may bill the patient for coinsurance and deductibles but may not collect amounts higher than the Medicare amount allowed by the fee schedule. NonPAR providers who do not accept assignment are subject to Medicare's charge limits and therefore must agree to the limiting charge. NonPar providers may not charge a Medicare patient more than 115 percent of the fee listed in the nonPAR MFS.

3. For coverage under Medicare, an item or service must be in a benefit category established by law and not otherwise excluded. Excluded services, which change yearly, are not covered under any circumstances.

Services that Medicare does not consider generally medically necessary are not covered unless certain conditions are met, such as the relation of the procedure, treatment, or service to the diagnosis. Providers must use a standard ABN to notify patients in advance about services they think may be determined to be medically unnecessary.

4. Medicare offers two basic options for prescription drug coverage. The first option is under the Original Medicare Plan, where participants can join a Medicare PDP, and the second option is to join a Medicare Advantage plan that includes drug coverage. Plans vary by cost, coverage, and convenience, and patients elect the most suitable plans based on these criteria. Many health care companies with competing services offer Medicare prescription drug coverage through several different methods.

5. Medicare beneficiaries owe payments for the prescriptions they receive based on several factors. Predetermined coinsurance and copayment standards affect patient fees, as do a drug's status as a brand-name or generic medication and whether it is listed in a formulary. Patients fall into a coverage gap if their Medicare drug plan's predetermined amount of financial coverage for drugs has been met, at which time they become responsible for the cost of all their prescription drugs for the remainder of the year.

Chapter Review

Multiple Choice

Read the question and select the best response.

1. Medicare enrollees' health insurance cards do *not* list which of the following?
   A. the beneficiary's name
   B. the beneficiary's Medicare number
   C. the beneficiary's sex
   D. the beneficiary's diseases

2. Which Medicare plans give patients financial incentives to use doctors within a network, but allow them to choose to go outside the network?
   A. preferred provider organization plans
   B. Medicare managed care plans
   C. private fee-for-service plans
   D. medical savings account plans

3. What is a group of practicing doctors and other health care experts working to check and improve Medicare called?
   A. medication therapy management
   B. Medicare managed care plan
   C. hospice
   D. Quality Improvement Organization

4. Which program allows private health insurance companies to contract with CMS to offer Medicare benefits through their own policies?
   A. Medicare Part A
   B. Medicare Part B

C. Medicare Part C

D. Medicare Part D

5. Which program offers benefits that include both regular services and preventive services?

A. Medicare Part A

B. Medicare Part B

C. Medicare Part C

D. Medicare Part D

6. Which program makes prescription drugs available through private insurance plans?

A. Medicare Part A

B. Medicare Part B

C. Medicare Part C

D. Medicare Part D

7. Which program helps pay for hospice care?

A. Medicare Part A

B. Medicare Part B

C. Medicare Part C

D. Medicare Part D

8. Which of the following types of plans is *not* an option for a beneficiary to enroll in instead of the Original Medicare Plan?

A. Medicare private fee-for-service plans

B. Medicare insurance coverage

C. medical savings accounts

D. Medicare preferred provider organizations

9. In 2007, what was the most a patient would ever have to pay out-of-pocket before leaving the coverage gap?

A. $2,400

B. $3,150

C. $3,850

D. $4,500

10. What is a person covered by Medicare called?

A. prescriber

B. Medicare beneficiary

C. Medi-Medi beneficiary

D. MTM beneficiary

11. Which of the following categories in a tiered system under Medicare Part D would offer the lowest copayment?

A. tier 1

B. tier 2

C. tier 3

D. specialty tier

12. Which service is performed for a patient who does not have symptoms, abnormal findings, or any past history of the disease?

A. diagnostic service

B. outpatient hospital service

C. screening service

D. surgical service

13. Which of the following is *not* required for someone to enroll in a Medicare drug plan?

A. permanent street address

B. information found on the Medicare card

C. personal identification information

D. personal health history

14. What minimum number of Medicare Part D plans offered by different sponsors is required to be available in every region?

A. zero

B. one

C. two

D. three

15. Which of the following is *not* a primary goal of medication therapy management?

A. improve health outcomes and cost reduction

B. encourage retirees to enroll in a Medicare drug plan

C. reduce the risk of adverse drug effects

D. optimize therapeutic outcomes through quality medication use

16. Medicare Part B does *not* provide coverage for which of these?

A. prescription drug services

B. kidney dialysis

C. braces

D. prosthetic devices

17. What percent of their allowed charges are patients required to pay after they have met their annual deductibles under Medicare Part B?

A. 10 percent

B. 15 percent

C. 20 percent

D. 25 percent

18. Which of the following treatments would not be considered medically necessary?

A. an appropriate treatment for the symptoms or diagnoses of an illness

B. an experimental or investigational procedure

C. a treatment that is not elective

D. an essential treatment

19. Medicare special needs programs would *not* service people in which of the following circumstances?

    A. people eligible under both Medicare and Medicaid

    B. people living in a nursing home

    C. people looking for an alternative method for getting Medicare benefits

    D. people with at least one specific chronic or disabling condition

20. Which of the following groups of people would *not* be eligible to receive benefits under Medicare Part A?

    A. disabled adults

    B. people age sixty-five or older

    C. people with end-stage renal disease

    D. none of the above

Matching

Match the key term with the appropriate definition.

_____ 1. Helps pay for physician services, outpatient hospital services, durable medical equipment, and other services and supplies

_____ 2. Offers pharmacists free education to improve medication use and reduce the number of adverse drug events

_____ 3. The maximum amount a nonPar provider can charge a Medicare patient based on the Medicare nonparticipating fee schedule

_____ 4. Enables private health insurance companies to contract with CMS to offer Medicare benefits through their own policies

_____ 5. Term for individuals who are eligible for both Medicaid and Medicare

_____ 6. Group of practicing doctors and other health care experts paid by the federal government to check and improve the care given to people with Medicare

_____ 7. Policies from federally approved private insurance carriers to fill gaps in Medicare coverage

_____ 8. The Medicare online eligibility and enrollment system

_____ 9. Helps pay for inpatient hospital services, care in a skilled nursing facility, home health care, and hospice care

_____ 10. Provides voluntary Medicare prescription drug plans to people who are eligible for Medicare

A. Medicare Part A

B. Medicare Part B

C. Medicare Part C

D. Medicare Part D

E. medication therapy management

F. TrOOP Facilitator

G. Quality Improvement Organization

H. limiting charge

I. Medi-Medi beneficiary

J. Medigap insurance

True/False

Indicate whether the following statements are true or false.

_____ 1. Prescription drug plans offered by private insurance plans are not available under Medicare Part D.

_____ 2. At least two prescription drug plans offered by different sponsors are required to be available in every region.

_____ 3. Medicare providers may charge patients when filing claims on their behalf.

_____ 4. Medicare is not the primary payer if a beneficiary has Medigap insurance.

_____ 5. Medication therapy management is a service or group of services that increases the likelihood of positive therapeutic outcomes for patients.

_____ 6. All prescribers, dispensers, and other providers are required to implement electronic prescribing.

_____ 7. A hospice is a public or private organization that provides services for terminally ill patients and their families.

_____ 8. Everyone who is eligible for Medicare Part A may choose to enroll in Part B.

_____ 9. There is no limit to the amount of money a beneficiary may spend on prescription drugs when in the coverage gap.

_____ 10. The Medicare Fee Schedule (MFS) is the basis for payments for all Original Medicare Plan services.

Short Answer

Think carefully about the following questions, and write your answers in the space provided.

1. What advantages might a participating provider in the Medicare program have over a nonPAR provider?

_____

_____

2. Nearly all retail pharmacies participate in at least one prescription drug plan, and more than two-thirds of them offer beneficiaries the choice of all available plans in their region. Why do you think pharmacies are so eager to participate?

_____

_____

3. How do you think electronic prescribing will make the process of filling prescriptions safer and more accurate for patients?

_____

_____

Internet Activities

1. Visit the AARP website at **https://www.aarpmedicarerx.com/** and explore the Medicare Part D plans AARP offers in more detail. What factors do you think patients would consider the most when making a choice?

2. Explore the information about Medigap insurance on the Medicare website at **http://www.medicare.gov/medigap/default.asp.** Read about some of the factors patients should consider when selecting this insurance.

Medicaid, TRICARE, CHAMPVA, Workers' Compensation, and Discount Card Programs

chapter

5

 Learning Outcomes

After completing this chapter, you will be able to define the key terms and:

5-1. Identify two ways Medicaid programs vary from state to state.

5-2. Discuss Medicaid prescription coverage.

5-3. Explain who is eligible for TRICARE and CHAMPVA and how to verify eligibility.

5-4. Discuss the prescription benefit programs offered to TRICARE and CHAMPVA beneficiaries.

5-5. Describe the coverage that employees have under workers' compensation insurance and the possible drug benefits.

5-6. Briefly discuss discount programs that assist individuals in paying for prescriptions.

 Chapter Outline

Medicaid

TRICARE and CHAMPVA

Workers' Compensation

Discount Card Programs

Key Terms

catastrophic cap
categorically needy
CHAMPVA
Defense Enrollment Eligibility Reporting System (DEERS)
discount card
Early and Periodic Screening, Diagnosis, and Treatment (EPSDT)
Federal Medicaid Assistance Percentage (FMAP)
fiscal agent
Medicaid
medically indigent/needy
military treatment facility (MTF)
payer of last resort
sponsors
State Children's Health Insurance Program (SCHIP)
Temporary Assistance for Needy Families (TANF)
TRICARE
TRICARE Extra
TRICARE for Life
TRICARE Prime
TRICARE Reserve Select (TRS)
TRICARE Standard
Welfare Reform Act
workers' compensation insurance

Medicaid assistance program that pays for health care services for people with incomes below the national poverty level

Federal Medicaid Assistance Percentage (FMAP) payments made by the federal government based on a state's average per capita income in relation to the national income average

fiscal agent organization that processes claims for a government program

Medicaid

Medicaid is an assistance program, not an insurance program. It pays for health care services for people with incomes below the national poverty level. Both the federal and state governments pay for Medicaid, and in some areas local taxes support it as well. The federal government makes payments to states under the **Federal Medicaid Assistance Percentage (FMAP).** The amount of the payment is based on the state's average per capita income in relation to the national income average. States with high per capita incomes receive less federal funding than do states with low per capita incomes. In each state, Medicaid is administered by a **fiscal agent,** an organization that processes claims for a government program. The Center for Medicaid and State Operations, a department of the Centers for Medicare and Medicaid Services (CMS), oversees the programs that are administered by the states.

The first Medicaid programs were required by federal law as part of the Social Security Act of 1965. Under the legislation, the federal government determines which kinds of medical services are covered and paid for by the federal portion of the program. States participate in their Medicaid programs in two ways: (1) they may authorize additional kinds of services or make additional groups eligible, and (2) they determine eligibility within federal guidelines. Because of this participation by state governments, Medicaid programs change often and vary widely from state to state. Pharmacy technician insurance specialists must become familiar with their own state's rules and requirements; only general information is covered in this chapter.

Medicaid Coverage

According to federal guidelines, Medicaid pays for the following types of health care:

- Physician services
- Laboratory and X-ray services
- Inpatient hospital services
- Outpatient hospital services
- Rural health clinic services
- Home health care
- Family planning services
- Federally qualified health-center (FQHC) services
- Skilled care at a public nursing facility
- Prenatal and nurse-midwife services
- Early and Periodic Screening, Diagnosis, and Treatment (EPSDT) services
- Emergency care

The state portion of a Medicaid program often includes a number of additional services under its federally funded Medicaid program. Some examples of extra assistance enacted by individual states are:

- Clinic services
- Emergency room care
- Eyeglasses and eye refraction

- Ambulance services
- Prescription drugs
- Chiropractic services
- Prosthetic devices
- Mental health services
- Private-duty nursing
- Certain cosmetic procedures
- Other diagnostic, screening, preventive, and rehabilitative services
- Allergy services
- Dermatology services
- Dental care
- Podiatry services

Family planning services include counseling, diagnosis, treatment, drugs, and supplies related to planning the number and spacing of children. **Early and Periodic Screening, Diagnosis, and Treatment (EPSDT)** is a prevention, early-detection, and treatment program for children under the age of twenty-one who are enrolled in Medicaid. Covered services include medical history, physical exam, assessment of development and immunization status, and screening for anemia, lead absorption, tuberculosis, sickle cell trait and disease, and dental, hearing, and vision problems. States must pay for all services identified in an EPSDT exam, even if they do not pay for the services for other eligible individuals.

The **State Children's Health Insurance Program (SCHIP),** part of the Balanced Budget Act of 1997, requires states to develop and implement plans for health insurance coverage for uninsured children. The more than 5 million children served by SCHIP come from low-income families whose incomes are not low enough to qualify for Medicaid. The program is funded jointly by the federal government and the states. It provides coverage for many preventive services and covers children up to age nineteen.

Early and Periodic Screening, Diagnosis, and Treatment (EPSDT) prevention, early detection, and treatment program for children under the age of twenty-one who are enrolled in Medicaid

State Children's Health Insurance Program (SCHIP) program that requires states to develop and implement plans for health insurance coverage for uninsured children

> **EXAMPLE**
>
> The state of Arkansas offers a health insurance program for children known as ARKids First. The program offers two types of health insurance for children who might otherwise not have any coverage. ARKids A offers a comprehensive package of benefits for low-income families, while ARKids B is designed to provide coverage for families with higher incomes.

The Ticket to Work and Work Incentives Improvement Act of 1999 (TWWIIA) expanded the availability of health care services for workers with disabilities. Previously, persons with disabilities often had to choose between health care and a job. TWWIIA gives states the option of allowing individuals with disabilities to purchase Medicaid coverage that is necessary to enable them to maintain employment.

In recent years, however, because of large state budget deficits, state laws have cut back on some of these benefits—for example, prescription drug benefits and hearing, vision, and dental benefits for adults. Many states have also had to restrict eligibility for Medicaid and to reduce Medicaid payments to doctors, hospitals, nursing homes, and other providers.

In each state, the Medicaid and/or social services agency can provide a list of services and limits or preauthorization requirements for those services. Any additional services, such as those just listed, are paid entirely from state funds.

Medicaid Eligibility

Generally, Medicaid recipients are people with low incomes who have children or are over the age of sixty-five, are blind, or have permanent disabilities. Within federal guidelines, states determine income levels and other qualifications for eligibility.

One group of Medicaid recipients is known as **categorically needy.** The needs of these beneficiaries are addressed under the Personal Responsibility and Work Opportunity Reconciliation Act of 1996 (P.L. 104-193), commonly known as the **Welfare Reform Act,** which created **Temporary Assistance for Needy Families (TANF).** Eligibility for TANF is determined at the county level. This program helps with living, in contrast to medical, expenses.

Some states extend Medicaid eligibility to include another group of people classified as **medically needy** or **medically indigent.** These individuals earn enough money to pay for basic living expenses, but they cannot afford high medical bills. In some cases, Medicaid recipients in the medically needy classification must pay deductibles before they receive benefits. Some Medicaid recipients in this category must pay coinsurance for medical services. States choose their own names for the programs. For example, California calls its program MediCal.

Once Medicaid eligibility is determined, the recipient gets an identification card or coupon explaining effective dates and additional information such as a coinsurance requirement, if any. An example of a Medicaid card is shown in Figure 5.1.

Different states authorize coverage for different lengths of time. Some states issue cards twice a month, some once a month, and others every two months or every six months. Most states, however, are moving to electronic verification of eligibility under the Electronic Medicaid Eligibility Verification System (EMEVS). Eligibility is determined through electronic or telephone verification each time a patient has a prescription filled.

categorically needy special group of Medicaid recipients whose needs are addressed under the Welfare Reform Act

Welfare Reform Act law that addresses the needs of categorically needy Medicaid recipients

Temporary Assistance for Needy Families (TANF) program that helps with living expenses

medically indigent/needy individuals who earn enough money to pay for basic living expenses but cannot afford high medical bills

Figure 5.1 Medicaid Identification Card

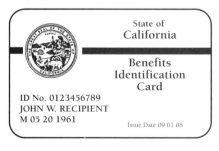 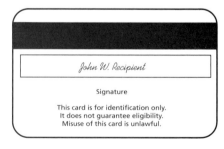

Front   Back

Because of this changing eligibility, the pharmacy technician insurance specialist is alert to checking these three points:

1. *Eligibility:* Medicaid eligibility varies from month to month if the recipient's income fluctuates. Comply with the state's requirements for verifying eligibility. The patient should present a Medicaid identification card at each visit.

2. *Preauthorization:* Most states require preauthorization for specified services. Check with the state's fiscal agent to find out how to get preauthorization by telephone and whether a written confirmation form must also be filed. If the state requires preauthorization, charges for services that did not get prior approval will not be paid. In emergencies, such as emergency room situations, authorization may be obtained after the treatment.

3. *Other insurance coverage:* If a patient who is eligible for Medicaid has additional health care coverage through an insurance plan or another government program such as Medicare, the patient's Medicaid eligibility does not relieve the other program or plan of its responsibility. In fact, the other program or insurance carrier is the primary carrier in these cases. Medicaid is the secondary carrier. File the claim first with the primary carrier, and file for Medicaid benefits last. Because of this sequence, Medicaid is referred to as the **payer of last resort.**

payer of last resort term for Medicaid, which pays after all other insurance carriers

Medicaid Drug Programs

As states have their own guidelines for Medicaid, the prescription drug plans that they offer through Medicaid are unique. The covered and noncovered drugs under Medicaid, steps required for beneficiaries to receive these drugs, options for obtaining information and registering for a program, and expected reimbursement practices for pharmacies vary by state. Some state Medicaid plans require copayments at the point of sale; the copayment amount varies with the price of the prescription. For example, in Arkansas a prescription that costs $70.00 would have a copayment of $3.00, and a prescription that costs $5.00 would have a copayment of $0.50.

EXAMPLE

The Texas Medicaid Program, run by the Texas Health and Human Services Commission (HHSC), seeks to improve health care for people who otherwise might go without medical care. The program offers a free help phone number with staff available at all times, easy to use applications, and benefits offices, as well as online resources to get information.

In early 2008, the Texas Vendor Drug Program announced the implementation of a Medicaid Preferred Drug List (PDL). Under PDL guidelines, preferred drugs are immediately available to beneficiaries, while nonpreferred drugs require prior authorization. All drugs already available to Medicaid beneficiaries continue to be available. If a nonpreferred drug is deemed medically necessary, a seventy-two-hour emergency supply is available. Visit the Texas Medicaid website at http://www.hhsc.state.tx.us/medicaid/med_info.html for more information on the program.

In 2008, the state of New Jersey announced a new plan to increase coverage for uninsured patients. New discount drug cards have been distributed to doctors and hospital clinics through one of the state's largest HMO plans, QualCare Inc., to be given to uninsured patients. Some pharmacies are offering the discounts as a way to bring more customers into their stores.

EXAMPLE

The New York State Medicaid Pharmacy program covers medically necessary FDA-approved prescription drugs. The program covers most over-the-counter products, but requires a fiscal order with the same information found on a prescription. The New York State Medicaid program also offers pharmacy reimbursement for prescription drugs. The dollar amount of reimbursement a pharmacy can expect to receive is regulated by the type of drug, federal pricing structures, estimated acquisition costs, and average wholesale prices.

New York State also uses the Medicaid Preferred Drug Program (PDP) to promote the use of less expense but equally effective prescription drugs when appropriate. All drugs covered by Medicaid are still available under the PDP, and medications are available regardless of their status as preferred or nonpreferred. Visit the New York State Department of Health website at http://www.health.state.ny.us/ for more information on the program.

 Tech Check

Medicaid pays for the health care services of people who fall under what financial qualification?

What entities are responsible for determining income levels and other qualifications for eligibility within the federal guidelines?

TRICARE and CHAMPVA

TRICARE and CHAMPVA are government medical insurance plans primarily for families of members of the U.S. uniformed services.

TRICARE

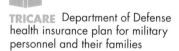

TRICARE Department of Defense health insurance plan for military personnel and their families

TRICARE is the Department of Defense health insurance plan for military personnel and their families. It offers several different health care plans to its beneficiaries in the Army, Navy, Air Force, Marine Corps, Coast Guard, Public Health Service, and National Oceanic and Atmospheric Administration. TRICARE replaced the program known as CHAMPUS (Civilian Health and Medical Program of the Uniformed Services).

TRICARE benefits spouses and children of active-duty service members, who are called **sponsors.** The health care for the service members themselves is automatically provided or paid for by their branch of service. TRICARE also serves military retirees and their families, some former spouses, and survivors of deceased military members.

A TRICARE beneficiary must be listed in the Department of Defense's **Defense Enrollment Eligibility Reporting System (DEERS).** A worldwide database of people covered by TRICARE, DEERS helps the Department of Defense track the use of medical services to better plan for beneficiaries' needs. It also helps eliminate fraudulent use of military benefits.

TRICARE Standard

TRICARE Standard is a fee-for-service program that covers medically necessary services provided by a civilian physician when an individual cannot obtain treatment from a **military treatment facility (MTF),** which is a military-operated medical facility. Military families may receive services at an MTF, but the services offered vary by facility, and first priority is given to active-duty service members.

Individuals must first seek care at a military treatment facility. If an individual lives within a certain proximity to a military hospital, generally within a forty-mile radius, a nonavailability statement (NAS) must be filed by the local military hospital before the patient can be treated at a civilian hospital for inpatient nonemergency care. The NAS is an electronic document stating that the service the patient requires is not available at the nearby military treatment facility. The form is electronically transmitted to the DEERS database. If it is not filed, TRICARE will not pay the hospital claim. If the patient has other insurance that is primary to TRICARE, an NAS is not required. In addition, emergency services do not require nonavailability statements.

Under TRICARE Standard, medical expenses are shared between TRICARE and the beneficiary. The TRICARE program uses the term *cost-share* for the patient's coinsurance. Patient cost-share payments are subject to an annual **catastrophic cap,** a limit on the total medical expenses that the patient must pay in one year. Once this cap has been met, TRICARE pays 100 percent of additional charges for that coverage year.

TRICARE Prime

TRICARE Prime is a managed care plan similar to an HMO. After enrolling in the plan, each individual is assigned a *primary care manager (PCM)* who coordinates and manages that patient's medical care. The PCM may be a single military or civilian provider or a group of providers. In addition to most of the benefits offered by TRICARE Standard, the program offers preventive care, including routine physical examinations. Active-duty service members are automatically enrolled in TRICARE Prime. TRICARE Prime enrollees receive the majority of their health care services from military treatment facilities, and they receive priority at these facilities.

An individual must pay an annual enrollment fee to join the TRICARE Prime program. Under TRICARE Prime, there is no deductible, and no payment is required for outpatient treatment at a military facility. For active-duty family members, no payment is required for visits to civilian

sponsors active-duty service members whose spouses and children benefit under TRICARE

Defense Enrollment Eligibility Reporting System (DEERS) worldwide database of people covered by TRICARE

TRICARE Standard fee-for-service program that covers medical services provided by a civilian physician

military treatment facility (MTF) military-operated medical facility

catastrophic cap limit on the total medical expenses a patient must pay in one year

TRICARE Prime managed care plan similar to an HMO

network providers, but different copayments apply for other beneficiaries, depending on the type of visit. For example, for retirees and their family members, an outpatient visit with a civilian provider requires a $12 copayment.

TRICARE Extra

TRICARE Extra alternative managed care plan for individuals who want to receive services primarily from civilian facilities and physicians rather than from military facilities

TRICARE Extra is an alternative managed care plan for individuals who want to receive services primarily from civilian facilities and physicians rather than from military facilities. Since it is a managed care plan, individuals must receive health care services from a select network of health care professionals. They may also seek treatment at military facilities, but active-duty personnel and other TRICARE Prime enrollees receive priority at those facilities, so care may not always be available. TRICARE Extra is more expensive than TRICARE Prime but less costly than TRICARE Standard. There is no enrollment fee, but there is an annual deductible.

TRICARE Reserve Select

TRICARE Reserve Select (TRS) premium-based health plan available for purchase by certain members of the National Guard and Reserve activated on or after September 11, 2001

Due to the large number of military reservists who have been called up for active duty, the Department of Defense has implemented **TRICARE Reserve Select (TRS).** This program is a premium-based health plan available for purchase by certain members of the National Guard and Reserve activated on or after September 11, 2001. TRS provides members and their covered family members with comprehensive health care coverage similar to TRICARE Standard and TRICARE Extra.

TRICARE for Life

TRICARE for Life program offered to military personnel to fulfill a promise that they would receive lifelong health care

TRICARE for Life (TFL) was initiated in October 2001 to fulfill a promise made to many military personnel at the time of enrollment that they would receive lifelong health care. TFL provides military health care coverage to TRICARE beneficiaries who are sixty-five years of age or older. In situations with multiple potential payers, Medicare pays first, followed by any other health insurance, and the remaining beneficiary liability may then be paid by TFL.

CHAMPVA

CHAMPVA program that helps pay health care costs for families of veterans who are totally and permanently disabled because of service-related injuries

CHAMPVA is the Civilian Health and Medical Program of the Veterans Administration, which is now known as the Department of Veterans Affairs. This government program helps pay health care costs for families of veterans who are totally and permanently disabled because of service-related injuries. It also covers the surviving spouse and children of a veteran who died from a service-related disability. Some surviving spouses of service members who died on active duty may be eligible for CHAMPVA.

The Veterans Health Care Eligibility Reform Act of 1996 requires veterans with a 100 percent disability to be enrolled in the program to receive benefits. Prior to this legislation, enrollment was not required. The Department of Veterans Affairs determines eligibility. CHAMPVA enrollees do not need to obtain nonavailability statements, as they are not eligible to receive service in military treatment facilities. A VA hospital is not considered a military treatment facility.

Figure 5.2 Sample Military Health Insurance
Identification Card

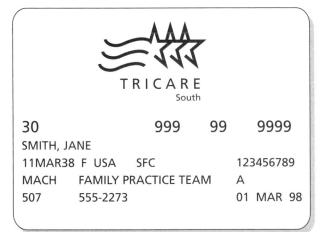

Beneficiary Identification

People who qualify for TRICARE or CHAMPVA are called beneficiaries. Beneficiaries get identification cards that contain information needed for claims (see Figure 5.2). When a patient qualifies for one of these programs, the pharmacy technician insurance specialist checks the effective and expiration dates to be sure that the card authorizes civilian medical care. Then a photocopy of the front and back of the identification card is filed in the patient's medical record. If the patient is a child under the age of ten, the parent's card is checked; beneficiaries under the age of ten usually do not get identification cards.

Although the claim processor needs eligibility information from the DEERS system, there are times when a beneficiary is not listed. For example, even though military sponsors must enroll their families in DEERS, sometimes they do not keep up with changes in family status or location. Also, new service members may not have had time to enroll their families.

The insurance specialist should ask all TRICARE and CHAMPVA patients whether they are enrolled in DEERS. Patients can check their status through the nearest personnel office of any branch of service or through the toll-free number of the DEERS center.

 HIPAA Tip

Sponsors may telephone DEERS to verify eligibility; providers may not contact DEERS directly because the information is protected by the HIPAA Privacy Rule.

TRICARE Drug Programs

TRICARE provides many options and services to beneficiaries to meet their prescription drug needs. This pharmacy benefit is available to all eligible U.S. uniformed service members, including TFL beneficiaries entitled to Medicare Part A and B based on their age, disability, and/or end-stage renal disease. In order to fill a prescription, beneficiaries must have a valid Uniformed Services identification card and a written prescription.

The amount a TRICARE beneficiary pays toward the cost of medication is based on whether the prescription is a generic, formulary, or nonformulary pharmaceutical. Copayments are equal for all beneficiaries (except active-duty service members, who receive free medications), depending on where the prescription is filled. TRICARE beneficiaries can fill prescriptions at military treatment facility pharmacies, through the TRICARE Mail Order Pharmacy, at TRICARE Retail Network Pharmacies, or at non-network pharmacies for a higher cost.

Military Treatment Facility Pharmacies

TRICARE offers pharmacies at military treatment facilities as a convenient and inexpensive option to beneficiaries. Prescriptions that are on the MTF formulary may be filled (usually up to a ninety-day supply) at no cost to the beneficiary. TRICARE has a basic core formulary that lists all the medications that must be made available at all full-service military pharmacies.

TRICARE Mail Order Pharmacy

The TRICARE Mail Order Pharmacy (TMOP), administered by Express Scripts, Inc. (ESI), is available for prescriptions that beneficiaries take on a regular basis, and is often a more cost-effective method of receiving prescriptions. Prescription refills may be requested by mail, phone, or online, giving beneficiaries flexibility. In order to use the TMOP, completion of a registration form is required, after which beneficiaries are able to mail written prescriptions to ESI and receive their medications through the mail in ten to fourteen working days. A beneficiary can receive up to a ninety-day supply for most medications through the TMOP. The TMOP may not be used by beneficiaries who have prescription drug coverage under another health plan unless the medication is not covered by that plan or the beneficiary exceeds the amount of coverage the other plan provides.

TRICARE Retail Network Pharmacies

Beneficiaries in the United States and its territories may fill prescriptions through the TRICARE Retail Network Pharmacies (TRRx), a nationwide network of over fifty-four thousand retail pharmacies. Beneficiaries who use pharmacies in the ESI network do not have to file claims for reimbursement if the pharmacies are outside their primary region.

Non-network Pharmacies

Not all retail pharmacies are part of the TRICARE network; those that are not are known as non-network pharmacies. While beneficiaries can fill prescriptions at non-network pharmacies, doing so is the most expensive option; they have to pay for the entire amount initially and then file a claim to receive partial reimbursement. Beneficiaries can check with TRICARE to determine whether a pharmacy is in its network.

Tech Check

Who is eligible for benefits under the various TRICARE programs?

Health care costs for families of veterans who are totally and permanently disabled because of service-related injuries are covered under what program?

What do TRICARE beneficiaries need to have in order to fill prescriptions?

Workers' Compensation

When someone is injured accidentally in the course of performing work or a work-related duty or becomes ill as a result of the employment environment, the cost of medical care for the injury or illness is covered by a federal or state plan known as **workers' compensation insurance.** Such a plan also provides benefits for lost wages and permanent disabilities.

Workers' compensation covers two kinds of situations that require medical care. A *traumatic injury* is caused by a specific event or series of events within a single workday or shift. An example is a broken leg caused by a fall from a catwalk in a warehouse. *Occupational disease or illness* (also known as *nontraumatic injury*) is caused by the work environment over a longer period of time. An example of occupational disease is a lung condition caused by repeated exposure to fumes in the workplace.

Compensation for work-related illnesses and injuries may be one of five types:

1. Medical treatment
2. Lost wages (temporary disability)
3. Permanent disability payments (either partial or full disability)
4. Compensation for dependents of employees who are fatally injured
5. Vocational rehabilitation

Federal Programs, Forms, and Procedures

Work-related illnesses or injuries suffered by civilian employees of federal agencies, including volunteers in the Peace Corps and AmeriCorps programs, are covered under the Federal Employees' Compensation Act (FECA). Other federal workers' compensation laws include the Federal Coal Mine Health and Safety Act (which includes the Black Lung Benefits Act), the Longshore and Harbor Workers' Compensation Act, and the Energy Employees Occupational Illness Compensation Program Act. All these plans are administered by the Office of Workers' Compensation Programs (OWCP), except for the Longshore and Harbor Workers' Compensation Act, which is administered by the Division of Longshore and Harbor Workers. Both the OWCP and the Division of Longshore and Harbor Workers are part of the U.S. Department of Labor.

workers' compensation insurance plan that provides benefits for someone who is injured accidentally in the course of performing work or a work-related duty or becomes ill as a result of the employment environment

Workers' Compensation Drug Programs

Individuals who receive prescription coverage as a result of workers' compensation may be provided with third-party prescription cards to pay for their prescriptions. The pharmacy technician insurance specialist should verify a patient's coverage under workers' compensation by contacting the patient's employer and asking for the name of the insurance carrier. The carrier should then be contacted to find out what information is needed in order to process the claim for the prescription.

 Tech Check

Name the two kinds of situations covered by workers' compensation that require medical care.

Individuals who receive prescription drug coverage as a result of workers' compensation may have what type of card to pay for their prescriptions?

Discount Card Programs

discount card offered by states to people who cannot afford prescription drugs

A number of states offer a **discount card** for people who cannot afford prescription drugs. For example, in the state of Florida, people sixty and older who do not have prescription drug coverage or who are covered by Medicare but fall into the program's prescription drug coverage gap are eligible for a discount card. The program is also available to people under age sixty without prescription drug coverage if their income is below a certain level. For individuals, the threshold is $30,636 a year. For a family of four, the cutoff is $61,956.

Discount cards offer savings that depend on the drugs. Average savings for commonly prescribed drugs are from 5 percent to more than 40 percent.

 Tech Check

Who might be offered a discount card?

Chapter Summary

1. Medicaid programs vary from state to state in a number of ways. The sources of a state's Medicaid funding, the different types of programs that are available, and the payment systems, types of coverage, and eligibility for beneficiaries all vary among state Medicaid programs. States make decisions about their Medicaid programs within the boundaries of established federal guidelines.

2. State Medicaid programs offer varying options with regard to covered and noncovered drugs, steps required for beneficiaries to receive drugs, options for obtaining information and registering for a program, and the expected reimbursement practices for pharmacies. States generally also offer information about approved drug lists and pricing structures, customer service features,

and other various programs and plans to provide prescription drug coverage.

3. TRICARE and CHAMPVA are government medical insurance plans primarily for families of members of the U.S. uniformed services. Eligible beneficiaries are generally enrolled in DEERS and carry identification cards with information needed for claims. TRICARE offers several different programs to fit the varying needs of military personnel. CHAMPVA helps families of veterans who are totally and permanently disabled because of service-related injuries and the surviving spouses and children of deceased veterans.

4. Under TRICARE and CHAMPVA, many options and services are provided to beneficiaries to meet their prescription drug needs, with this pharmacy benefit being available to all eligible U.S. uniformed service members. TRICARE beneficiaries can fill prescriptions at MTF pharmacies, through the TMOP, at TRRx pharmacies, or at non-network pharmacies.

Beneficiary payments vary based on the status of the medication prescribed and where the prescription is filled.

5. Employees who are accidentally injured in their work or working environment may be covered by workers' compensation insurance for medical care for their injury or illness. Benefits provided by these plans may include payment for lost wages and compensation for medical treatment, permanent disability, dependents of fatally injured employees, and vocational rehabilitation. Employees who receive prescription drug coverage may be provided with a third-party prescription card to pay for their prescriptions.

6. Several states offer discount cards to people who cannot afford prescription drugs. Savings depend on the drugs, with average savings for commonly prescribed drugs ranging from 5 percent to more than 40 percent. Types of coverage and patient eligibility in the programs vary by state.

Chapter Review

Multiple Choice

Read the question and select the best response.

1. The first Medicaid programs were required by federal law as part of which government action?
   A. HIPAA Privacy Rule
   B. Social Security Act of 1965
   C. Veterans Health Care Eligibility Reform Act of 1996
   D. Longshore and Harbor Workers' Compensation Act

2. A TRICARE beneficiary must be listed in which government system?
   A. CHAMPVA
   B. Defense Enrollment Eligibility Reporting System (DEERS)
   C. Medicaid
   D. none of the above

3. Which program requires states to develop and implement plans for health insurance coverage for uninsured children?
   A. Social Security Act of 1965
   B. TRICARE Reserve Select
   C. CHAMPVA
   D. State Children's Health Insurance Program

4. In the TRICARE health plans, what is the name of the electronic document that states that the service the patient requires is not available at the nearby military treatment facility?
   A. out-of-network approval statement
   B. prior authorization form
   C. nonavailability statement
   D. authorization statement

5. What is the name of the program that offers a premium-based health plan available for purchase by certain members of the National Guard and Reserve activated on or after September 11, 2001?
   A. TRICARE Prime
   B. TRICARE Standard
   C. TRICARE Reserve Select
   D. TRICARE Extra

6. What is the name of the program that assigns a primary care manager to coordinate and manage the patient's medical care?
   A. TRICARE Prime
   B. TRICARE Standard
   C. TRICARE Reserve Select
   D. TRICARE Extra

7. What is the name of the program that applies to individuals who want to receive services primarily from civilian facilities and physicians rather than from military facilities?

A. TRICARE Prime

B. TRICARE Standard

C. TRICARE Reserve Select

D. TRICARE Extra

8. Discount cards for people who cannot afford prescription drugs are offered on which level?

A. national

B. county

C. state

D. neighborhood

9. According to federal guidelines, Medicaid will not pay for which of these types of health care?

A. cosmetic surgery

B. home health care

C. physician services

D. family planning services

10. Which of the following methods may be used by a beneficiary to request a prescription refill through the TRICARE Mail Order Pharmacy?

A. online

B. mail

C. phone

D. all of the above

11. Which of these groups of people would not necessarily qualify for Medicaid?

A. people with permanent disabilities

B. blind people

C. people with children

D. people who are over the age of sixty-five with low incomes

12. Which of the following are examples of extra assistance enacted by some states under Medicaid?

A. prosthetic devices

B. prescription drugs

C. dental care

D. all of the above

13. Which of the following is *not* a valid type of compensation for work-related illnesses and injuries?

A. vocational rehabilitation

B. placement in a new job

C. medical treatment

D. lost wages

14. What is the name of the government program that helps pay health care costs for families of veterans who are totally and permanently disabled because of service-related injuries?

A. CHAMPVA

B. TRICARE for Life

C. Medicaid

D. workers' compensation

15. Which organization is referred to as the payer of last resort?

A. TRICARE

B. Medicare

C. CHAMPVA

D. Medicaid

Matching

Match the key term with the appropriate definition.

_____ 1. A managed care plan that is similar to an HMO

_____ 2. Fee-for-service program covering medical services provided by a civilian physician

_____ 3. An organization that processes claims for a government program

_____ 4. Plan for individuals who want to receive services primarily from civilian facilities and physicians rather than from military facilities

_____ 5. A term for Medicaid as it relates to other insurance carriers

A. TRICARE Extra

B. TRICARE for Life

C. TRICARE Prime

D. TRICARE Reserve Select

E. TRICARE Standard

F. discount card

G. fiscal agent

H. catastrophic cap

I. payer of last resort

J. categorically needy

_____ 6. A group whose needs are addressed under the Welfare Reform Act

_____ 7. Plan available for purchase by certain members of the National Guard and Reserve activated on or after September 11, 2001

_____ 8. States may offer this to people who cannot afford prescription drugs

_____ 9. The limit on the total medical expenses a patient must pay in one year

_____ 10. Offered to military personnel to fulfill a promise about receiving lifelong health care

True/False

Indicate whether the following statements are true or false.

F 1. According to federal guidelines, Medicare will not pay for emergency care.

_____ 2. Eligibility for TANF is determined at the state level.

_____ 3. Medicaid eligibility may vary from month to month if the recipient's income fluctuates.

_____ 4. The federal government makes payments to states under the Federal Medicaid Assistance Percentage (FMAP).

F 5. Workers' compensation will never cover a nontraumatic injury.

_____ 6. A TRICARE beneficiary must be listed in the Defense Enrollment Eligibility Reporting System (DEERS).

_____ 7. Medicaid is referred to as the payer of last resort.

T 8. TRICARE beneficiaries may not fill prescriptions at non-network pharmacies.

T 9. Generally, Medicaid recipients are people with low incomes who have children or are over the age of sixty-five, are blind, or have permanent disabilities.

T 10. No annual enrollment fee is required to join the TRICARE Prime program.

Short Answer

Think carefully about the following questions, and write your answers in the space provided.

1. What types of information do you think pharmacy technician insurance specialists should know about their state's Medicaid program? Why?

_____

_____

_____

2. Should customers who are filling prescriptions at a pharmacy receive different treatment based on the prescription drug plan they are enrolled in? Explain your answer.

_____

_____

_____

Internet Activities

1. Visit the website for Arkansas Medicaid at **https://www.medicaid.state.ar.us/,** and review the programs offered. In addition, search for a Medicaid Prior Authorization form.

2. Explore the official TRICARE Management Activity website at **http://www.tricare.mil** for more information about the various programs and services that TRICARE offers.

3. Use the health insurance website at **http://healthinsuranceinfo.net/** to learn about the Medicaid benefits for your state.

Claim Preparation and Transmission

Learning Outcomes

After completing this chapter, you will be able to define the key terms and:

6-1. List the major sections of information that are required to complete a pharmacy claim.

6-2. Discuss the procedure that is followed when a patient has more than one pharmacy benefit.

6-3. Describe the purpose of dispense as written (DAW) codes.

6-4. Discuss the ways in which the retail price of a prescription is established.

6-5. List the three methods of submitting claims.

6-6. Describe the HIPAA standard for electronic retail pharmacy drug claims.

6-7. Describe the process of real-time claim adjudication.

6-8. Explain the different functions of a drug utilization review (DUR) program.

6-9. Discuss billing for durable medical equipment (DME).

Chapter Outline

Claim Content
Creating Claims
Other Types of Pharmacy Billing

Key Terms

average wholesale price (AWP)

birthday rule

CMS-1500

compounding

coordination of benefits (COB)

dispense as written (DAW) codes

dispensing fee

durable medical equipment (DME)

maximum allowable cost (MAC)

National Council for Prescription Drug Programs (NCPDP) Telecommunications Standard Version 5.1 and Batch Standard 1.1

National Drug Code (NDC)

primary insurance

real-time claims management systems

secondary insurance

switch vendor

universal claim form (UCF)

usual and customary price (U&C)

Claim Content

When a patient fills a prescription with the aid of any type of medical insurance, a claim must be sent to the involved third party or parties. Pharmacy technician insurance specialists know how to complete claims, the appropriate methods used to send them, and their proper destinations based on the patient's medical insurance. The correct patient, prescriber, pharmacy, insurance, and prescription information must be recorded on the claim, and the correct insurance plan, codes, pricing, and fees need to be assigned. The proper filing of a claim will save the pharmacy from unnecessary penalties and delays in the process, and will also ensure that the maximum benefit is received. Today most claims are filed electronically through online claim submission, although paper claims are still sometimes used.

Patient Information

Recording the correct patient information is vital to a successful claim submission and is generally the beginning point for filing a claim. The pharmacy technician insurance specialist must verify for whom the prescription is being filed and record the information accordingly. The following components are recorded when completing the patient information portion of a claim:

- Patient name
- Date of birth
- Gender
- Patient address
- Patient phone number
- Relationship to cardholder
- Pharmacy/prescriber's internal patient ID

Figure 6.1 displays a screen from a pharmacy management (PM) program containing patient information.

Prescriber Information

In addition to completing the information about the patient, the pharmacy technician insurance specialist must also input the correct information about the prescribing physician. This information must be verified in order for a prescription to be valid. Three components are recorded when completing the prescriber information portion of a claim:

1. Prescriber ID (NPI or DEA)
2. Prescriber last name
3. Prescriber phone number

The prescriber ID number may comprise two different identifiers. The provider's National Provider Identifier (NPI), a ten-digit number required for all HIPAA-regulated claim submissions, is used to submit the claim. In addition, the Drug Enforcement Administration (DEA) number, which is designed to regulate drug prescriptions and identify the prescriber, may be used. Prescriber information in a PM program is illustrated in Figure 6.2.

Review Prescription Details, Part 1

Instructions: Double-click Activity 1 and follow the on-screen instructions. Answer the questions listed below.

1. When was the prescription written?
2. Who is the prescriber?

Pharmacy Information

Another component in submitting a valid claim is to record the information about the pharmacy that is filling the prescription and thus filing the claim. All this pharmacy information will be consistent for each prescription, except for the name of the pharmacist who fills the order. The following components are recorded when completing the prescriber information portion of a claim:

- Identifier (NPI), formerly known as the NABP number
- Pharmacy name
- Pharmacist name
- Pharmacy address information
- Pharmacy phone number

The NPI was formerly known as the NABP number and was a seven-digit code used to identify the pharmacy.

Figure 6.1 Patient Information in a Pharmacy Management Program

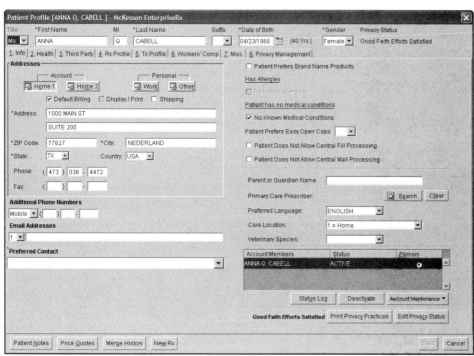

Your Turn 2

Review Prescription Details, Part 2

Instructions: Double-click Activity 2 and follow the on-screen instructions. Answer the questions listed below.

1. How many refills are allowed?
2. What phone number would you call if you had a question about a prescription written by this provider?

Insurance Information

Along with collecting the patient information, the pharmacy technician insurance specialist also records insurance information relevant to that patient. Figure 6.3 shows a screen from a PM program with insurance information. Not all patients have medical insurance, but for those who do, all the relevant information is collected, and proper steps are taken to determine how to file the claim based on the insurance. The following components are recorded when completing the prescriber information portion of a claim:

- Cardholder ID
- Group ID
- Patient relationship

Coordination of Benefits

Sometimes a patient has more than one insurance policy. A patient may have coverage under more than one group plan, such as a person who has

Figure 6.2 **Prescriber Information in a Pharmacy Management Program**

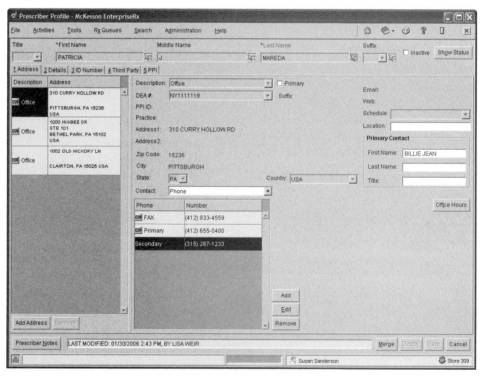

Your Turn 3

Review Prescription Details, Part 3

Instructions: Double-click Activity 3 and follow the on-screen instructions. Answer the questions listed below.

1. What is entered in the Dispense Qty field?
2. What is entered in the DAW Code field?

both employer-sponsored insurance and a policy from union membership. The primary plan is billed first; after adjudication, the second plan can be billed for any eligible unreimbursed amount.

Determining the primary policy is important because under state and/or federal law, insurance policies contain a provision called **coordination of benefits (COB).** This provision ensures that when a patient is covered under more than one policy, maximum appropriate benefits are paid, but without duplication. For example, federal regulations and applicable state laws require that third-party resources be billed before Medicaid is billed. Claims submitted to Medicaid for the member with other insurance on file will be denied until the claim is submitted with COB information.

Determining the Primary Plan A person may have **primary insurance** coverage from an employer and may also be covered as a dependent under a spouse's insurance, making the spouse's plan the person's **secondary insurance.** As noted above, primary insurance is the first insurance that the patient will use for claims, while secondary insurance is used afterward for

coordination of benefits (COB) a provision ensuring that maximum appropriate benefits are paid to a patient covered under more than one policy without duplication

primary insurance the first insurance that the patient will use for claims

secondary insurance the insurance used after primary insurance for any remaining expense

Figure 6.3 Insurance Information in a Pharmacy Management Program

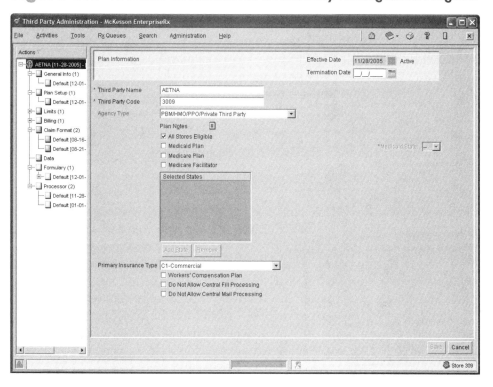

Your Turn 4

Review Third-Party Information

Instructions: Double-click Activity 4 and follow the on-screen instructions. Answer the questions listed below.

1. Which third party should be billed first?
2. What is the patient's copayment for a generic medication (under the primary plan)?

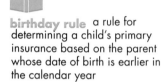

birthday rule a rule for determining a child's primary insurance based on the parent whose date of birth is earlier in the calendar year

any remaining expense. Some real-time claim submission includes review of recipient eligibility and commercial health insurance coverage. The real-time rejection response includes health insurance information to assist in claim submission to the insurance plan when recipient eligibility indicates other insurance coverage.

A common issue involves determining which of two parents' plans is primary for a child. If both parents cover dependents on their plans, the child's primary insurance is usually determined by the **birthday rule.** This rule states that the parent whose date of birth is earlier in the calendar year is primary. For example, Rachel Foster's mother and father both work and have employer-sponsored insurance policies with drug benefits. Her father, George Foster, was born on October 7, 1971, and her mother, Myrna, was born on May 15, 1972. Since the mother's date of birth is earlier in the calendar year (although the father is older), her plan is Rachel's primary insurance. The father's plan is secondary for Rachel.

Table 6.1 summarizes the facts that are used to determine which plan is primary.

Prescription Information

The final information that is required to submit a claim is information about the prescription itself (see Figure 6.4). This aspect is vital in determining how the medical insurance provider handles the claim and what benefits are assigned. The following components are recorded when completing the prescription information portion of a claim:

- Drug name
- Drug dosage
- DEA number (required for controlled medications)

Dispense as Written (DAW) Codes

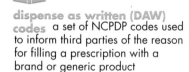

dispense as written (DAW) codes a set of NCPDP codes used to inform third parties of the reason for filling a prescription with a brand or generic product

Dispense as written (DAW) codes are a set of NCPDP codes used to inform third parties of the reason why a brand or generic product was used to fill a prescription. Prescribers and pharmacies must prescribe and dispense the generic form of a drug whenever possible. In most cases, prior authorization is required when a brand name drug is prescribed instead of a generic equivalent. For example, if a physician prescribes Coumadin and indicates that the generic version of the drug (warfarin) should not be substituted, the pharmacy must obtain authorization from the insurance company before providing the Coumadin. If a brand name drug is provided when a generic is available and authorization is not obtained, the claim will not be paid correctly.

Table 6.1 Determining Primary Coverage

1. If the patient has only one policy, it is primary.

2. If the patient has coverage under two plans, the plan that has been in effect for the patient for the longest period of time is primary. However, if an active employee has a plan with the present employer and is still covered by a former employer's plan as a retiree or a laid-off employee, the current employer's plan is primary.

3. If the patient is also covered as a dependent under another insurance policy, the patient's plan is primary.

4. If an employed patient has coverage under the employer's plan and additional coverage under a government-sponsored plan, such as Medicare, the employer's plan is primary.

5. If a retired patient is covered by a spouse's employer's plan and the spouse is still employed, the spouse's plan is primary, even if the retired person has Medicare.

6. If the patient is a dependent child covered by both parents' plans and the parents are not separated or divorced (or if the parents have joint custody of the child), the primary plan is determined by the birthday rule.

7. If two or more plans cover dependent children of separated or divorced parents who do not have joint custody of their children, the children's primary plan is determined in this order:
   - The plan of the custodial parent
   - The plan of the spouse of the custodial parent (if the parent has remarried)
   - The plan of the parent without custody

Figure 6.4 Prescription Information in a Pharmacy Management Program

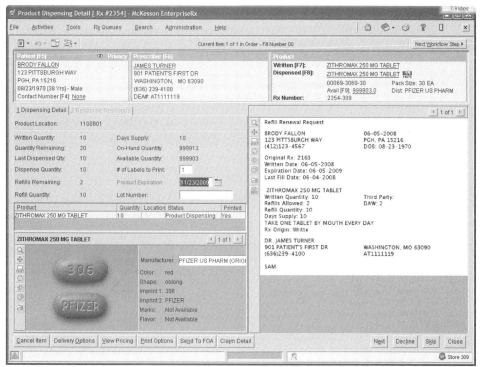

In a pharmacy claim, the DAW code indicates whether the prescriber's instructions regarding generic substitution were followed. Acceptable codes include the following:

0   This is the field default code that is appropriately used for prescriptions in which product selection is not an issue. Examples include prescriptions written for single-source brand products and prescriptions written using the generic name for which a generic product is dispensed.

1   Prescriber has indicated, in a manner specified by prevailing law, that the product is to be dispensed as written.

2   Prescriber has indicated, in a manner specified by prevailing law, that generic substitution is permitted, but the patient requests the brand product. This situation can occur when the prescriber writes the prescription using either the brand or generic name and the product is available from multiple sources.

3   Prescriber has indicated, in a manner specified by prevailing law, that generic substitution is permitted, but the pharmacist determines that the brand product should be dispensed. This can occur when the prescriber writes the prescription using either the brand or generic name and the product is available from multiple sources.

4   This code is used when the prescriber has indicated, in a manner specified by prevailing law, that generic substitution is permitted, but the brand product is dispensed because a currently marketed generic is not stocked in the pharmacy. This situation is caused by the buying habits of the pharmacist, not by the unavailability of the generic product in the marketplace.

5   The prescriber has indicated, in a manner specified by prevailing law, that generic substitution is permitted, but the pharmacist is utilizing the brand product as the generic entity.

6   This code is used when the prescriber has specified that the brand product is medically necessary and requires prior authorization in most cases.

7   Prescriber has indicated, in a manner specified by prevailing law, that generic substitution is permitted, but prevailing law or regulation prohibits the substitution of a brand product even though generic versions may be available in the marketplace.

8   Prescriber has indicated, in a manner specified by prevailing law, that generic substitution is permitted, but the brand product is dispensed because the generic is not currently manufactured or distributed or is temporarily unavailable.

9   Other situation.

National Drug Code (NDC)

National Drug Code (NDC)
an eleven-digit code assigned to all prescription drug products by the labeler or distributor of the product under FDA regulations

All outpatient prescription drugs are billed using the drug's **National Drug Code (NDC),** which is an eleven-digit code assigned to all prescription drug products by the labeler or distributor of the product under FDA regulations. Figure 6.5 displays a partial page from the FDA's National Drug Code Directory. Services for pharmaceuticals must be submitted using NDCs eleven-digit format.

Your Turn 5

Verify a Patient's Medicare Part D Eligibility

Instructions: Double-click Activity 5 and follow the on-screen instructions. Answer the questions listed below.

1. What third party plans are listed in the Medicare Part D Eligibility Check and Billing Priority Results area of the screen?
2. Which plan should be billed first?

For NDC code 12345-6789-10:

12345 is the labeler code

6789 is the product code

10 is the package size

Claims must accurately report the NDC dispensed, the number of units dispensed, the number of days' supply, and the date of dispensing. Provider records are audited on a random basis to assure accurate NDC reporting. Payments for incorrect NDC coded claims may be retroactively recovered, the provider may be required to rebill using accurate NDC information.

Pricing Prescriptions

A number of methods are used to price pharmacy prescriptions in the retail setting:

- Usual and customary (also known as UCR for usual, customary, and reasonable)
- Maximum allowable cost (MAC)
- Average wholesale price (AWP)

Figure 6.5 A Partial Listing from the FDA's National Drug Code Directory

Trade Name	NDC Number	Appl No	Strength	Firm Name
ALBUTEROL SULFATE SYRUP	00472-0825	074454	2MG/5 ML	ACTAVIS MID ATLANTIC LLC
ALBUTEROL SULFATE TABLETS	13411-*279	072637	4MG	ADVANCED PHARMACEUTICAL SERVICES INC
ALBUTEROL SULFATE INHALATION SOLUTION	13411-*277	074543	0.5%	ADVANCED PHARMACEUTICAL SERVICES INC
ALBUTEROL TABLETS	13411-*439	072636	2MG	ADVANCED PHARMACEUTICAL SERVICES INC
ALBUTEROL SULFATE SYRUP	13411-*278	074749	2MG/5ML	ADVANCED PHARMACEUTICAL SERVICES INC
ALBATUSSIN DM DROPS PEDIATRIC	10023-*236	Other	3;50MG/1ML;MG/	ALBA PHARMACAL
ALBATUSSIN EX DROPS PEDIATRIC	10023-*239	Other	50MG/1ML	ALBA PHARMACAL
ALBATUSSIN CF DROPS PEDIATRIC	10023-*245	Other	3;45;2MG/1ML;MG/	ALBA PHARMACAL
ALBATUSSIN PE LIQUID DROPS PEDIATRIC	10023-*242	Other	45;2MG/ML;MG/M	ALBA PHARMACAL
ALBATUSSIN LIQUID PEDIATRIC DROPS SUGAR FREE ALCOHOL FREE	10023-*230	Other	5;2.5MG/ML;MG/M	ALBA PHARMACAL
ALBAFORT INJECTION	10023-*100	Other	100;50;20;MCG;MG;%	ALBA PHARMACAL
ALBA LYBE SYRUP	10023-*101	Other		ALBA PHARMACAL
ALBATUSSIN NN LIQUID	10023-*104	Other	10;5;75;8.3MG/5ML;MG/	ALBA PHARMACAL
ALBA 3 OPHTHALMIC SOLUTION	10023-*186	064047	0.025;1.75MG;MG;UNT	ALBA PHARMACAL
ALBATUSSIN SR TABLETS	10023-*301	Other		ALBA PHARMACAL
ALBATUSSIN SR CAPLETS	10023-*361	Other		ALBA PHARMACAL
ALBALON OPHTHALMIC SOLUTION	11980-*154	080248	0.1%	ALLERGAN AMERICA
ALBUTEROL SULFATE TABLETS	54569-3409	072779	2MG	ALLSCRIPTS LLC
ALBUTEROL TABLETS	54569-2874	072780	4MG	ALLSCRIPTS LLC
ALBUTEROL SULFATE INHALATION	54569-3899	072652	0.083%	ALLSCRIPTS LLC
ALBUTEROL SUFATE SOLUTION	54569-3900	019243	0.5%	ALLSCRIPTS LLC
ALBUTEROL SUFATE SOLUTION	54569-3900	075050	0.5%	ALLSCRIPTS LLC
ALBUTEROL SULFATE SYRUP	54569-4899	074454	2MG/5ML	ALLSCRIPTS LLC
ALBUTEROL SULFATE INHALER	54569-5777	021457	90MCG/INH	ALLSCRIPTS LLC
ALBUTEIN	49669-5211	Other	5%	ALPHA THERAPEUTIC CORP
ALBUTEIN	49669-5213	Other	25%	ALPHA THERAPEUTIC CORP
ALBUTEIN	49669-5212	Other	20%	ALPHA THERAPEUTIC CORP
ALBUMIN SOLUTION HUMAN	63546-*310	Other	5%	ALPINE BIOLOGICS INC

In finding the appropriate price for a prescription, pharmacy technician insurance specialists sometimes need to perform mathematical calculations. Quantities of drugs are always represented numerically, and pricing can require the use of decimals, fractions, percentages, and even equations. The use of mathematics may also be required to determine the proper medicinal dosage for children. Familiarity with systems of measurement (primarily the metric system) is also sometimes required for proper pricing.

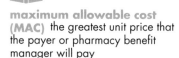

usual and customary price (U&C) the price the provider most frequently charges the general public for a drug

Usual, Customary, and Reasonable Payment Structure The **usual and customary price (U&C)** is the price a provider most frequently charges the general public for a specified drug. Such a price is generally determined at the corporate level by the provider, but a formula is sometimes used when the prescription is filled. Computers in pharmacies are often programmed to calculate U&C prices automatically.

Maximum Allowable Cost Pharmacies serve many customers who are covered by prescription drug benefits. When the pharmacy has a contract as a network member of a health plan run by a third-party payer and/or a PBM (pharmacy benefit manager), charges for prescriptions filled by covered customers are based on the terms of that contract. The **maximum allowable cost (MAC)** is the greatest unit price that the payer or PBM will pay.

maximum allowable cost (MAC) the greatest unit price that the payer or pharmacy benefit manager will pay

average wholesale price (AWP) the average price at which a wholesaler sells prescription drugs to pharmacies, physicians, and other consumers

Average Wholesale Price The **average wholesale price (AWP)** of a prescription drug is the average price at which a wholesaler (such as a drug manufacturer) sells the drug to pharmacies, physicians, and other consumers. This pricing information is based on data obtained from various distributors, manufacturers, and other suppliers. The AWP is generally used as a drug pricing benchmark by payers, as the actual cost of the drugs varies based on the circumstances of purchase.

compounding the preparation or mixing of combinations of drugs prior to purchase

Pricing Compounded Drugs Pharmacists are sometimes required to create medications and combinations specific to individual patients. **Compounding** is the process of mixing or adjusting drug ingredients to customize a medication to meet a patient's individual needs. Compounding may require a pharmacist to utilize medication knowledge and expertise to mix, assemble, package and label, and prepare drugs (and any other necessary components) in a specific manner. The pricing structure for compounds is generally U&C, and there is no reimbursement from insurance carriers under the normal schedule. Compounding fees are generally higher, as more time and effort is required from the pharmacist and multiple drugs are used.

Compounding pharmacists play an essential role in patient's lives by allowing physicians to prescribe customized medication therapy to best meet patients' needs. For the growing number of people with unique health care needs that cannot be addressed with commercially available products, compounded products may be the only viable treatment option.

Compounding has been a significant component of the practice of pharmacy and medicine for time immemorial. Virtually all practicing pharmacists are involved with compounding activities at some point during their careers. Pharmacists are the only health care professionals who have studied chemical compatibilities and can prepare alternate dosage forms. In fact, each state requires pharmacy schools to instruct students in the compounding of pharmaceutical ingredients as part of the core curriculum. Compounding pharmacies are licensed and regulated in the fifty states and the District of Columbia by their respective state boards of pharmacy. The U.S. Pharmacopeia (USP) is the government organization responsible for setting standards and guidelines relating to pharmacy compounding.

Dispensing Fees The fee for a pharmacy's professional services is known as the **dispensing fee** (or professional fee). Determining these fees depends on several factors specific to a pharmacy, including the following components of pharmacy operating costs:

dispensing fee the fee for a pharmacy's professional services

- Staffing (salaries and licensing expenses)
- Store operations and overhead (including rent, utilities, insurance, and marketing)
- Prescription preparation (including dispensing materials, packaging, and supplies)
- Assurance of proper medication use (including drug review, counseling, and education)
- Allowing for a reasonable profit

Additional variables affect the dispensing fee, including the AWP of a particular drug. Dispensing fees are generally regulated on a state level, and states may collect data to determine the average cost pharmacies incur when dispensing a drug. Currently, state Medicaid programs pay a $4 dispensing fee on average, despite the fact that a recent national study shows the average cost to dispense a medication to be between $10 and $12.70.

Copayments

Patients with health insurance are often required to make out-of-pocket payments, generally known as copayments, for prescriptions. Different providers use different copayment plans.

The cost-sharing agreement for health insurance between the provider and the patient is known as coinsurance. Coinsurance involves several payment methods. Two common types are the copay and dual copay. A copay is the amount of the price of a prescription that the patient is required to pay. Dual copays have two different prices, one for a generic medication, and the other for the brand name medication.

Compliance Guideline

Under HIPAA, covered entities are required to show a National Provider Identifier (NPI) in the prescriber ID field on the NCPDP HIPAA transaction. A non-NPI is entered as a default only in the rare case in which a prescriber does not have an NPI.

Average Wholesale Cost Versus Wholesale Acquisition Cost

According to federal and state officials who review pricing structures, although pharmacies charge patients based on the AWP and a dispensing fee, some pharmaceutical companies supply the drugs under a different wholesale acquisition cost price structure. These government officials indicate that the wholesale distributors can be seen as illegally inflating wholesale costs for brand name drugs and creating profits based on overpayments by patients and state-funded health care programs.

Your Turn 6

Review a Price Quote for a Prescription

Instructions: Double-click Activity 6 and follow the on-screen instructions. Answer the questions listed below.

1. How much would the patient's payment be for a brand-name drug?
2. What is the amount of money saved by selecting the generic drug?

 About the NCPDP Pharmacy Database

The NCPDP Provider Identification Number (NCPDP Provider ID), formerly known as the NABP number, was developed over twenty-five years ago to provide pharmacies with unique national identifiers that would assist them in their interactions with pharmacy payers and claim processors. The NCPDP Provider ID is a seven-digit numbering system that is assigned to every licensed pharmacy and qualified non-pharmacy dispensing site (NPDS) in the United States. The NCPDP pharmacy database lists more than seventy thousand pharmacies. NCPDP currently maintains and updates information inn the database.

Non-Pharmacy Dispensing Sites

NCPDP also enumerates licensed dispensing sites in the United States as part of its Non-Pharmacy Dispensing Site Numbering System (NPDS). The purpose of this system is to enable a site to identify itself to prescription drug benefit claim processors.

Subscribing to the Pharmacy Database

The NCPDP pharmacy database is currently licensed by many claim processors, health plans, pharmaceutical manufacturers, health informatics companies, and clearinghouses, among others. It is also available through licensed NCPDP distributors for mailings and other list-related purposes.

 Tech Check

What components are recorded when completing the prescriber information portion of a claim?

What type of insurance is used first when submitting a claim?

What term refers to the price that the provider most frequently charges the general public for a drug?

What is the name for the amount of the price of a prescription that the patient is required to pay?

Creating Claims

Within the pharmacy system, three claim submission options are in use:

1. Electronic (real-time)
2. Electronic (batch)
3. Paper

Electronic Claims

In pharmacy billing, electronic claims can be adjudicated in real time or in several batches throughout the day. **Real-time claims management systems** enable providers to submit electronic pharmacy claims in an online real-time environment. When a prescription is filled, the pharmacy enters the prescription data into the internal system through a personal computer, a terminal, or some other point-of-sale device. The pharmacy system then formats and sends the claim to the payer's claim system for adjudication. Within seconds of submitting a real-time claim, a patient's eligibility is confirmed and the provider receives an electronic response indicating payment or denial.

In some cases, the claim is routed to a switch vendor before being sent on to the payer. The **switch vendor** verifies that the claim conforms to NCPDP transaction standards before forwarding it to the payer's claim system. Switch vendors typically receive claims from hundreds of different claim processors, many with different electronic formats. The switch vendor is able to reformat the data to conform to HIPAA standards.

In addition to verifying eligibility and adjudicating the claim, real-time systems perform such other functions as:

- Checking the patient's benefit plan
- Enforcing formulary compliance
- Pricing the claim and providing copay and reimbursement amounts
- Determining whether a drug is appropriate based on the diagnosis code, patient drug history, clinical guidelines, and other factors before filling the prescriptions
- Evaluating the claim for cost-effectiveness

Claims that are sent in batches are processed through the pharmacy system but do not result in real-time claim responses to the provider.

National Council for Prescription Drug Programs Standards

The **National Council for Prescription Drug Programs (NCPDP) Telecommunications Standard Version 5.1 and Batch Standard 1.1** is the HIPAA standard for electronic retail pharmacy drug claims. The telecommunications standard defines the record layout for prescription claim transactions between providers and adjudicators. Providers include retail pharmacies, mail-order pharmacies, doctors' offices, clinics, hospitals, long-term care facilities, and other entities that dispense prescription drugs and submit drug claims to payers for reimbursement. An adjudicator, or processor, is often a third-party administrator of prescription drug programs acting on behalf of insurers. The adjudicator may be an insurer, a government program, or another entity that receives prescription drug claims.

Table 6.2 lists the data segments and some of the fields available in a billing request transaction. Not all fields are required by every payer; each payer has its own payer sheets, making the transmission of claims slightly different for different payers.

Table 6.3 shows sample claim data in a billing request, followed by the same data in the NCPDP format.

real-time claims management systems a program that enables providers to submit electronic pharmacy claims in an online real-time environment

switch vendor service used to verify that a claim conforms to NCPDP transaction standards before it is forwarded to the payer's claim system

National Council for Prescription Drug Programs (NCPDP) Telecommunications Standard Version 5.1 and Batch Standard 1.1 the HIPAA standard for electronic retail pharmacy drug claims

Table 6.2 Data Segments and Fields in a Billing Request Transaction*

Billing Request (NCPDP Transaction Code B1)

Transaction Header Segment (Mandatory)
BIN Number
Version/Release Number
Transaction Code
Processor Control Number
Transaction Count
Service Provider ID Qualifier
Service Provider ID
Date of Service
Software Vendor/Certification ID

Insurance Segment (Mandatory)
Cardholder ID
Cardholder First Name
Cardholder Last Name
Person Code
Group Number
Plan ID
Eligibility Clarification Code
Patient Relationship Code
Home Plan

Patient Segment (Optional)
Date of Birth
Patient Gender Code
Patient First Name
Patient Last Name
Patient Location

Claim Segment (Mandatory)
Prescription/Service Reference Number Qualifier
Prescription/Service Reference Number
Product/Service ID Qualifier
Product/Service ID
Date Prescription Written
Fill Number
Other Coverage Code
Days' Supply
Quantity Dispensed
Unit Dose Indicator
Compound Code
Number of Refills Authorized
Prescription Origin Code
Level of Service
Submission Clarification Code
Dispense as Written (DAW)

Prior Authorization Type Code
Prior Authorization Number Submitted

Pharmacy Provider Segment

Prescriber Segment (Required)
Prescriber ID Qualifier
Prescriber ID

COB/Other Payments Segment
COB Count
Other Coverage Type
Other Payer ID Qualifier
Other Payer ID
Other Payer Date
Other Payer Paid Count
Other Payer Amount Qualifier
Other Payer Amount Paid
Other Payer Reject Count
Other Payer Reject Code

Workers' Compensation Segment
Date of Injury
Carrier ID

DUR/PPS Segment
DUR/PPS Code Counter
Reason for Service Code
Professional Service Code
Result of Service Code

Pricing Segment (Mandatory)
Ingredient Cost Submitted
Dispensing Fee Submitted
Patient Paid Amount Submitted
Flat Sales Tax Amount Submitted
Percentage Sales Tax Amount Submitted
Percentage Sales Tax Rate Submitted
Percentage Sales Tax Basis Submitted
Usual and Customary Charge
Gross Amount Due
Incentive Fee
Basis of Cost Determination

Coupon Segment

Compound Segment
Compound Dosage Form Description Code
Compound Dispensing Unit Form Indicator

Table 6.2 Data Segments and Fields in a Billing Request Transaction (*cont.*)

Billing Request (NCPDP Transaction Code B1)

Compound Route of Administration Compound Ingredient Component (Count) Compound Product ID Qualifier Compound Product ID Compound Ingredient Quantity Compound Ingredient Drug Cost Compound Ingredient Basis of Cost Determination	**Prior Authorization Segment** **Clinical Segment** Diagnosis Code Count Diagnosis Code Qualifier Diagnosis Code

*Does not include all fields

Table 6.3 Sample Billing Request Claim

Field Number	Field Name	Field Value
102	Version/Release Number	51
103	Transaction Code	B1
109	Transaction Count	1
202	Service Provider ID Qualifier	05
201	Service Provider ID	AAAPROV00007
401	Date of Service (CCYYMMDD)	19931121
110	Software Vendor/Certification ID	XXX0100
302	Cardholder ID Number	333224444931101
304	Date of Birth (CCYYMMDD)	19220402
305	Patient Gender Code	1
307	Patient Location	00
455	Prescription/Service	1
402	Prescription	0234567
436	Product	03
407	Product/Service	00078010409
442	Quantity Dispensed	0000100000 or 100000*
405	Days Supply	030 or 30
406	Compound Code	1
420	Submission Clarification Code	00
308	Other Coverage Code	2
461	Prior Auth Type Code	01

Table 6.3 Sample Billing Request Claim (*cont.*)

Field Number	Field Name	Field Value
462	Prior Auth Number (TCN)	11111111111
433	Patient Paid Amount	00001000 or 1000[†]
430	Gross Amount Due	00002200 or 2200[‡]
423	Basis of Cost Determination	00
466	Prescriber ID Qualifier	08
411	Prescriber ID	123456 or 123456
337	Coordination of Benefits	1
338	Other Payer Cov. Type	99
341	Other Payer Amt. Paid Count	1
342	Other Payer Amt. Paid Qualifier	08
431	Other Payer Amount	00001100 or 1100[§]

61044251B1..........105AAAPROV00007...19931121XXX0100.....AM04.
C2333224444931101..AM01.C419220402.C51.C700~..AM07.EM1.
D20234567.E102.D700078010409.E70000100000.D5030.D61.DK00.C802.
EU01.EV11111111111..AM11.DX00001000.DU00002200.DN00..AM02.EZ08.
DB123456....AM05.4C1.5C99.HB1.HC08.DV00001100

OR

61044251B1..........105AAAPROV00007...19931121XXX0100.....AM04.
C2333224444931101..AM01.C419220402.C51.C700~..AM07.EM1.
D20234567.E102.D700078010409.E7100000.D530.D61.DK00.C802.EU01.
EV11111111111..AM11.DX1000.DU2200.DN00..AM02.EZ08.DB123456.
AM05.4C1.5C99.HB1.HC08.DV1100

*Quantity: 100
[†]$10.00
[‡]$22.00
[§]$0.00

universal claim form (UCF)
a two-sided document that the pharmacy technician completes and submits for paper claims

CMS-1500 the prescribed paper form for health care claims prepared and submitted by physicians and suppliers

Paper Claims

The majority of pharmacy claims are sent electronically. If paper claims are submitted, most payers require the NCPDP **universal claim form (UCF),** an example of which appears in Figure 6.6. Paper claims are processed through the pharmacy system but do not result in real-time claim responses to the provider. (Some paper claims must be filed on the **CMS-1500** form; this is addressed later in the chapter.)

The UCF is a two-sided document. The pharmacy technician fills out the first section of the document, providing patient information (including employment information, if applicable), the patient's health care information, and the acting pharmacy; the patient's signature is also required.

Figure 6.6 NCPDP Universal Claim Form (UCF)

NCPDP UNIVERSAL CLAIM FORM (UCF)

TYPE OR PRINT ALL INFORMATION NEATLY AND COMPLETELY IN APPROPRIATE SPACES

I.D. ____ GROUP I.D. ____

NAME ____ PLAN NAME ____

PATIENT NAME ____ OTHER COVERAGE CODE (1) ____ PERSON CODE (2) ____

PATIENT DATE OF BIRTH ___ MM ___ DD ___ CCYY ___ PATIENT (3) GENDER CODE ____ PATIENT (4) RELATIONSHIP CODE ____

PHARMACY NAME ____

ADDRESS ____ SERVICE PROVIDER I.D. ____ / QUAL (5) ____

FOR OFFICE USE ONLY

CITY ____ PHONE NO. ( ) ____

STATE & ZIP CODE ____ FAX NO. ( ) ____

WORKERS COMP. INFORMATION

EMPLOYER NAME ____

ADDRESS ____

CITY ____ **STATE** ____ **ZIP CODE** ____

CARRIER I.D. (6) ____ **EMPLOYER PHONE NO.** ____

DATE OF INJURY ___ MM ___ DD ___ CCYY **CLAIM (7) REFERENCE I.D.** ____

I have hereby read the Certification Statement on the reverse side. I hereby certify to and accept the terms thereof. I also certify that I have received 1 or 2 (please circle number) prescription(s) listed below.

PATIENT / AUTHORIZED REPRESENTATIVE ____

ATTENTION RECIPIENT PLEASE READ CERTIFICATION STATEMENT ON REVERSE SIDE

1

PRESCRIPTION / SERV. REF. #	QUAL. (8)	DATE WRITTEN MM DD CCYY	DATE OF SERVICE MM DD CCYY	FILL#	QTY DISPENSED (9)	DAYS SUPPLY

PRODUCT / SERVICE I.D.	QUAL. (10)	DAW CODE	PRIOR AUTH # SUBMITTED	PA TYPE (11)	PRESCRIBER I.D.	QUAL. (12)

DUR/PPS CODES (13)	BASIS COST (14)	PROVIDER I.D.	QUAL. (15)	DIAGNOSIS CODE	QUAL. (16)

OTHER PAYER DATE MM DD CCYY	OTHER PAYER I.D.	QUAL. (17)	OTHER PAYER REJECT CODES	USUAL & CUST. CHARGE

1

	INGREDIENT COST SUBMITTED
	DISPENSING FEE SUBMITTED
	INCENTIVE AMOUNT SUBMITTED
	OTHER AMOUNT SUBMITTED
	SALES TAX SUBMITTED
	GROSS AMOUNT DUE SUBMITTED
	PATIENT PAID AMOUNT
	OTHER PAYER AMOUNT PAID
	NET AMOUNT DUE

2

PRESCRIPTION / SERV. REF. #	QUAL. (8)	DATE WRITTEN MM DD CCYY	DATE OF SERVICE MM DD CCYY	FILL#	QTY DISPENSED (9)	DAYS SUPPLY

PRODUCT / SERVICE I.D.	QUAL. (10)	DAW CODE	PRIOR AUTH # SUBMITTED	PA TYPE (11)	PRESCRIBER I.D.	QUAL. (12)

DUR/PPS CODES (13)	BASIS COST (14)	PROVIDER I.D.	QUAL. (15)	DIAGNOSIS CODE	QUAL. (16)

OTHER PAYER DATE MM DD CCYY	OTHER PAYER I.D.	QUAL. (17)	OTHER PAYER REJECT CODES	USUAL & CUST. CHARGE

2

	INGREDIENT COST SUBMITTED
	DISPENSING FEE SUBMITTED
	INCENTIVE AMOUNT SUBMITTED
	OTHER AMOUNT SUBMITTED
	SALES TAX SUBMITTED
	GROSS AMOUNT DUE SUBMITTED
	PATIENT PAID AMOUNT
	OTHER PAYER AMOUNT PAID
	NET AMOUNT DUE

(PERF) 1A5

1842-1108-9227

SCREENS: BOX 10%, TEXT 11%.

Figure 6.6 NCPDP Universal Claim Form (UCF) *(cont.)*

IMPORTANT I certify that the patient information entered on the front side of this form is correct, that the patient named is eligible for the benefits and that I have received the medication described. If this claim is for a workers compensation injury, the appropriate section on the front side has been completed. I hereby assign the provider pharmacy any payment due pursuant to this transaction and authorize payment directly to the provider pharmacy. I also authorize release of all information pertaining to this claim to the plan administrator, underwriter, sponsor, policyholder and the employer.

PLEASE SIGN CERTIFICATION ON FRONT SIDE FOR PRESCRIPTION(S) RECEIVED

INSTRUCTIONS
1. Fill in all applicable areas on the front of this form.
2. Enter COMPOUND RX in the Product Service ID area(s) and list each ingredient, name, NDC, quantity, and cost in the area below. Please use a separate claim form for each compound prescription.
3. Worker's Comp. Information is conditional. It should be completed only for a Workers Comp. Claim.
4. Report diagnosis code and qualifier related to prescription (limit 1 per prescription).
5. Limit 1 set of DUR/PPS codes per claim.

DEFINITIONS / VALUES

1. OTHER COVERAGE CODE
0=Not Specified	1=No other coverage identified	2=Other coverage exists-payment collected
3=Other coverage exists-this claim not covered	4=Other coverage exists-payment not collected	5=Managed care plan denial
6=Other coverage denied-not a participating provider	7=Other coverage exists-not in effect at time of service	8=Claim is billing for a copay

2. PERSON CODE: Code assigned to a specific person within a family.

3. PATIENT GENDER CODE
0=Not Specified	1=Male	2=Female

4. PATIENT RELATIONSHIP CODE
0=Not Specified	1=Cardholder	2=Spouse
3=Child	4=Other	

5. SERVICE PROVIDER ID QUALIFIER
Blank=Not Specified	01=National Provider Identifier (NPI)	02=Blue Cross
03=Blue Shield	04=Medicare	05=Medicaid
06=UPIN	07=NCPDP Provider ID	08=State License
09=Champus	10=Health Industry Number (HIN)	11=Federal Tax ID
12=Drug Enforcement Administration (DEA)	13=State Issued	14=Plan Specific
99=Other		

6. CARRIER ID: Carrier code assigned in Worker's Compensation Program.

7. CLAIM/REFERENCE ID: Identifies the claim number assigned by Worker's Compensation Program.

8. PRESCRIPTION/SERVICE REFERENCE # QUALIFIER
Blank=Not Specified	1=Rx billing	2=Service billing

9. QUANTITY DISPENSED: Quantity dispensed expressed in metric decimal units (shaded areas for decimal values).

10. PRODUCT/SERVICE ID QUALIFIER: Code qualifying the value in Product/Service ID (407-07)
Blank=Not Specified	00=Not Specified	01=Universal Product Code (UPC)
02=Health Related Item (HRI)	03=National Drug Code (NDC)	04=Universal Product Number (UPN)
05=Department of Defense (DOD)	06=Drug Use Review/Professional Pharm. Service (DUR/PPS)	07=Common Procedure Terminology (CPT4)
08=Common Procedure Terminology (CPT5)	09=HCFA Common Procedural Coding System (HCPCS)	10=Pharmacy Practice Activity Classification (PPAC)
11=National Pharmaceutical Product Interface Code (NAPPI)	12=International Article Numbering System (EAN)	13=Drug Identification Number (DIN)
99=Other		

11. PRIOR AUTHORIZATION TYPE CODE
0=Not Specified	1=Prior authorization	2=Medical Certification
3=EPSDT (Early Periodic Screening Diagnosis Treatment)	4=Exemption from copay	5=Exemption from Rx limits
6=Family Planning Indicator	7=Aid to Families with Dependent Children (AFDC)	8=Payer Defined Exemption

12. PRESCRIBER ID QUALIFIER: Use service provider ID values.

13. DUR/PROFESSIONAL SERVICE CODES: Reason for Service, Professional Service Code, and Result of Service. For values refer to current NCPDP data dictionary.
A=Reason for Service	B=Professional Service Code	C=Result of Service

14. BASIS OF COST DETERMINATION
Blank=Not Specified	00=Not Specified	01=AWP (Average Wholesale Price)
02=Local Wholesaler	03=Direct	04=EAC (Estimated Acquisition Cost)
05=Acquisition	06=MAC (Maximum Allowable Cost)	07=Usual & Customary
09=Other		

15. PROVIDER ID QUALIFIER
Blank=Not Specified	01=Drug Enforcement Administration (DEA)	02=State License
03=Social Security Number (SSN)	04=Name	05=National Provider Identifier (NPI)
06=Health Industry Number (HIN)	07=State Issued	99=Other

16. DIAGNOSIS CODE QUALIFIER
Blank=Not Specified	00=Not Specified	01=International Classification of Diseases (ICD9)
02=International Classification of Diseases (ICD10)	03=National Criteria Care Institute (NDCC)	04=Systemized Nomenclature of Human and Veterinary Medicine (SNOMED)
05=Common Dental Term (CDT)	06=Medi-Span Diagnosis Code	07=American Psychiatric Association Diagnostic Statistical Manual of Mental Disorders (DSM IV)
99=Other		

17. OTHER PAYER ID QUALIFIER
Blank=Not Specified	01=National Payer ID	02=Health Industry Number (HIN)
03=Bank Information Number (BIN)	04=National Association of Insurance Commissioners (NAIC)	09=Coupon
99=Other		

COMPOUND PRESCRIPTIONS - LIMIT 1 COMPOUND PRESCRIPTION PER CLAIM FORM.

Name	NDC	Quantity	Cost

1842-1108-9227

REGULAR BACKER, SCREEN 10%

B 1A1

Before signing the UCF, the patient is required to read the Certification Statement on the back page of the document. The bottom half of the front page requests details about the prescriptions being filled and all accompanying relevant information. The back of the document contains directions for filling out the form and a list of codes that may be used. The last section on the back of the document allows for the recording of compounded prescriptions.

After completing the UCF, the pharmacy technician should also:

- Verify that the recipient information is correct and that the patient is eligible for benefits
- Check to be sure the patient signed the front of the form
- Verify that the appropriate codes have been assigned and that no information is missing

Drug Utilization Review

Once a claim has been submitted, whether electronically or on paper, it is subjected to editing for drug utilization review. Drug utilization review (DUR) is the process by which prescribed medications are evaluated against explicit criteria to improve the quality of drug therapy and reduce unnecessary expenditures. Examples of DUR issues include the following:

- *Early refill:* Prescription refill occurs before a previous fill of the same prescription is sufficiently exhausted. Early refills are identified by the number of early refill days, by percentage of drug used, or by a combination of the two.
- *High dose:* Prescription is checked against a preset standard for the maximum daily dosage that should be administered for a specified drug based on the patient's age or age group to determine if the dosage exceeds the maximum standard dosing range.
- *Low dose:* Prescription is checked against a preset standard for the minimum daily dosage that should be administered for a specified drug based on the patient's age or age group to determine if the dosage falls below the minimum standard dosing range.
- *Ingredient duplication:* Ingredient duplication occurs when one or more drugs in the new prescription have ingredients and routes of administration that are similar to those of one or more drugs in an active prescription.
- *Therapeutic duplication:* A therapeutic duplication occurs when the patient has two or more active prescriptions that contain one or more drugs in the same therapeutic class.
- *Maximum duration:* The number of days the drug has been prescribed on the new prescription is added to the number of days prescribed on any current prescription or within a specified date range to determine if the total days exceed the maximum number of days the drug should be taken.
- *Drug-drug interaction:* The prescription is checked against all active prescriptions in the patient's drug history profile for any drug-drug interaction.
- *Pregnancy precaution:* The pregnancy precaution targets female patients within a predefined age range to detect drugs that may be inappropriate in pregnancy.

- *Pediatric precaution:* The pediatric precaution targets patients within a predefined age range to detect drugs that may be inappropriate for that age group.
- *Geriatric precaution:* The geriatric precaution targets patients within a predefined age range to detect drugs that may be inappropriate for that age group.
- *Drug-gender precaution (SX):* The drug-gender precaution looks for drugs not indicated for a specific gender.
- *Late refill monitoring (LR):* This targets a refill of a chronic maintenance drug requested at an interval longer than that directed by the prescriber.

 Tech Check

Claims are sometimes routed to switch vendors before they go to what destination?

What term describes an entity that dispenses prescription drugs and submits claims to a payer for reimbursement, such as a retail pharmacy, mail-order pharmacy, doctor's office, clinic, hospital, or long-term care facility?

What type of claims cannot generate real-time claim responses?

Other Types of Pharmacy Billing

Pharmacy technician insurance specialists need to familiarize themselves with a variety of different billing procedures and types. While the majority of claims are filed for patients who fill prescriptions at the pharmacy, other types occur from time to time. Pharmacies sometimes need to bill for additional medical equipment and other services.

Durable Medical Equipment

durable medical equipment (DME) certain medical equipment that is ordered by a doctor for use in the home

Durable medical equipment (DME) comprises certain medical equipment that is ordered by a doctor for use in the home. Examples are walkers, wheelchairs, and hospital beds. Durable Medical Equipment Regional Carriers (DMERCs) manage claims for durable medical equipment, prosthetic devices and related supplies, orthotics, home dialysis supplies and equipment, surgical dressings and other devices, some immunosuppressive drugs, and other items or services.

More than 14 million pharmacy claims for supplies are processed through pharmacies each year via NCPDP standards, representing approximately $447 million. NCPDP standards are used when billing for products consumed or used during, or as a consequence of, the administration of a drug therapy or commonly dispensed via the retail pharmacy.

EXAMPLE

DME associated with prescription drugs includes empty gelatin capsules that may be prescribed with prednisone or other hard-to-swallow tablets. The patient pulls a capsule apart, places one or more tablets into half of it, rejoins the halves, and swallows the whole capsule with water. These capsules are considered supplies dispensed by the pharmacy with the prescription, and they are billed in the same manner as the prescription, using NCPDP standards. Plan coverage may be contingent on a patient's receiving both the supply and the corresponding drug concurrently.

Chapter Summary

1. Many components and requirements are involved in submitting a pharmacy claim, including patient, prescriber, pharmacy, insurance, and prescription information. The patient's primary insurance must also be determined, along with the appropriate coordination of benefits procedures.

2. Dispense as written (DAW) codes are used to inform third parties of the reason why a brand or generic product was used to fill a prescription. The codes, with values ranging from 0 to 9, indicate whether the prescriber's instructions regarding generic substitution were followed.

3. The retail price of a prescription is determined using four major methods. The usual and customary price, maximum allowable cost, average wholesale price, and pending AMC price are all considered. The act of compounding drugs and the pharmacy's dispensing fee also affect the amount of money a patient owes.

4. Three claim submission options are in use within the pharmacy system. Electronic claims, either real-time or through a batch method, allow the pharmacy to confirm a patient's eligibility and give the provider an electronic response indicating payment or denial. Paper claim options are also available.

5. Drug utilization review (DUR) programs exist to evaluate prescribed medications and thereby improve the quality of drug therapy and reduce unnecessary expenditures. DUR issues may include drug dosage matters, occurrences of ingredient and/or therapeutic duplication, drug-drug interaction, and various case-specific safety precautions.

6. Durable medical equipment (DME) is medical equipment that is ordered by a doctor for use in the home. Examples are walkers, wheelchairs, and hospital beds. Durable Medical Equipment Regional Carriers (DMERCs) manage claims for durable medical equipment.

Chapter Review

Multiple Choice

Read the question and select the best response.

1. What provider's ten-digit number is required for all HIPAA-regulated claims submissions?
   A. NABP number
   B. National Provider Identifier (NPI)
   C. cardholder ID number
   D. all of the above

2. In a pharmacy claim, which DAW code is the field default value used for prescriptions for which product selection is not an issue?
   A. 0
   B. 1
   C. 2
   D. 3

3. Which of the following components is not recorded when completing the patient information portion of a claim?
   A. gender
   B. date of birth
   C. employer
   D. phone number

4. Which of the following is not an example of a type of durable medical equipment?
   A. medication
   B. walker
   C. hospital bed
   D. wheelchair

5. Which of these components is recorded when completing the prescriber information portion of a claim?
   A. prescriber phone number
   B. prescriber ID (NPI or DEA)
   C. prescriber last name
   D. all of the above

6. Which of the following components is not recorded when completing the prescription information portion of a claim?
   A. drug dosage
   B. drug name
   C. NABP number
   D. DEA number

7. Which group processes claims for durable medical equipment?
   A. PBMs17.25
   B. DMEPs
   C. PBMDEs
   D. DMERCs

8. If two or more plans cover dependent children of separated or divorced parents who do not have joint custody of the children, which option is first used to determine the children's primary plan?
   A. the plan of the parent without custody
   B. the plan of the custodial parent
   C. the plan of the spouse of the custodial parent (if the parent has remarried)
   D. the birthday rule

9. The usual and customary price (U&C) is the price the provider
   A. pays when the drug is purchased from a manufacturer
   B. always charges members of its health plan
   C. pays when the drug is purchased from a wholesaler
   D. most frequently charges the general public for the drug

10. If both parents are custodial and have insurance coverage for a child, what rule is used to determine the primary plan?
    A. the birthday rule
    B. the primary plan rule
    C. the birthright rule
    D. the insurance rule

11. The fee for a pharmacy's professional services is known as the
    A. copayment fee
    B. prescription fee
    C. dispensing fee
    D. staffing fee

12. Which of these claim submission options is in use within the pharmacy system?
    A. paper only
    B. electronic (real-time) only
    C. electronic (batch) only
    D. all of the above

13. Properly filing a claim will help the pharmacy
    A. avoid unnecessary penalties
    B. ensure that the maximum benefit is received
    C. avoid delays
    D. all of the above

14. Which of the following is not a segment of the eleven-digit National Drug Code?
    A. product code
    B. health plan code
    C. package size
    D. labeler code

15. Compounding may require the pharmacist to perform what practices with a drug?
    A. assembling the drug
    B. packaging and labeling the drug
    C. inventing the drug
    D. mixing the drug

Matching

Match the key term with the appropriate definition.

_____ 1. The average price at which a wholesaler sells prescription drugs to pharmacies, physicians, and other consumers

A. switch vendor

B. dispensing fee

_____ 2. The prescribed paper form for health care claims prepared and submitted by physicians and suppliers

_____ 3. The greatest unit price that the payer or pharmacy benefit manager will pay

_____ 4. The fee for a pharmacy's professional services

_____ 5. The practice of creating combinations of drugs that are prepared or mixed prior to purchase

_____ 6. The process by which prescribed medications are evaluated against explicit criteria to improve the quality of drug therapy and reduce unnecessary expenditures

_____ 7. An eleven-digit code assigned to all prescription drug products by the labeler or distributor of the product under FDA regulations

_____ 8. A provision ensuring that maximum appropriate benefits are paid to a patient covered under more than one policy without duplication

_____ 9. Service used to verify that a claim conforms to NCPDP transaction standards before it is forwarded to the payer's claims system

_____ 10. The price the provider most frequently charges the general public for a drug

C. maximum allowable cost (MAC)

D. coordination of benefits (COB)

E. drug utilization review (DUR)

F. National Drug Code (NDC)

G. usual and customary price (U&C)

H. universal claim form (UCF)

I. average wholesale price (AWP)

J. compounding

True/False

Indicate whether the following statements are true or false.

_____ 1. Prescribers and pharmacies must prescribe and dispense the generic form of a drug whenever possible.

_____ 2. The maximum allowable cost method is used to find the maximum amount of payment for a particular prescription.

_____ 3. Paper claims are not processed through the pharmacy system.

_____ 4. All prescription claims are now filed electronically through online claim submission.

_____ 5. Claims for durable medical equipment (DME) are processed by the same payers as prescription drugs.

_____ 6. The birthday rule is used to determine which parent's primary health insurance plan covers a child.

_____ 7. Within seconds of submitting a real-time claim, a patient's eligibility is confirmed and the provider receives an electronic response indicating payment or denial.

_____ 8. Dispensing fees are generally regulated on a national level.

_____ 9. Because drug costs do not vary, the average wholesale price is used for exact pricing by payers.

_____ 10. All outpatient prescription drugs are billed using the drug's National Drug Code (NDC).

Short Answer

Think carefully about the following questions.

1. Do you think that the birthday rule is an effective means of determining a child's primary health insurance? Why?

_____

_____

2. Describe the controversy regarding wholesale acquisition cost. Do you think wholesale distributors should be forced to adopt average wholesale prices (AWP)? Why?

_____

_____

Internet Activities

1. Investigate dispensing fees using an online search engine. Do they vary from one pharmacy to another? Does Medicare Part D coverage mandate a specific dispensing fee?

2. Use an online search engine to look for more information about switch vendors.

Processing Claims and Reconciling Accounts

chapter
7

Payer Processing of Claims

After the pharmacy technician insurance specialist enters the patient, prescriber, medication, and insurance information in the computer, a claim is submitted to the appropriate payer for reimbursement. A number of criteria must be met for a payer to provide reimbursement for a prescription. The payer's claim processing program reviews the incoming claims against these criteria. The process that a payer follows to examine claims and determine the correct payments is known as adjudication. With today's high-speed computers and networks, the entire process takes seconds, and the pharmacy's computer screen displays a response from the payer. If the claim is approved for payment, the computer displays the price of the medication, the patient's copayment or coinsurance, and other relevant information, such as reimbursement based on the contracted rate. The processing of the prescription continues, and the medication is soon ready to be dispensed to the customer. If the claim is not approved, the response contains information about the reason for the denial.

During the initial processing of the claim, the payer's system checks incoming claims against the reimbursement criteria using a series of edits. **Edits** are checks that evaluate prescription claims for errors and missing information and that ensure compliance with the benefit plan and industry standards. For example, edits are performed to check the eligibility of the individual and whether the drug is covered by the patient's plan. Edits are also performed to check the accuracy and safety of information contained in the claim. Most large chain pharmacies perform similar computerized reviews of claim transactions prior to submission to the third-party payer. Figure 7.1 shows a pre-edit screen from a pharmacy management

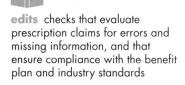

adjudication the process that a payer follows to examine claims and determine correct payments

edits checks that evaluate prescription claims for errors and missing information, and that ensure compliance with the benefit plan and industry standards

Figure 7.1 Pre-edit Screen in a Pharmacy Management Program

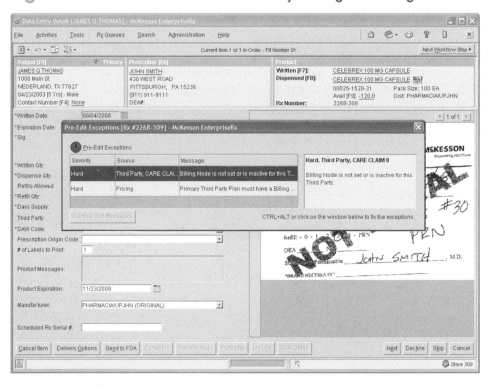

Your Turn 7

View Pre-Edit Exceptions

Instructions: Double-click Activity 7 and follow the on-screen instructions. Answer the questions listed below.

1. What is the cause of the pre-edit exception?
2. What is done to resolve the problem?

(PM) program. These built-in reviews optimize reimbursement and reduce the number of denials and rejected claims.

Administrative and Safety Edits

Edits fall into two categories: administrative and safety. **Administrative edits** are checks that typically indicate that additional information is required to process the claim or that some information has been entered incorrectly. Common administrative edits include the following:

- *Eligibility:* The date of birth or insurance identification number submitted does not match the information in the payer's claim processing system.
- *Dosage:* Specific drugs are checked for high dose, low dose, and age-appropriate dose. This alert provides a safety check for members.
- *Duplicate claim:* This edit checks to discover whether a claim submitted for a prescription was already paid on the submitted fill date.
- *Refill-too-soon:* Customers who attempt to refill prescriptions too soon will not have their prescription claims approved. For example, a plan may require a patient to wait until 75 percent of their current supply has been used before it will authorize a refill. This edit can alert the pharmacist that a customer may be taking medications incorrectly—such as two a day rather than one a day—and thus needs a refill too soon.
- *Coordination of benefits:* The online claim processing system rejects claims when the payer is not designated as the primary payer and the claim has not yet been submitted to the primary payer.
- *High dollar:* The pharmacist will receive an online message when a claim reaches a predetermined cost or quantity limit. This edit prevents claims that exceed a normally expected dollar threshold from continuing to be processed without correction of data from the pharmacy or an override for special circumstances. The alert assists in identification and correction of pharmacy keying errors.
- *Non-formulary products:* Most health plans have formularies that are used to encourage use of preferred drugs. Drugs in a plan's formulary are selected for their safety, quality, efficacy, and cost-effectiveness. If a claim is submitted for a drug that is not in the formulary, the pharmacist receives a message suggesting a comparable drug that is in the formulary.
- *Step therapy:* **Step therapy** edits are used to encourage the use of less-expensive, similarly effective generic medications before considering coverage of a higher-cost brand-name product. For example, a patient may be required to use the generic paroxetine instead of the branded antidepressant Paxil. After trying the generic drug, a patient may be

administrative edits checks that typically indicate that additional information is required to process the claim or that some information has been entered incorrectly

step therapy edits used to encourage the use of less-expensive, similarly effective generic medications before considering coverage of higher-cost brand-name products

Figure 7.2 Safety Edits in a Pharmacy Management Program

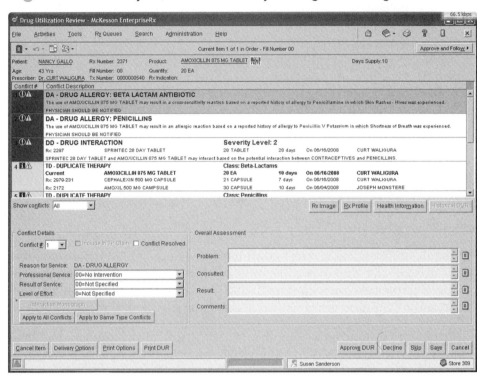

approved for the higher-cost drug depending on the circumstances. For example, if a patient is found to be allergic to an ingredient in the generic product, the plan may pay for the branded medication.

The majority of claim edits are for administrative edits, but claims may also be rejected for safety edits. Certain prescription drugs that may otherwise be covered by the plan could result in potential harm to the patient's health. **Safety edits** are checks that are required when a prescription request exceeds a certain quantity limit or dosage, there is a potentially dangerous drug interaction, or there are other concerns for the patient's health. If the pharmacy believes that the prescribed medication is safe for the patient, it can override the edit and provide the payer with the reason for the override. A sample safety edit in a PM program is displayed in Figure 7.2. Examples of safety edits include the following:

- *Drug-drug interactions:* When a potential drug-drug interaction is detected, the pharmacist is notified. This edit is particularly useful when a patient fills prescriptions at multiple pharmacies, so one pharmacist may not know all of the medications that the patient currently takes.
- *Age/gender contraindications:* Claims submitted for health plan customers may be screened to determine whether the drug and/or its dosage is consistent with the age and/or gender of the customer.
- *Days' supply/maximum quantity:* The quantity of the medication requested should not exceed the days' supply limit or the maximum quantity limit as specified in the benefit plan. An edit is performed that compares the days' supply submitted on the claim with the maximum quantity and the daily dosage in a drug database. If quantities are deliberately

safety edits checks required when a prescription request exceeds a certain quantity limit or dosage, there is potentially dangerous drug interaction, or there are other concerns for the patient's health

Your Turn 8

View a Drug Utilization Review (DUR) Conflict

Instructions: Double-click Activity 8 and follow the on-screen instructions. Answer the questions listed below.

1. What conflict is listed in the Conflict Description field?
2. Who is the prescriber for this order?

Figure 7.3 Claim Rejection in a Pharmacy Management Program

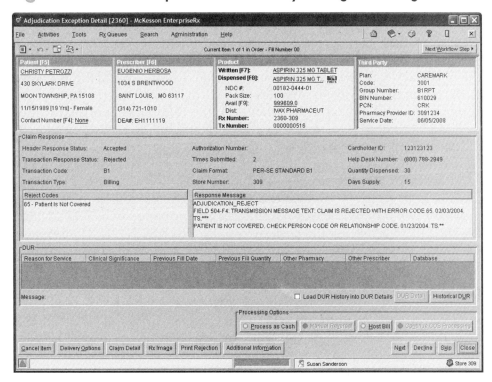

exceeded, rather than resulting from a data submission error, it is necessary to obtain prior authorization for the claim to be processed.

- *Therapeutic duplication:* Prescription claims are screened to identify possible therapeutic duplication—the prescription of a new drug in the same therapeutic class as an existing prescription. Therapeutic duplications may cause toxicity, side effects, and customer confusion.

- *Time interval:* This check reviews the quantity (amount), duration (length), and/or dosage of a drug or drug class based on established clinical guidelines. If the edit is not the result of a data submission error, it is necessary to obtain prior authorization for the claim to be processed.

Before a prescription can be dispensed, edits—whether administrative or safety—must be resolved and the claim must be resubmitted. Once the reason for the claim rejection is identified, the technician can evaluate whether any actions can be taken to revise and resubmit the claim. If the edits cannot be resolved, either the prescription will not be processed or it will be processed and the patient will be responsible for the full cost. A claim rejection in a PM program is illustrated in Figure 7.3.

Tech Check

What is the name of the process that a payer follows to examine claims and determine the correct payments?

What are the two categories of edits?

What status must edits have before a prescription can be dispensed?

Remittance Advice

Once a claim has been processed by the payer and the amount of the reimbursement has been determined, the payer must provide the pharmacy with documentation of the decision. The document sent from the payer to the pharmacy explaining the actions taken and status of a claim is known as the remittance advice. It provides the pharmacy with the results of claim adjudication and indicates the amount of the reimbursement that will be paid. Additionally, it indicates the reason for any full or partial rejection by the payer. Remittances are mailed and electronically transmitted to pharmacies, using the HIPAA compliant standard format known as the **ASC X12N 835 Pharmacy Remittance Advice Template.**

While both electronic and paper remittances provide similar information, they look very different. Paper remittances are formatted to be read and understood by pharmacies and customers alike. The ASC X12N 835 format is intended for the transfer of electronic information; the data are not easily readable. A remittance in this format consists of strings of numbers, letters, and symbols, making it difficult to locate key data (see Table 7.1). For this reason, some payers also provide their own remittance advices in addition to the electronic version. Medicare offers free software, Medicare Remit Easy Print (MREP), that permits pharmacies and other providers to print the electronic remittance in a format that can be easily understood.

Adjustments

An adjustment occurs when the amount charged on a claim is not equal to the amount paid. The following sets of codes are used to report payment adjustments in electronic remittance advice transactions:

- Claim Adjustment Group Code
- Claim Adjustment Reason Code
- Remittance Advice Remark Code

The **Claim Adjustment Group Codes** describe the type of adjustment:

- PR (patient responsibility)
- CO (contractual obligation)
- CR (corrections and reversals)
- PI (payer initiated)
- OA (other adjustment)

Claim Adjustment Reason Codes (CARC) are mandatory codes used to specify a reason for an adjustment to a claim. The **Remittance Advice Remark Codes (RARC)** can be used to provide further explanation of the

---

remittance advice document sent by the payer to the pharmacy explaining the actions taken and status of a claim

ASC X12N 835 Pharmacy Remittance Advice Template the HIPAA-compliant standard format used for transmitting remittances electronically

Claim Adjustment Group Codes codes that describes the type of needed claim adjustment

Claim Adjustment Reason Codes (CARC) mandatory codes used to specify reasons for adjustments to claims

Remittance Advice Remark Codes (RARC) non-mandatory codes used to provide further explanation of the basic information provided by the other codes

Table 7.1 Sample Data from Electronic Remittance Advice

ISA*00* *00* *ZZ*100000 *ZZ*114674 *031030*1818*U*00401
*000000001*0*T*: GS*HP*77047*114674*20031030*18183724*1
*X*004010X091A1

ST*835*000000001

BPR*I*1038865*C*ACH*CCP*01*011000138*DA*500202890*1046002284
**01*211370299*DA*0980800

0185*20031024

TRN*1*297D0004194*1046002284

REF*EV*2222418

DTM*405*20031016

N1*PR*Commonwealth of Massachusetts/MassHealth

N3*600 WASHINGTON ST

N4*BOSTON*MA*02111

REF*EO*77047

PER*CX*DMA EDI support*TE*8006724972*EM*pbm.edisupport@acs-inc.com

N1*PE*YOUR LOCAL DRUGSTORE*FI*042624919

N3*ANY STREET

N4*ANY CITY*MA*02745

REF*D3*1234567

LX*196

CLP*006329363*4*18409*0**MC*20328400003013021

NM1*QC*1*JANE DOE****34*013168944

NM1*82*2*YOUR LOCAL DRUGSTORE*****MC*0405663

SVC*N4:00173069700:::::ADVAIR 500/50 DISKUS*18409*0**0**60

DTM*472*20030905

CAS*OA*16*18409

LQ*RX*79

PLB*0405663*20031231* *0

SE*1510*000000001

GE*1*1

IEA*1*000000001

Your Turn 9

Resolve a Drug Utilization Review (DUR) Conflict

Instructions: Double-click Activity 9 and follow the on-screen instructions. Answer the questions listed below.

1. What is entered in the Consulted field?
2. What button is selected to resolve the conflict and continue processing the prescription?

basic information provided by the other codes, but their use is not mandatory. Codes are updated regularly, and current code lists are available at www.wpc-edi.com/codes. Table 7.2 illustrates examples of CARC and RARC codes used in pharmacy transactions.

 Tech Check

What provides the pharmacy with the results of claim adjudication and indicates the amount of the claim reimbursement that will be paid?

When do adjustments occur?

Table 7.2 Examples of Adjustment Codes Used in Pharmacy Transactions

DATE OF BIRTH INVALID	
CARC 16	Claim/service lacks information which is needed for adjudication. At least one Remark Code must be provided (may be either the Remittance Advice Remark Code or NCPDP Reject Reason Code).
RARC N329	Missing/incomplete/invalid patient birth date.

DISPENSE AS WRITTEN CODE INVALID	
CARC 16	Claim/service lacks information which is needed for adjudication. At least one Remark Code must be provided (may be either the Remittance Advice Remark Code or NCPDP Reject Reason Code).
RARC M123	Missing/incomplete/invalid name, strength, or dosage of the drug furnished.

RECIPIENT INELIGIBLE (COVERAGE CODE IS EQUAL TO 18 (FAMILY PLANNING))	
CARC 96	Non-covered charge(s). At least one Remark Code must be provided (may be either the Remittance Advice Remark Code or NCPDP Reject Reason Code).
RARC N30	Patient ineligible for this service.

DRUG INVALID FOR RECIPIENT SEX	
CARC 188	This product/procedure is only covered when used according to FDA recommendations.

PRESCRIBING PROVIDER PROFESSION CODE INVALID FOR ISSUING PRESCRIPTION	
CARC 184	The prescribing/ordering provider is not eligible to prescribe/order the service billed.

Collecting Patient Point-of-Sale Payment

The information received from the payer also includes information about the payment required from the patient. The patient may owe a copayment, which is a fixed fee, for the prescription in accordance with the agreement between the payer and patient. Similarly, the terms may indicate that a coinsurance payment is due, in which case the patient pays an established percentage of the amount owed for the prescription. A patient may also have to satisfy a deductible before the plan pays anything toward the prescription. If multiple payers have submitted remittance advices, the coordination of benefits process is followed, and the patient's payment may be affected.

For the convenience of the patient, most pharmacies accept various payment methods, including cash, checks, major credit cards, and other options. Pharmacy technician insurance specialists are familiar with the options offered by their pharmacies and the methods used to process the payments. A pharmacy must have good patient point-of-sale collections practices in order to have a steady cash flow and a smoothly operating business. A portion of the pharmacy's income will come from payments due from patients when they pick up their prescriptions. This face-to-face interaction with the patient is the most convenient time to collect the funds owed, and doing so gives the pharmacy the greatest chance of receiving those funds. During this exchange, it is important for the pharmacy technician insurance specialist to clearly express the patient's financial obligation for the prescription. While customers are always treated with respect, they are made aware of their obligations.

Customer Relations

One of the primary roles of the pharmacy technician insurance specialist in processing, resubmitting, and finalizing claims is to provide good customer service to the patient. The ability to provide sound customer relations begins with development of a firm understanding of the processes involved with payer adjudication and the steps that follow. Beyond possessing technical proficiency in these matters, the pharmacy technician must be patient and communicative with patients. Many patients may not immediately understand the reason claims are rejected, or that they are responsible for payment on prescriptions, and may require clear explanations.

Sample Dialogue

The following is a sample conversation between the pharmacy technician insurance specialist and a patient regarding questions that may arise as the result of payer adjudication and the processes that follow.

Technician: I am sorry to inform you that the original claim our pharmacy submitted to your health insurance company has been rejected.

Patient: Why was the claim rejected?

Technician: The claim was rejected because your health insurance company has stated that you have already exceeded your prescription coverage for this year.

Patient: They are incorrect. I have been trying to straighten this misunderstanding out with them for the last few days. Can I still receive my medication?

Technician: If you believe there is an error, you should contact your health insurance company to resolve the problem. Our pharmacy can then appeal your claim and resubmit it for further review. However, until the claim is approved, you are personally responsible for the amount owed on the prescription.

Patient: I understand. I will pay the full amount for the prescription today and then request the form to be resubmitted once I contact my health insurance company.

Technician: Thank you. Please contact our pharmacy once you have resolved the issue.

 Tech Check

What payment methods are generally offered to patients by pharmacies?

What is one of the primary roles of the pharmacy technician insurance specialist in processing, resubmitting, and finalizing claims?

Account Reconciliation

A payer may send payment with the remittance advice or separately. In addition, the payment may be directly mailed to the pharmacy in the form of a check, or it may be deposited in the pharmacy's bank account via an electronic funds transfer (EFT). Whichever method is used, the pharmacy needs to ensure that the payment and remittance advice are reconciled in the accounting system. **Account reconciliation** is the act of comparing the total charges and amount owed with the reimbursement received from the insurer and the patient. This act is also referred to as balancing the account. If reconciliation is not done, the pharmacy has no way of knowing whether it was paid the right amount and no way of following up if the payment was not correct.

In some pharmacies, reconciliation is performed automatically; the electronic funds transfer data are imported into the pharmacy program, enabling matching a claim already processed in the pharmacy with its portion of the payment check. Any discrepancies between the amount expected and the amount received are identified on a report generated by the program. Smaller pharmacies may rely on external companies that provide claim reconciliation services for a fee, or they may do the reconciliation manually. An example of a manual claim reconciliation log is illustrated in Figure 7.4.

Resubmitting and Appealing Claims

When the pharmacy concludes that a payer has mistakenly rejected a valid claim, it may resubmit the claim. Using the information from the payer's claim edits and codes listed on the remittance advice, the pharmacy revises the claim before resubmitting it to the payer. Once the pharmacy has resubmitted the claim, the payer reviews the adjusted claim and make a decision about whether to pay or deny it.

account reconciliation the act of comparing the total charges and amount owed with the reimbursement received from the insurer and the patient

Your Turn 10

Resolve an Adjudication Exception

Instructions: Double-click Activity 10 and follow the on-screen instructions. Answer the questions listed below.

1. In the Claim Response section of the window, what is the Transaction Response Status?

2. How is the exception resolved?

Figure 7.4 Sample Claim Reconciliation Log

Patient Name	Date of Birth	Insurance ID Number	Claim ID Number	Service from/to Date	Claim Amount Billed	Claim Amount Paid	Actions Taken

Not all claims that are resubmitted to payers are accepted on the second attempt. The payer may still decide that it has met the obligations of its agreement with the patient and determine that no further reimbursement is due. When this occurs, the pharmacy should once again review the reasoning for the payer's decision, which will again be documented on the denied claim. If the pharmacy still believes there is an error, it may appeal the payer's decision. While the process for filing an appeal varies from payer to payer, the first step is usually to submit a form detailing the denied claim. If the matter is not resolved satisfactorily, another appeal may be filed, or in some cases a grievance can be filed with a neutral third party. Most payers place a limit on the length of time a pharmacy has to file an appeal, such as six months after the claim was originally filed. Pharmacies must keep records of all claim submissions and denials until the final resolution of the claim is reached.

The desired outcome after claim resubmission is that the payer's original decision is reversed. This means that the payer decides to accept the resubmitted claim and issues the appropriate reimbursement to the pharmacy. The patient may still be responsible for a copayment or coinsurance, but the payer has accepted the claim as valid. The pharmacy documents the approved claim and completes the transaction with the patient.

aging reports documents used to identify patient accounts with overdue outstanding balances

Payment Follow-up and Collections

At times it will be necessary for the pharmacy, or a contracted agency, to contact patients about bills or prescriptions that have not been paid in full. **Aging reports** are used to identify patient accounts with outstanding balances that are overdue. An aging report groups unpaid claims by time, in such categories as current claims, 0 to 30 days since processing, 31 to 60 days, 60 to 90 days, 90 to 120 days, and over 120 days.

Patients may not pay some or all of a bill for many reasons. Some common reasons include the following:

- The patient believes the bill is incorrect.
- The patient does not think that the bill matches the service or product provided.
- The patient did not receive the bill.
- The patient cannot afford to pay the bill.

Regardless of the reason for the lack of payment, the pharmacy attempts to collect the funds it is owed. Efforts made to collect payments by the pharmacy, or any organization representing the pharmacy, must follow the guidelines of the Fair Debt Collection Practices Act of 1977 (FDCPA) and the Telephone Consumer Protection Act of 1991. Pharmacy technician insurance specialists are sometimes involved in these processes and need to familiarize themselves with the laws and methods that are used in contacting patients and collecting overdue funds. The most important point to remember is to treat the patient with respect, but to clearly state that the money is owed.

Pharmacies may employ several tactics in collecting overdue funds, including sending collection letters and making collection phone calls. Some larger pharmacies hire collection agencies to professionally represent them and perform these procedures. A patient with particularly large bills may be offered a payment plan or similar arrangement to help accommodate his or her limited ability to pay. At times, skip tracing techniques may be used to locate a patient who has been unresponsive or has not been able to be contacted. Sometimes the pharmacy is unable to collect the money owed, and some patient accounts become write-offs to indicate that the money is no longer expected to be collected.

 Tech Check

What is another term for the act of balancing an account?

What can a pharmacy do if it concludes that a payer has mistakenly rejected a valid claim?

By what method do aging reports group unpaid claims?

Audits

Rising prescription drug costs and the complexity of prescription benefit plans have led to an increased focus on pharmacy fraud. Most private payers, as well as government plans such as Medicare, include programs that

Figure 7.5 A Page from the Medicare Part D Manual on Fraud, Waste, and Abuse

Prescription Drug Benefit Manual

Chapter 9 – Part D Program to Control Fraud, Waste and Abuse

Last Updated – Rev.2, 04-25-2006

Table of Contents

10 – Part D Program to Control Fraud, Waste and Abuse
- 10.1 – Definition of Terms Used in this Chapter

20 – Overview of Fraud, Waste and Abuse Chapter
30 – CMS' Use of MEDICs to Detect Fraud, Waste and Abuse
40 – Part D Sponsor Accountability and Oversight of Subcontractors
- 40.1 – Delegating Compliance Functions to a Subcontractor
- 40.2 – Contracts Executed Between Sponsors and Subcontractors

50 – The Basics of a Program to Control Fraud, Waste and Abuse
- 50.1 – Benefits of an Effective Fraud, Waste and Abuse Program
- 50.2 – Components of a Comprehensive Program to Detect, Prevent and Control Part D Fraud, Waste and Abuse as Part of the Genearl General Compliance Plan Requirements
  - 50.2.1 – Written Policies and Procedures
    - 50.2.1.1 – Code of Conduct/Ethics
    - 50.2.1.2 – Policies and Procedures
    - 50.2.1.3 – Distribution of Code of Conduct and Policies and Procedures
  - 50.2.2 – Compliance Officer and Committee
    - 50.2.2.1 – Compliance Officer
    - 50.2.2.2 – Compliance Committee
  - 50.2.3 – Training and Education
    - 50.2.3.1 – General Compliance Training
    - 50.2.3.2 – Specialized Compliance Training
    - 50.2.3.3 – Methods of Training
  - 50.2.4 – Effective Lines of Communication
    - 50.2.4.1 – Effective Lines of Communication Between the Compliance Officer, Employees and Subcontractors
    - 50.2.4.2 – Establishing a Mechanism to Field Compliance Questions and Concerns from Employees and Subcontractors
  - 50.2.5 – Enforcement of Standards
    - 50.2.5.1 – Involvement of Chief Executive Officer (CEO) and other Senior Management
    - 50.2.5.2 – Methods of Publicize Disciplinary Guidelines
    - 50.2.5.3 – Enforcing Standards of Conduct
  - 50.2.6 – Monitoring and Auditing

control fraud and abuse. A sample page from the manual for Medicare's Part D Prescription Drug Benefit that addresses fraud, waste, and abuse is pictured in Figure 7.5.

Examples of pharmacy fraud include:

- Providing the patient with less than the prescribed quantity of a drug and billing for the full amount
- Billing for brand-name drugs when generic drugs are dispensed
- Billing multiple payers for the same prescriptions (except when doing so is part of coordination of benefits)

- Dispensing expired prescription drugs
- Billing for prescriptions that are never picked up (not reversing claims that were processed when prescriptions that are never picked up were filled)
- Altering prescriptions
- Refilling prescriptions erroneously

To detect possible fraud, payers conduct audits. Audits evaluate a pharmacy's compliance with payer contracts and plan guidelines, as well as with applicable federal and state laws. Audits are generally performed to prevent or identify fraud, to correct billing errors, and to ensure the quality of the service provided to customers. Most contracts between pharmacies and payers allow the payer to audit the pharmacy's records. Pharmacies also are subject to audits conducted by state and federal licensing agencies.

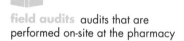

desk audits computerized audits performed off-site

Desk audits are computerized audits performed off-site by computer programs that search through thousands of claims to find irregularities. Examples of the types of data that a desk audit may discover include duplicate and early refills, quantities that exceed plan limits, utilization overrides, and billing issues.

field audits audits that are performed on-site at the pharmacy

Field audits are performed on-site at the pharmacy. They typically include the review of computerized claim records, signature logs, record retention practices, inventory, and policies and procedures, among other things.

In 2007, the Vermont State Auditor's Office reported the results of a field audit that found that over $2 million in Medicaid pharmacy payments may have been billed or paid in error. This finding was the result of sophisticated computer analyses of millions of claims. The pharmacies have the opportunity to provide documentation that justifies the suspected improper claims.

After an audit is complete, the pharmacy is given a report of the findings. It is provided with a period of time to respond to the results of the audit, which may involve providing additional documentation. If the negative findings are not resolved, the pharmacy may be subject to:

- Repayment of any improperly obtained payments
- Termination of the contract with the payer
- Referral to law enforcement agencies and/or state and federal agencies

 Tech Check

What can payers do to detect possible fraud?

What are the types of audits performed off-site and on-site, respectively?

Chapter Summary

1. The process that a payer follows to examine claims and determine the correct payments is known as adjudication. A number of criteria must be met for a payer to provide reimbursement for a prescription, and various edits may be performed to help the payer determine whether to pay or deny the claim. Edits are performed to check the eligibility of the individual, whether the drug is covered by the patient's plan, and the accuracy and safety of the information contained in the claim.

2. The two categories of edits used to evaluate prescription claims are administrative and safety edits. Administrative edits typically indicate that additional information is required to process the claim or that some information has been entered incorrectly. Safety edits determine that a prescription request exceeds a certain quantity limit or dosage, that there is potentially dangerous drug interaction, or that other concerns for the patient's health exist.

3. A pharmacy must have good patient point-of-sale payment collections practices in order to have a steady cash flow and a smoothly operating business. This face-to-face interaction with the patient is the most convenient time to collect the funds owed, and it is important for the pharmacy technician insurance specialist to clearly express the patient's financial obligation for the prescription. Most pharmacies offer various payment methods including cash, checks, and major credit cards for the convenience of the patient.

4. Once a claim has been processed by the payer and the amount of reimbursement has been determined, the payer must provide the pharmacy with documentation of the decision by means of a remittance advice. The remittance advice provides the pharmacy with the results of claim adjudication and indicates the amount of the claim reimbursement that will be paid. It is transmitted electronically using the ASC X12N 835 Pharmacy Remittance Advice Template.

5. Several sets of codes are used to report payment adjustments in electronic remittance advice transactions. The Claim Adjustment Group Codes describe the type of adjustment. The Claim Adjustment Reason Codes (CARC) are mandatory codes used to specify a reason for an adjustment to a claim. The Remittance Advice Remark Codes (RARC) can be used to provide further explanation of the basic information provided by the other codes, but they are not mandatory.

6. Pharmacies sometimes need to contact patients who have not met their financial obligations. Patients may have a number of reasons for not paying their bills, including not having received the bills. Aging reports are used to identify patient accounts with overdue outstanding balances. Collections phone calls and letters may be necessary to convince patients to pay. The pharmacy may also sometimes need to use skip tracing techniques or hire a collection agency to collect on overdue bills.

7. When the pharmacy concludes that a payer has mistakenly rejected a valid claim, it may resubmit the claim. Sometimes claims will be denied a second time, at which point the pharmacy reviews the claim again to see if there is agreement with the payer. If the pharmacy still believes there is an error, it may appeal the payer's decision. Pharmacies must keep records of all claim submissions and denials until a final resolution is reached.

8. Account reconciliation, or balancing the account, is the act of comparing the total charges and amount owed with the reimbursement received from the insurer and the patient. It is performed to ensure that the pharmacy knows whether it was paid the right amount for a claim and so that it can follow up if the payment is not correct.

9. Rising prescription drug costs and the complexity of prescription benefit plans have led to an increased focus on pharmacy fraud and the implementation of audits to evaluate the compliance of pharmacies. Two common types of pharmacy audits are desk audits and field audits. Desk audits are computerized audits performed off-site, while field audits are performed on-site at the pharmacy.

Chapter Review

Multiple Choice

Read the question and select the best response.

1. Which of the following is a common reason a patient may not pay a bill?
   A. the patient believes the bill is incorrect
   B. the patient cannot afford to pay the bill
   C. the patient does not think that the bill matches the service or product provided
   D. all of the above

2. The act of comparing the total charges and amount owed with the reimbursement received from the insurer and the patient is referred to as
   A. account reconciliation
   B. balancing the account
   C. adjudication
   D. both A and B

3. Checks that typically indicate that additional information is required to process the claim or

that some information has been entered incorrectly are called

A. edits

B. administrative edits

C. safety edits

D. dosage checks

4. Checks that are required when the prescription request exceeds a certain quantity limit or dosage, there is potentially dangerous drug interaction, or there are any other concerns for the patient's health are called

A. edits

B. administrative edits

C. safety edits

D. dosage checks

5. What is the general term for checks that evaluate prescription claims for errors and missing information and ensure compliance with the benefit plan and industry standards?

A. edits

B. administrative edits

C. safety edits

D. dosage checks

6. What are aging reports used for by the pharmacy?

A. summarizing the average age of the pharmacy's customers

B. identifying patient accounts with outstanding balances that are overdue

C. summarizing the average age of the pharmacy's employees

D. identifying patients who may be in need of new prescriptions

7. What edits are used to encourage the use of less-expensive, similarly effective generic medications before considering coverage of a higher-cost brand-name product?

A. step therapy edits

B. administrative edits

C. safety edits

D. all of the above

8. What type of audits are computerized and performed off-site?

A. field audits

B. off-site audits

C. desk audits

D. pharmacy audits

9. Which of the following is an example of a safety edit?

A. refill-too-soon

B. dosage check

C. therapeutic duplication

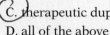

D. all of the above

10. Beyond technical proficiency, what should pharmacy technicians possess to help in dealing with customers?

A. the ability to answer drug usage questions a pharmacist normally handles

B. patience and good communication

C. an aggressive tone and manner

D. a clever wit

11. What technique would a pharmacy *not* use in trying to collect overdue funds from patients?

A. shouting and intimidation

B. hiring a collection agency

C. appropriate skip tracing measures

D. collections phone calls and letters

12. The process that a payer follows to examine claims and determine the correct payments is known as

A. account reconciliation

B. adjudication

C. step therapy

D. auditing

13. Which of the following is a common administrative edit?

A. duplicate claim

B. step therapy

C. high dollar

D. all of the above

14. Which of the following is the HIPAA-compliant standard format used for transmitting remittances electronically?

A. ACS N12X 835 Pharmacy Remittance Advice Template

B. ASC X835N 12 Pharmacy Remittance Advice Template

C. ASC X12N 835 Pharmacy Remittance Advice Template

D. ASC X12 N835 Pharmacy Remittance Advice Template

15. Which of the following is a set of mandatory codes used to specify a reason for an adjustment to a claim?

A. Claim Adjustment Reason Codes (CARC)

B. Claim Adjustment Group Codes

C. Remittance Advice Remark Codes (RARC)

D. none of the above

Matching

Match the key term with the appropriate definition.

_____ 1. Audits that are performed on-site at the pharmacy

_____ 2. The document sent from the payer to the pharmacy explaining the actions taken and status of a claim

_____ 3. The act of comparing the total charges and amount owed with the reimbursement received from the insurer and the patient

_____ 4. Edits that are used to encourage the use of a less-expensive, similarly effective generic medication before considering coverage of a higher-cost brand-name product

_____ 5. The process that a payer follows to examine claims and determine the correct payments

_____ 6. The codes that describes the type of needed claim adjustment

_____ 7. Computerized audits performed off-site

_____ 8. Inquiries done to evaluate a pharmacy's compliance with payer contracts, plan guidelines, and applicable federal and state laws

_____ 9. The HIPAA-compliant standard format used for transmitting remittances electronically

_____ 10. Checks that evaluate prescription claims for errors and missing information, and ensure compliance with the benefit plan and industry standards

A. remittance advice

B. audits

C. field edits

D. desk edits

E. edits

F. ASC X12N 835 Pharmacy Remittance Advice Template

G. account reconciliation

H. Claim Adjustment Group Codes

I. adjudication

J. step therapy

....

True/False

Indicate whether the following statements are true or false.

_____ 1. An adjustment occurs when the amount charged on a claim is not equal to the amount paid.

_____ 2. Before a prescription can be dispensed, edits must be resolved, and the claim must be resubmitted.

_____ 3. Pharmacies usually do not attempt to collect the funds they are owed when a patient refuses to pay.

_____ 4. The majority of claim edits are safety edits, but claims may also be rejected for administrative edits.

_____ 5. Rising prescription drug costs and the complexity of prescription benefit plans have led to an increased focus on pharmacy fraud.

_____ 6. It is sufficient for a pharmacy technician to possess only technical proficiency in dealing with customers.

_____ 7. If a claim is not approved, the response contains information about the reason for the denial.

_____ 8. Today, most remittance advices are printed and mailed to pharmacies.

_____ 9. In some pharmacies, account reconciliation is performed automatically.

_____ 10. The information received from the payer does not include information about payment required from the patient.

Short Answer

Think carefully about the following question.

1. What role do you think pharmacy technician insurance specialists might play in field edits performed on-site at the pharmacy? How might they help the process?

   _____

   _____

Internet Activities

1. Using an online search engine, perform searches for collection agencies that offer their services to pharmacies. Examine what these agencies offer the pharmacy and the costs for their services.

2. Using an online search engine, check for recent news stories about pharmacies that are being processed with fraud charges. Think about the charges they are facing and how they might have been avoided.

The CMS-1500 claim contains thirty-three form locators (FLs), or information boxes, as shown in Figure A.1a. Form locators 1through 13 refer to the patient and the patient's insurance coverage. Form locators 14 through 33 contain information about the provider and the patient's condition, including diagnoses, procedures, and charges.

Patient Information

The items in this part of the CMS-1500 claim form identify the patient and the insured, the health plan, and assignment of benefits/release information.

Form Locator 1: Type of Insurance

Form locator 1 is used to indicate the patient's type of insurance coverage.

Form Locator 1a: Insured's ID Number

The insured's ID number is the identification number of the person who holds the policy. Form locator 1a records the insurance identification number that appears on the insurance card of the person who holds the policy (who may or may not be the patient).

Form Locator 2: Patient's Name

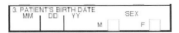

The patient's name is the name of the person who received the treatment or supplies, listed exactly as it appears on the insurance card. Do not change the spelling, even if the card is incorrect. The order in which the name should appear is last name, first name, and middle initial.

Form Locator 3: Patient's Birth Date/Sex

The patient's birth date and sex (gender) helps identify the patient; this information distinguishes persons with similar names. Enter the patient's date of birth in eight-digit format (MM/DD/CCYY). Note that all four digits for the year are entered, even though the printed form indicates only two

Figure A.1a   CMS-1500 Claim

1500

HEALTH INSURANCE CLAIM FORM

APPROVED BY NATIONAL UNIFORM CLAIM COMMITTEE 08/05

☐☐ PICA   PICA ☐☐

CARRIER

1. MEDICARE MEDICAID TRICARE CHAMPUS CHAMPVA GROUP HEALTH PLAN FECA BLK LUNG OTHER	1a. INSURED'S I.D. NUMBER (For Program in Item 1)
☐ (Medicare #) ☐ (Medicaid #) ☐ (Sponsor's SSN) ☐ (Member ID#) ☐ (SSN or ID) ☐ (SSN) ☐ (ID)	

2. PATIENT'S NAME (Last Name, First Name, Middle Initial)	3. PATIENT'S BIRTH DATE MM DD YY SEX M ☐ F ☐	4. INSURED'S NAME (Last Name, First Name, Middle Initial)
5. PATIENT'S ADDRESS (No., Street)	6. PATIENT RELATIONSHIP TO INSURED Self ☐ Spouse ☐ Child ☐ Other ☐	7. INSURED'S ADDRESS (No., Street)
CITY STATE	8. PATIENT STATUS Single ☐ Married ☐ Other ☐	CITY STATE
ZIP CODE TELEPHONE (Include Area Code) ( )	Employed ☐ Full-Time Student ☐ Part-Time Student ☐	ZIP CODE TELEPHONE (INCLUDE AREA CODE) ( )

PATIENT AND INSURED INFORMATION

9. OTHER INSURED'S NAME (Last Name, First Name, Middle Initial)	10. IS PATIENT'S CONDITION RELATED TO:	11. INSURED'S POLICY GROUP OR FECA NUMBER
a. OTHER INSURED'S POLICY OR GROUP NUMBER	a. EMPLOYMENT? (CURRENT OR PREVIOUS) ☐ YES ☐ NO	a. INSURED'S DATE OF BIRTH MM DD YY SEX M ☐ F ☐
b. OTHER INSURED'S DATE OF BIRTH MM DD YY SEX M ☐ F ☐	b. AUTO ACCIDENT? ☐ YES ☐ NO PLACE (State)	b. EMPLOYER'S NAME OR SCHOOL NAME
c. EMPLOYER'S NAME OR SCHOOL NAME	c. OTHER ACCIDENT? ☐ YES ☐ NO	c. INSURANCE PLAN NAME OR PROGRAM NAME
d. INSURANCE PLAN NAME OR PROGRAM NAME	10d. RESERVED FOR LOCAL USE	d. IS THERE ANOTHER HEALTH BENEFIT PLAN? ☐ YES ☐ NO If yes, return to and complete item 9 a-d.

READ BACK OF FORM BEFORE COMPLETING & SIGNING THIS FORM.

12. PATIENT'S OR AUTHORIZED PERSON'S SIGNATURE I authorize the release of any medical or other information necessary to process this claim. I also request payment of government benefits either to myself or to the party who accepts assignment below. SIGNED _____ DATE _____	13. INSURED'S OR AUTHORIZED PERSON'S SIGNATURE I authorize payment of medical benefits to the undersigned physician or supplier for services described below. SIGNED _____

14. DATE OF CURRENT: MM DD YY ◄ ILLNESS (First symptom) OR INJURY (Accident) OR PREGNANCY(LMP)	15. IF PATIENT HAS HAD SAME OR SIMILAR ILLNESS. GIVE FIRST DATE MM DD YY	16. DATES PATIENT UNABLE TO WORK IN CURRENT OCCUPATION MM DD YY MM DD YY FROM TO
17. NAME OF REFERRING PHYSICIAN OR OTHER SOURCE	17a. 17b. NPI	18. HOSPITALIZATION DATES RELATED TO CURRENT SERVICES MM DD YY MM DD YY FROM TO
19. RESERVED FOR LOCAL USE		20. OUTSIDE LAB? ☐ YES ☐ NO $ CHARGES
21. DIAGNOSIS OR NATURE OF ILLNESS OR INJURY. (Relate Items 1,2,3 or 4 to Item 24e by Line) 1. L__.__ 3. L__.__ 2. L__.__ 4. L__.__		22. MEDICAID RESUBMISSION CODE ORIGINAL REF. NO. 23. PRIOR AUTHORIZATION NUMBER

24. A. DATE(S) OF SERVICE From To MM DD YY MM DD YY	B. PLACE OF SERVICE	C. EMG	D. PROCEDURES, SERVICES, OR SUPPLIES (Explain Unusual Circumstances) CPT/HCPCS MODIFIER	E. DIAGNOSIS POINTER	F. $ CHARGES	G. DAYS OR UNITS	H. EPSDT Family Plan	I. ID. QUAL.	J. RENDERING PROVIDER ID.#
1									NPI
2									NPI
3									NPI
4									NPI
5									NPI
6									NPI

PHYSICIAN OR SUPPLIER INFORMATION

25. FEDERAL TAX I.D. NUMBER SSN EIN ☐ ☐	26. PATIENT'S ACCOUNT NO.	27. ACCEPT ASSIGNMENT? (For govt. claims, see back) ☐ YES ☐ NO	28. TOTAL CHARGE $	29. AMOUNT PAID $	30. BALANCE DUE $
31. SIGNATURE OF PHYSICIAN OR SUPPLIER INCLUDING DEGREES OR CREDENTIALS (I certify that the statements on the reverse apply to this bill and are made a part thereof.) SIGNED _____ DATE _____	32. SERVICE FACILITY LOCATION INFORMATION a. NPI b.		33. BILLING PROVIDER INFO & PHONE # ( ) a. NPI b.		

NUCC Instruction Manual available at: www.nucc.org

characters (YY). Use zeros before single digits. Enter an X in the correct box to indicate the sex of the patient.

Form Locator 4: Insured's Name

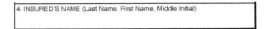

In FL 4, enter the full name of the person who holds the insurance policy (the insured). If the patient is a dependent, the insured may be a spouse, parent, or other person. If the insured is the patient, enter SAME.

Form Locator 5: Patient's Address

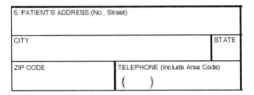

Form locator 5 contains the patient's address and telephone number. The address includes the number and street, city, state, and ZIP code. The first line is for the street address; the second line, the city and state; the third line, the ZIP code and phone number. Use a two-digit state abbreviation and a nine-digit ZIP code if it is available.

Note that the patient's address refers to the patient's permanent residence. A temporary address or school address should not be used.

Form Locator 6: Patient's Relationship to Insured

In FL 6, enter the patient's relationship to the insured who is listed in FL 4. Choosing *self* indicates that the insured is the patient. *Spouse* indicates that the patient is the husband or wife or qualified partner as defined by the insured's plan. *Child* means that the patient is the minor dependent as defined by the insured's plan. *Other* means that the patient is someone other than the insured, the spouse, or the child, which may include employee, ward, or dependent as defined by the insured's plan.

Form Locator 7: Insured's Address

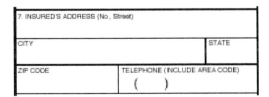

The insured's address refers to the insured's permanent residence, which may be different from the patient's address (FL 5). Enter the address and telephone number of the person who is listed in FL 4. If the insured's address is the same as the patient's, enter SAME. This form locator does not need to be completed if the patient is the insured person.

Form Locator 8: Patient Status

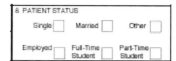

Enter an X in the box for the patient's marital status and for the patient's employment or student status. Choosing *employed* indicates that the patient has a job. *Full-time student* means that the patient is registered as a full-time student as defined by the postsecondary school or university. *Part-time student* means that the patient is registered as a part-time student as defined by the postsecondary school or university.

Form Locator 9: Other Insured's Name

An entry in the other insured's name box indicates that there is a holder of another policy that may cover the patient. When additional group health coverage exists, enter the insured's name (the last name, first name, and middle initial of the enrollee in another health plan if it is different from that shown in FL 2). Otherwise, use SAME.

Example: If a husband is covered by his employer's group policy and also by his wife's group health plan, enter the wife's name in FL 9.

Form Locator 9a: Other Insured's Policy or Group Number

Enter the policy or group number of the other insurance plan.

Form Locator 9b: Other Insured's Date of Birth

Enter the eight-digit date of birth (MM/DD/CCYY) and the sex of the other insured indicated in FL 9.

Form Locator 9c Employer's Name or School Name

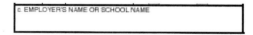

Enter the name of the other insured's employer or school. This box identifies the name of the employer or school attended by the other insured indicated in FL 9.

Form Locator 9d: Insurance Plan Name or Program Name

Enter the other insured's insurance plan or program name. This box identifies the name of the plan or program of the other insured indicated in FL 9.

Form Locators 10a–10c: Is Patient Condition Related to:

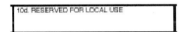

This information indicates whether the patient's illness or injury is related to employment, auto accident, or other accident. Choosing *employment* (current or previous) indicates that the condition is related to the patient's job or workplace. *Auto accident* means that the condition is the result of an automobile accident. *Other accident* means that the condition is the result of any other type of accident.

Form Locator 10d: Reserved for Local Use

The content of FL 10d varies with the insurance plan. Check instructions from the applicable public or private payer regarding the use of this field.

Form Locator 11: Insured's Policy Group or FECA Number

Enter the insured's policy or group number as it appears on the insured's health care identification card. If FL 4 is completed, this entry should also be completed.

Form Locator 11a: Insured's Date of Birth/Sex

The insured's date of birth and sex (gender) refers to the birth date and gender of the insured as indicated in FL 1a. It is used when the insured and the patient are different individuals. Enter the insured's eight-digit birth date (MM/DD/CCYY) and sex if different from FL 3 (patient's birth date and sex).

Form Locator 11b: Employer's Name or School Name

Enter the name of the insured's employer or the school attended by the insured who is indicated in FL 1a.

Form Locator 11c: Insurance Plan Name or Program Name

c. INSURANCE PLAN NAME OR PROGRAM NAME

Enter the insurance plan or program name of the insured who is indicated in FL 1a. Note that some payers require the payer identification number of the primary insurer in this field.

Form Locator 11d: Is There Another Health Benefit Plan?

d. IS THERE ANOTHER HEALTH BENEFIT PLAN?
☐ YES   ☐ NO   *If yes, return to and complete item 9 a-d.*

Select Yes if the patient is covered by additional insurance. If the answer is Yes, form locators 9a through 9d must also be completed. If the patient does not have additional insurance, select No. If not known, leave 11d blank.

Form Locator 12: Patient's or Authorized Person's Signature

READ BACK OF FORM BEFORE COMPLETING & SIGNING THIS FORM.
12. PATIENT'S OR AUTHORIZED PERSON'S SIGNATURE I authorize the release of any medical or other information necessary to process this claim. I also request payment of government benefits either to myself or to the party who accepts assignment below.

SIGNED_____   DATE _____

Enter "Signature on File," "SOF," or legal signature. When legal signature is entered, also enter the date an authorization was signed. This entry means that there is an authorization on file for the release of any medical or other information necessary to process the claim.

Form Locator 13: Insured or Authorized Person's Signature

13. INSURED'S OR AUTHORIZED PERSON'S SIGNATURE I authorize payment of medical benefits to the undersigned physician or supplier for services described below.

SIGNED _____

Enter "Signature on File," "SOF," or legal signature.

Physician or Supplier Information

The items in this part of the CMS-1500 claim form identify the health care provider, describe the services performed, and give the payer additional information to process the claim.

Form Locator 14: Date of Current Illness or Injury or Pregnancy

14. DATE OF CURRENT: ILLNESS (First symptom) OR
    MM | DD | YY   INJURY (Accident) OR
                        PREGNANCY(LMP)

Enter the date for the first date of the present illness, injury, or pregnancy. For pregnancy, use the date of the last menstrual period (LMP) as the first date. This date refers to the first date of onset of illness, the actual date of injury, or the LMP for pregnancy.

Form Locator 15: If Patient Has Had Same or Similar Illness

Enter the first date the patient had the same or a similar illness. Leave blank if unknown.

Form Locator 16: Dates Patient Unable to Work in Current Occupation

```
16. DATES PATIENT UNABLE TO WORK IN CURRENT OCCUPATION
        MM   DD   YY              MM   DD   YY
   FROM                        TO
```

If the patient is employed and is unable to work in his or her current occupation, a date must be shown as the "from–to" dates that the patient is unable to work.

Form Locator 17: Name of Referring Provider or Other Source

```
17. NAME OF REFERRING PROVIDER OR OTHER SOURCE
```

The name of the referring provider, ordering provider, or other source must be shown if the service or item was ordered or referred by a provider.

Form Locator 17a and 17b: ID Number of Referring Provider (split field)

```
17a.
17b. NPI#
```

The non-NPI ID number (for 17a) of the referring provider, ordering provider, or other source is the payer-assigned unique identifier of the physician or other health care provider and is put above the dotted line. The qualifier (a code indicating what the number represents) should also be reported above the dotted line and on the left side of the box before the Other ID# is entered. The NPI—as described in Chapter 2—is entered in 17b.

Form Locator 18: Hospitalization Dates Related to Current Services

```
18. HOSPITALIZATION DATES RELATED TO CURRENT SERVICES
        MM   DD   YY              MM   DD   YY
   FROM                        TO
```

The hospitalization dates related to current services refer to an inpatient stay and indicate the admission and discharge dates associated with the services on the claim.

Form Locator 19: Reserved for Local Use

19. RESERVED FOR LOCAL USE

Refer to instructions from the payer regarding the use of this field.

Form Locator 20: Outside Lab? $ Charges

"Outside lab? $ charges" indicates that services have been rendered by an independent provider as indicated in FL 32 and shows the related costs.

Form Locator 21: Diagnosis or Nature of Illness or Injury (relate items 1, 2, 3, or 4 to item 24e by line)

21. DIAGNOSIS OR NATURE OF ILLNESS OR INJURY. (RELATE ITEMS 1,2,3 OR 4 TO ITEM 24E BY LINE)

1. |___.__   3. |___.__

2. |___.__   4. |___.__

ICD-9-CM codes (see Chapter 2) that describe the patient's condition are entered in priority order. The first code listed is the primary diagnosis. Additional codes for secondary diagnoses are used only when the diagnoses are directly related to the services being provided. Relate lines 1, 2, 3, and 4 to the lines of service in FL 24e by line number. The codes used should specify the highest level of detail possible, including the use of a fifth digit when appropriate.

Form Locator 22: Medicaid Resubmission

This form locator is left blank for all claims other than those for Medicaid plans that require a resubmission number and the original claim reference number.

Form Locator 23: Prior Authorization Number

Some procedures and diagnostic tests require preauthorization. If it is required, enter the preauthorization number assigned by the payer.

Section 24

The term *service line information* describes section 24 of the claim, the part that reports the procedures—that is, the services—performed for the patient. Each item of service line information has a procedure code and a charge, with additional information as detailed below.

Form Locator 24A: Dates of Service

Date(s) of service indicate the actual month, day, and year the service was provided. "Grouping services" refers to a charge for a series of identical services without listing each date of service.

Enter the from and to date(s) of service: If there is only one date of service, enter that date under From. Leave To blank or reenter the From date. If grouping services, the place of service, procedure code, charges, and individual provider for each line must be identical for that service line. Grouping is allowed only for services on consecutive days. The number of days must correspond to the number of units in FL 24G.

Form Locator 24B: Place of Service

In 24B, enter the appropriate two-digit code from the place of service code list for each item used or service performed. A *place of service (POS)* code describes the location where the service was provided, as shown below:

Code	Definition
11	Office
12	Home
22	Outpatient hospital
23	Emergency room—hospital
24	Ambulatory surgical center
31	Skilled nursing facility
81	Independent laboratory

Form Locator 24C: EMG

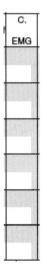

The form locator is EMG, for emergency indicator, as defined by federal or state regulations or programs, payer contracts, or HIPAA claim rules.

Form Locator 24D: Procedures, Services, or Supplies

D. PROCEDURES, SERVICES, OR SUPPLIES
(Explain Unusual Circumstances)
CPT/HCPCS	MODIFIER

Enter the CPT or HCPCS code(s) (see Chapter 2) from the appropriate code set in effect on the date of service. State-defined procedure and supply codes are needed for workers' compensation claims.

Form Locator 24E: Diagnosis Pointer

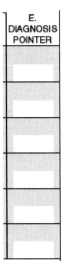

The diagnosis pointer refers to the line number from FL 21 that provides the link between diagnosis and treatment. In FL 24E, enter the diagnosis code reference number (pointer) as shown in FL 21 to relate the date of service and the procedures performed to the primary diagnosis. When multiple services are performed, the primary reference number for each service should be listed.

Form Locator 24F: $ Charges

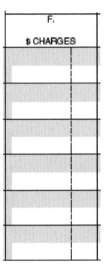

Form locator 24F lists the total billed charges for each service line in FL 24D. A charge for each service line must be reported. The numbers should be entered without dollar signs and decimals. If the services are for multiple days or units, the number of days or units must be multiplied by the charge to determine the entry in FL 24F. This is done automatically when a billing program is used to create the claim.

Form Locator 24G: Days or Units

Enter the number of days or units for the service line. This field is most commonly used for multiple visits, units of supplies, anesthesia units or minutes, or oxygen volume. If only one service is performed, the numeral 1 must be entered.

Form Locator 24H: EPSDT Family Plan

The Medicaid EPSDT/family plan identifies certain services that may be covered under some state plans.

Form Locator 24I: ID Qualifier

I. ID. QUAL.	J. RENDERING PROVIDER ID. #
NPI #	
NPI #	
NPI #	
NPI #	
NPI #	
NPI #	

Form locator 24I works together with FL 24J. These boxes are used to enter an ID number for the *rendering provider*—the individual who is providing the service.

Form Locator 25: Federal Tax ID Number

25. FEDERAL TAX I.D. NUMBER	SSN EIN
	☐ ☐

Enter the physician's Social Security number or Employer Identification Number (EIN) in FL 25. Mark the appropriate box (SSI or EIN).

Form Locator 26: Patient's Account No.

Enter the patient account number used by the billing program to help identify the patient and post payments when working with RAs/EOBs.

Form Locator 27: Accept Assignment?

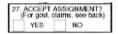

Enter a capital X in the correct box. Yes means that the provider agrees to accept Medicare's terms for payment and filing claims for the beneficiary.

Form Locator 28: Total Charge

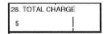

Form locator 28 lists the total of all charges in form locator 24F, lines 1 through 6. Do not use dollar signs or commas.

Form Locator 29: Amount Paid

Enter the amount that the patient has paid toward this claim. If no payment was made, enter "none" or 0.00.

Form Locator 30: Balance Due

Check with the payer regarding the use of this field.

Form Locator 31: Signature of Physician or Supplier Including Degrees or Credentials

Enter the provider's or supplier's signature, the date of the signature, and the provider's credentials (such as MD).

Form Locator 32: Service Facility Location Information

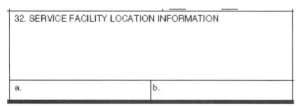

Enter the name, address, city, state, and ZIP code of the location where the services were rendered.

Form Locator 33: Billing Provider Information

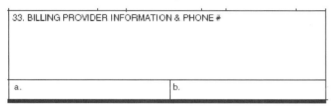

The *billing provider* is the organization or person transmitting the claim to the payer. This term is used to distinguish between a billing provider and the *pay-to provider*, the organization or person that should receive payment. (Note that if the pay-to provider is also the rendering provider, no rendering provider is reported.) This distinction is necessary because an outside firm such as billing services may be hired to send claims. Enter the provider's or supplier's billing name, address, ZIP code, phone number, and NPI (or non-NPI).

Table A.1 summarizes the information that is required for the correct completion of the CMS-1500 claim.

Table A.1 Summary of CMS-1500 Claim Completion

Form Locator	Content
1	**Medicare, Medicaid, CHAMPUS, CHAMPVA, FECA Black Lung, Group Health Plan, or Other:** Enter the type of insurance.
1a	**Insured's ID Number:** The insurance identification number that appears on the insurance card of the policyholder.
2	**Patient's Name:** As it appears on the insurance card.
3	**Patient's Birth Date/Sex:** Date of birth in eight-digit format; appropriate selection for male or female.
4	**Insured's Name:** The full name of the person who holds the insurance policy (the insured). If the patient is a dependent, the insured may be a spouse, parent, or other person. If the insured is the patient, enter "Same."
5	**Patient's Address:** Address includes the number and street, city, state, ZIP code, and telephone number.
6	**Patient's Relationship to Insured:** Self, spouse, child, or other. *Self* means that the patient is the policyholder.
7	**Insured's Address:** Address and telephone number of the person listed in FL 4. If the insured's address is the same as the patient's, enter "Same."

Table A.1 Summary of CMS-1500 Claim Completion (*cont.*)

Form Locator	Content
8	**Patient Status:** Marital status and employment status—employed, full-time student, or part-time student.
9	**Other Insured's Name:** If there is additional insurance coverage, the insured's name.
9a	**Other Insured's Policy or Group Number:** The policy or group number of the other insurance plan.
9b	**Other Insured's Date of Birth:** Date of birth and sex of the other insured.
9c	**Employer's Name or School Name:** Other insured's employer or school.
9d	**Insurance Plan Name or Program Name:** Other insured's insurance plan or program name.
10a–10c	**Is Patient Condition Related to:** To indicate whether the patient's condition is the result of a work injury, an automobile accident, or another type of accident.
10d	**Reserved for Local Use:** Varies with the insurance plan.
11	**Insured's Policy Group or FECA Number:** As it appears on the insurance identification card.
11a	**Insured's Date of Birth/Sex:** The insured's date of birth and sex if the patient is not the insured.
11b	**Employer's Name or School Name:** Insured's employer or school.
11c	**Insurance Plan Name or Program Name:** Of the insured.
11d	**Is There Another Health Benefit Plan?** Yes if the patient is covered by additional insurance. If yes, FL 9a–9d must also be completed.
12	**Patient's or Authorized Person's Signature:** If the patient's or authorized representative's signature authorizing release of information is on file, the words "Signature on file" or "SOF" are entered.
13	**Insured or Authorized Person's Signature:** The words "Signature on File" or "SOF" are entered to indicate that the patient or patient's representative authorizes payments from the insurance carrier to be made directly to the provider.
14	**Date of Current Illness or Injury or Pregnancy:** The date that symptoms first began for the current illness, injury, or pregnancy. For pregnancy, enter the date of the patient's last menstrual period (LMP).
15	**If Patient Has Had Same or Similar Illness:** Date when the patient first consulted the provider for treatment of the same or a similar condition.
16	**Dates Patient Unable to Work in Current Occupation:** Dates the patient has been unable to work.
17	**Name of Referring Physician or Other Source:** Name of the physician or other source who referred the patient to the billing provider.
17a	**ID Number of Referring Physician:** Identifying number(s) for the referring physician.

Table A.1 Summary of CMS-1500 Claim Completion (*cont.*)

Form Locator	Content
18	**Hospitalization Dates Related to Current Services:** If the services provided are needed because of a related hospitalization, the admission and discharge dates are entered. For patients still hospitalized, the admission date is listed in the From box, and the To box is left blank.
19	**Reserved for Local Use**
20	**Outside Lab? $Charges:** Completed if billing for outside lab services.
21	**Diagnosis or Nature of Illness or Injury:** ICD-9-CM codes in priority order.
22	**Medicaid Resubmission:** Medicaid-specific.
23	**Prior Authorization Number:** If required by payer, report the assigned number.
24A	**Dates of Service:** Date(s) service was provided.
24B	**Place of Service:** A place of service (POS) code describes the location at which the service was provided.
24C	**EMG:** Payer-specific code.
24D	**Procedures, Services, or Supplies:** CPT or HCPCS codes and applicable modifiers for services provided.
24E	**Diagnosis Pointer:** Using the numbers (1, 2, 3, 4) listed to the left of the diagnosis codes in FL 21, enter the diagnosis for the each service listed in FL 24D.
24F	**$ Charges:** For each service listed in FL 24D, enter charges without dollar signs and decimals.
24G	**Days or Units:** The number or days or units.
24H	**EPSDT Family Plan:** Medicaid-specific.
24I and J	ID Qualifier and ID Numbers.
25	**Federal Tax ID Number:** Physician's or supplier's Social Security number or Employer Identification Number (EIN).
26	**Patient's Account No.:** Patient account number used by the practice's accounting system.
27	**Accept Assignment?** For Medicare claims, if the physician accepts Medicare assignment, select Yes. If not, select No.
28	**Total Charge:** Total of all charges in FL 24F.
29	**Amount Paid:** Amount of the payments received for the services listed on this claim.
30	**Balance Due:** May be payer-specific; generally balance resulting from subtracting the amount in FL 29 from the amount in FL 28.
31	**Signature of Physician or Supplier Including Degrees or Credentials:** Provider's or supplier's signature, the date of the signature, and the provider's credentials (such as MD).
32	**Service Facility Location Information:** Name, address, and ID numbers of place of service.
33	**Billing Provider Information:** Billing office name, address, telephone number, and ID numbers.

Glossary

A

abuse action that misuses money that the government has allocated

account reconciliation the act of comparing the total charges and amount owed with the reimbursement received from the insurer and the patient

accounts receivable (AR) remaining balance due after an initial payment has been made

adjudication payer's processing of claim data to decide whether a drug is covered by the patient's plan and properly utilized

administrative edits checks that typically indicate that additional information is required to process the claim or that some information has been entered incorrectly

advance beneficiary notice (ABN) of noncoverage form given to a patient before treatment when a provider thinks that Medicare will deem a procedure not reasonable and necessary and will not cover it

aging reports documents used to identify patient accounts with overdue outstanding balances

any willing provider state laws requiring pharmacy benefit managers to contract with any pharmacy willing to accept their reimbursement rates

ASC X12N 835 Pharmacy Remittance Advice Template the HIPAA-compliant standard format used for transmitting remittances electronically

audit methodical examination of selected pharmacy records

authorization document a patient must sign for a covered entity to use or disclose information other than for TPO

average wholesale price (AWP) the average price at which a wholesaler sells prescription drugs to pharmacies, physicians, and other consumers

B

benefits payments made by a health plan for medical services

billing cycle ten-step work flow followed at a pharmacy to care for patients' financial matters

birthday rule a rule for determining a child's primary insurance based on the parent whose date of birth is earlier in the calendar year

business associates in HIPAA terms, agencies that must comply with the law in order to do business with covered entities

C

capitation fee usually paid monthly by a patient to the primary care physician regardless of the number of times the patient visits the physician

catastrophic cap limit on the total medical expenses a patient must pay in one year

categorically needy special group of Medicaid recipients whose needs are addressed under the Welfare Reform Act

Centers for Medicare and Medicaid Services (CMS) main federal government agency responsible for health care

CHAMPVA program that helps pay health care costs for families of veterans who are totally and permanently disabled because of service-related injuries

Claim Adjustment Group Codes codes that describes the type of needed claim adjustment

Claim Adjustment Reason Codes (CARC) mandatory codes used to specify reasons for adjustments to claims

clearinghouses companies that help providers handle electronic transactions such as pharmacy claims

closed formulary type of formulary that will not provide coverage for unlisted drugs without an authorized medical exception from a physician

CMS-1500 the prescribed paper form for health care claims prepared and submitted by physicians and suppliers

code set any group of codes used for encoding data elements

coinsurance percentage of the fees owed by the policyholder

compliance plans plans a pharmacy practice writes and implements to uncover compliance problems and correct them to avoid risking liability

compounded medications medications containing one or more ingredients that are prepared on-site by a pharmacist

compounding the preparation or mixing of combinations of drugs prior to purchase

consumer-driven health plan (CDHP) type of medical insurance that combines a high-deductible health plan with a medical savings plan that covers some out-of-pocket expenses

coordination of benefits (COB) a provision ensuring that maximum appropriate benefits are paid to a patient covered under more than one policy without duplication

copayment small fixed fee paid by a patient for a drug

corporate integrity agreement compliance action under which a provider's Medicare billing is monitored by the Office of the Inspector General

coverage gap point where a patient and the Medicare drug plan have spent a predetermined amount of money for covered drugs and the patient is responsible for the entire cost of the drugs

covered entities organizations that electronically transmit any information that is protected under HIPAA

covered expenses expenses incurred by or on behalf of a covered person for supplies that are ordered by a doctor, are medically necessary, and are not excluded by any provision of the policy

crossover claim claims submitted first to Medicare and then to Medicaid

Current Procedural Terminology (CPT) mandated code set for physician procedures and services under TCS

D

deductible amount paid by a policyholder each year before benefits from a health plan will start

Defense Enrollment Eligibility Reporting System (DEERS) worldwide database of people covered by TRICARE

de-identified health information health information that neither identifies nor provides a reasonable basis to identify an individual

designated record set (DRS) medication and billing records a pharmacy maintains

desk audits computerized audits performed off-site

diagnostic services treatment for a patient who has been diagnosed with a condition or with a high probability for it

discount card offered by states to people who cannot afford prescription drugs

disease management (DM) programs programs that are often provided by pharmacy benefit managers for common and potentially high-cost conditions such as asthma, diabetes, heart disease, and depression

dispense as written (DAW) codes a set of NCPDP codes used to inform third parties of the reason for filling a prescription with a brand or generic product

dispensing fee the fee for a pharmacy's professional services

drug utilization review tool used to ensure safety, improve care quality, and promote compliance with the formulary

durable medical equipment (DME) certain medical equipment that is ordered by a doctor for use in the home

E

Early and Periodic Screening, Diagnosis, and Treatment (EPSDT) prevention, early detection, and treatment program for children under the age of twenty-one who are enrolled in Medicaid

EDI (electronic data interchange) claims that are sent electronically between the pharmacy management system and the payer

edits checks that evaluate prescription claims for errors and missing information, and that ensure compliance with the benefit plan and industry standards

electronic prescribing (eRx) use of software by a physician to transmit an order

encryption process of encoding information in such a way that only the person or computer with the key can decode it

explanation of benefits (EOB) document that comes to a pharmacy showing the details for a claim (also known as a *remittance advice*)

F

family deductible deductible that can be met by the combined payments to providers for any covered members of the insured's family

Federal Medicaid Assistance Percentage (FMAP) payments made by the federal government based on a state's average per capita income in relation to the national income average

field audits audits that are performed on-site at the pharmacy

fiscal agent organization that processes claims for a government program

formulary list containing the Food and Drug Administration (FDA)-approved brand-name and generic medications a plan covers (also known as a *preferred drug list* or *prescription drug list*)

fraud act of deception used to take advantage of another person

G

group health plan (GHP) medical insurance coverage that employers buy from insurance companies for their employees

H

Healthcare Common Procedure Coding System (HCPCS) mandated code set for reporting supplies, orthotic and prosthetic devices, and durable medical equipment under TCS

Health Care Fraud and Abuse Control Program program created to uncover and prosecute fraud and abuse

Health Insurance Portability and Accountability Act (HIPAA) of 1996 law designed to protect people's private health information, ensure health coverage for workers and their families when they change or lose jobs, and uncover fraud and abuse

health maintenance organization (HMO) type of managed care organization where patients pay fixed premiums and very small (or no) copayments when they need services

health plan organization that offers financial protection in case of illness or accidental injury (also known as *insurance payer*)

HIPAA Electronic Health Care Transactions and Code Sets (TCS) code sets that make it possible for providers and health plans to exchange data using a standard format and standard code sets

HIPAA National Identifiers numbers of predetermined length and structure used for identification purposes

HIPAA Privacy Rule   the first comprehensive federal protection for the privacy of health information

HIPAA Security Rule   rule that requires covered entities to establish safeguards to protect a patient's protected health information

hospice   public or private organization that provides services for terminally ill patients and their families

I

ICD-9-CM   mandated code set for diagnoses under TCS

individual deductible   deductible that must be met for each individual—whether the policyholder or a covered dependent—who has an encounter

individual health plan (IHP)   medical insurance plan purchased by an individual

initial preventive physical examination (IPPE)   once-in-a-lifetime benefit under Medicare Part B that must be received in the first six months after the date of enrollment

insurance payers   organizations that offer financial protection in case of illness or accidental injury (also known as *health plans*)

L

limiting charge   maximum amount a nonPar provider can charge a Medicare patient based on the Medicare nonparticipating fee schedule

M

managed care   method of supervising medical care with the goal of ensuring that patients get needed services in the most appropriate, cost-effective setting

managed care organization (MCO)   plan that establishes links among provider, patient, and payer by combining the delivery of services with the financing and management of health care

maximum allowable cost (MAC)   the greatest unit price that the payer or pharmacy benefit manager will pay

maximum benefit limit   monetary amount after which a plan's benefits end

Medicaid   assistance program that pays for health care services for people with incomes below the national poverty level

medical insurance   agreement between a person and a health plan that enables individuals to be able to afford medical expenses

medically indigent/needy   individuals who earn enough money to pay for basic living expenses but cannot afford high medical bills

medically necessary   insurance term referring to appropriate medical treatment given under generally accepted standards of medical practice

medical records   patient's medication files and other clinical materials that are legal documents belonging to the pharmacy that created them

medical savings account (MSA)   program that combines a high-deductible fee-for-service plan with a tax-exempt trust to pay for qualified medical expenses

Medicare   federal health insurance program for people who are sixty-five and older and some people with disabilities and end-stage renal disease (ESRD)

Medicare administrative contractors (MACs)   insurance organizations the federal government contracts with to pay Medicare claims on its behalf

Medicare Advantage   new name for Medicare + Choice plans, with some changed rules to give Part C enrollees better benefits and lower costs

Medicare beneficiary   person covered by Medicare

Medicare Fee Schedule (MFS)   basis for payments for all Original Medicare Plan services

Medicare Part A   program that helps pay for inpatient hospital services, care in skilled nursing facilities, home health care, and hospice care

Medicare Part B   program that helps pay for physician services, outpatient hospital services, durable medical equipment, and other services and supplies

Medicare Part C   program that enables private health insurance companies to contract with CMS to offer Medicare benefits through their own policies

Medicare Part D   program that provides voluntary Medicare prescription drug plans to people who are eligible for Medicare

Medicare Remittance Notice (MRN)   notice sent to an office to show the amount of a patient's medical bills that has been applied to the annual deductible

Medicare Summary Notice (MSN)   notice sent to a patient to show the amount of his or her medical bills that has been applied to the annual deductible

medication therapy management (MTM)   provision of the Medicare Part D prescription drug plan that offers pharmacists free education to improve medication use and reduce the number of adverse drug events

Medigap insurance   policies from federally approved private insurance carriers to fill gaps in Medicare coverage

Medi-Medi beneficiary   individuals who are eligible for both Medicaid and Medicare

member pharmacy   pharmacy that falls within the network created by a managed care organization

military treatment facility (MTF)   military-operated medical facility

minimum necessary standard   precautions a covered entity must take to limit the usage of protected health information by taking reasonable safeguards to protect it from incidental disclosure

N

National Council for Prescription Drug Programs (NCPDP) Telecommunications Standard Version 5.1 and Batch Standard 1.1   the HIPAA standard for electronic retail pharmacy drug claims

National Drug Code (NDC)   an eleven-digit code assigned to all prescription drug products by the labeler or distributor of the product under FDA regulations

National Provider Identifier (NPI)   standard for the identification of providers when filing claims and other transactions

NCPDP Provider Identification Number   provides pharmacies with a unique national identifier for use in interactions with payers and claim processors

network   group of participating providers, including physicians, hospitals, and pharmacies, created by a managed care organization for its policyholders

noncovered (excluded) services   services that a medical insurance policy does not pay for

Notice of Privacy Practices (NPP)   document explaining how patients' protected health information may be used and describing their rights

O

Office for Civil Rights (OCR)   enforcer of HIPAA privacy regulations

Office of the Inspector General (OIG)   detects health care fraud and abuse and enforces all laws relating to them

open enrollment period   specific periods of time when employees choose a particular set of benefits for the coming benefit period

open formulary   least restrictive type of formulary, which will sometimes cover medications that are not listed

Original Medicare Plan   term used by Medicare to refer to its fee-for-service plan

out-of-network   term for physicians, hospitals, and pharmacies that are not part of the network created by a managed care organization for its policyholders

out-of-pocket expenses   amounts that a patient pays for medical expenses

P

password   key to information for individuals who have been granted access rights

payer of last resort   term for Medicaid, which pays after all other insurance carriers

pharmacy benefit   feature of a policy that provides coverage for selection of prescription medications

pharmacy benefit manager (PBM)   third-party administrator of prescription drug programs that processes and pays prescription drug claims

pharmacy claim   information transmitted to a payer that identifies the policyholder, the prescriber, the pharmacy sending the claim, and the medications being supplied

pharmacy management (PM) system   system that stores, processes, transmits, and receives billing data

pharmacy technician insurance specialist   job title that describes the vital job of getting paid for prescriptions, whether the setting is a large pharmacy practice where individuals specialize in various tasks or a small practice where the same individual may handle this role as well as others, such as filling prescriptions

point of sale (POS)   drug plan benefits received at the time the pharmacy technician insurance specialist processes a person's prescriptions

policyholder   individual who enters into an agreement with a health plan to receive medical insurance

preferred drug list   list containing the Food and Drug Administration (FDA)-approved brand-name and generic medications a plan covers (also known as a *formulary* or *prescription drug list*)

preferred provider organization (PPO)   most popular type of managed care organization that combines flexibility in patients' choice of physicians with reduced costs for medical services

premium   fee paid monthly to a health plan by a person who buys medical insurance

prescription drug deductible amount   term used to refer to a deductible in prescription benefit plans

prescription drug list (PDL)   list containing the Food and Drug Administration (FDA)-approved brand-name and generic medications a plan covers (also known as a *formulary* or *preferred drug list*)

Prescription Drug Plan (PDP)   basic Medicare option for offering prescription drug coverage

prescription legend drug   medication whose label is required to bear the legend "Caution: federal law prohibits dispensing without a prescription"

primary insurance   the first insurance that the patient will use for claims

prior authorization (preauthorization)   review required to be conducted by a plan before medications are dispensed and, ideally, before they are prescribed

protected health information (PHI)   individually identifiable health information that is transmitted or maintained by electronic media

provider   hospital, physician, and other medical staff members and facilities that offer medical services

Q

Quality Improvement Organization (QIO)   group of practicing doctors and other health care experts paid by the federal government to check and improve the care given to people with Medicare

qui tam   whistle-blower cases

R

real-time claims management systems   a program that enables providers to submit electronic pharmacy claims in an online real-time environment

relator   person who makes an accusation of suspected fraud

remittance advice (RA)   document that comes to a pharmacy showing the details for a claim (also known as an *explanation of benefits*)

Remittance Advice Remark Codes (RARC)   non-mandatory codes used to provide further explanation of the basic information provided by the other codes

respondeat superior   law stating that an employer is responsible for employees' actions

restricted formulary   type of formulary that limits the drugs listed to generics or limited medications within a drug class

S

safety edits   checks required when a prescription request exceeds a certain quantity limit or dosage, there is potentially dangerous drug interaction, or there are other concerns for the patient's health

screening service   treatment for a patient who does not have symptoms, abnormal findings, or any past history of a disease

secondary insurance   the insurance used after primary insurance for any remaining expense

special needs plans (SNP)   prescription drug coverage offered by Medicare to some patients with specific needs

specialty drug   category of medication including biotech and other drugs that are designed to treat serious diseases such as cancer, multiple sclerosis, and rheumatoid arthritis and other inflammatory maladies

sponsors   active-duty service members whose spouses and children benefit under TRICARE

State Children's Health Insurance Program (SCHIP)   program that requires states to develop and implement plans for health insurance coverage for uninsured children

step therapy   edits used to encourage the use of less-expensive, similarly effective generic medications before considering coverage of higher-cost brand-name products

subpoena   order of the court directing a party to appear and testify

subpoena *duces tecum*   order of the court directing a party to appear, testify, and bring specified documents or items

switch vendor   service used to verify that a claim conforms to NCPDP transaction standards before it is forwarded to the payer's claim system

T

Temporary Assistance for Needy Families (TANF)   program that helps with living expenses

therapeutic interchange   substitution of one drug for another in the same therapeutic class

tier   specific list of drugs within a formulary

transactions   electronic data that are regularly sent back and forth between providers, health plans, and employers

treatment, payment, and health care operations (TPO)   term referring to providing and coordinating a patient's medical care, the exchange of information with health plans, and general business management functions

TRICARE   Department of Defense health insurance plan for military personnel and their families

TRICARE Extra   alternative managed care plan for individuals who want to receive services primarily from civilian facilities and physicians rather than from military facilities

TRICARE for Life   program offered to military personnel to fulfill a promise that they would receive lifelong health care

TRICARE Prime   managed care plan similar to an HMO

TRICARE Reserve Select (TRS)   premium-based health plan available for purchase by certain members of the National Guard and Reserve activated on or after September 11, 2001

TRICARE Standard   fee-for-service program that covers medical services provided by a civilian physician

TrOOP Facilitator   Medicare online eligibility and enrollment system

U

universal claim form (UCF)   a two-sided document that the pharmacy technician completes and submits for paper claims

usual and customary price (U&C)   the price the provider most frequently charges the general public for a drug

W

Welfare Reform Act   law that addresses the needs of categorically needy Medicaid recipients

workers' compensation insurance   plan that provides benefits for someone who is injured accidentally in the course of performing work or a work-related duty or becomes ill as a result of the employment environment